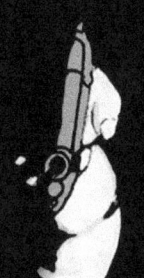

BOCAS

Volume 1
Written, Drawn By
Jake Estrada

Additional Grayscale Help By
Catherine Hill

Cover: Jake Estrada
Design assistant: Adriana Estrada
Editor in Chief: Beth Sipps
BOCAS created by Jake Estrada

Produced by
Jake Estrada & Beth Sipps

In memory of my father
Santiago "Chago" Estrada

www. estradamedia.net

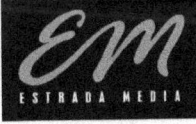

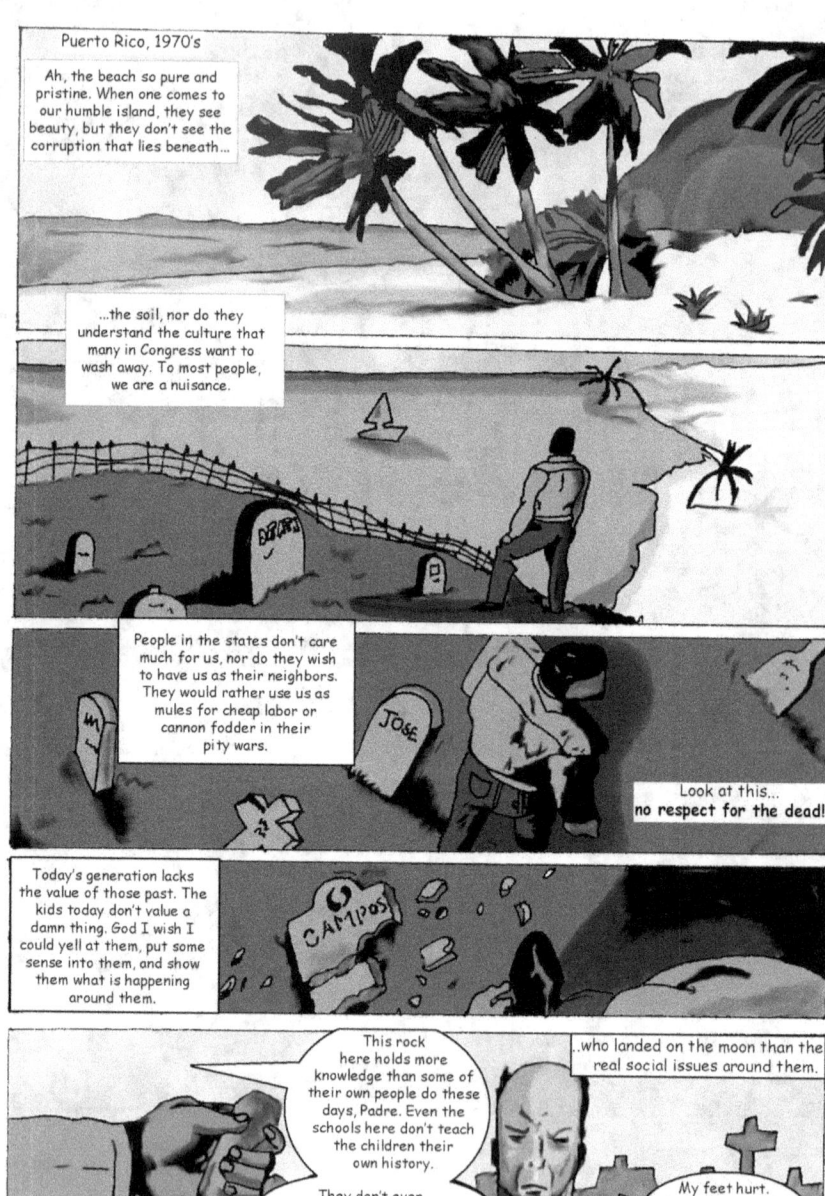

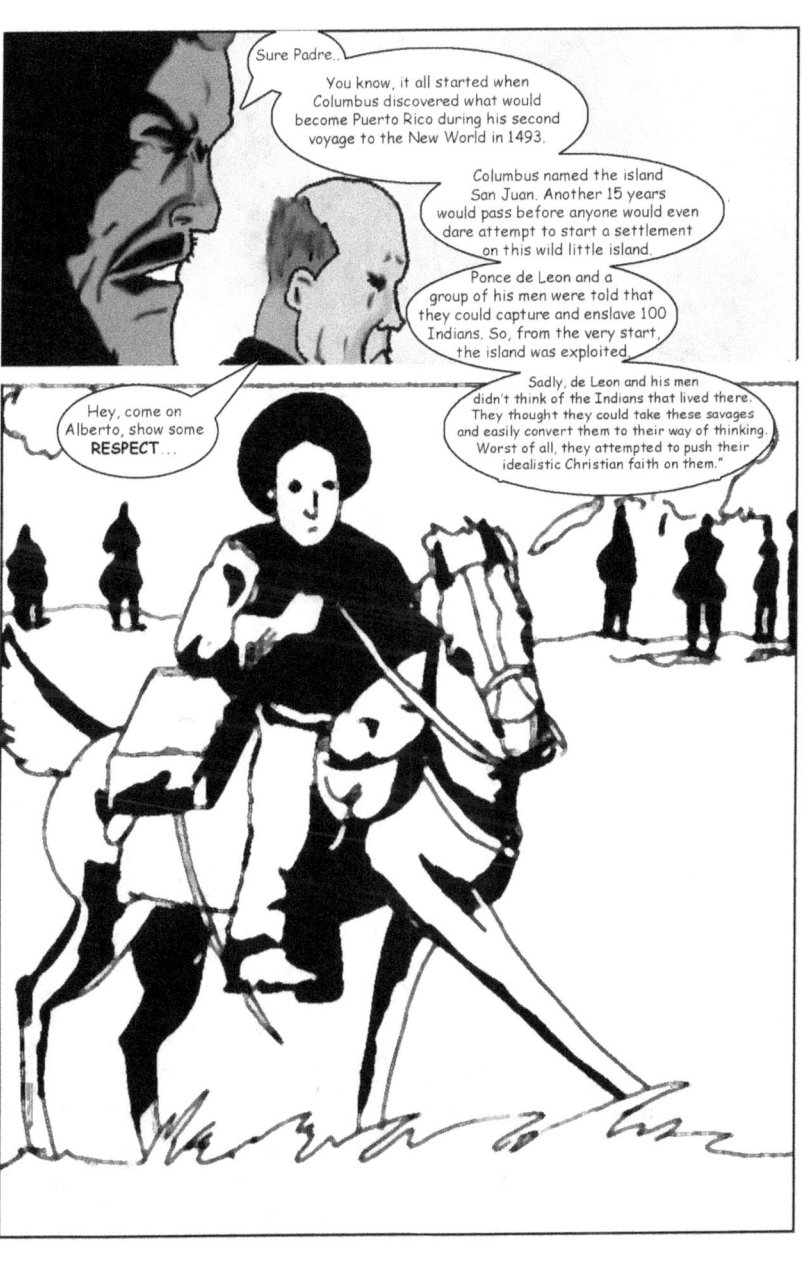

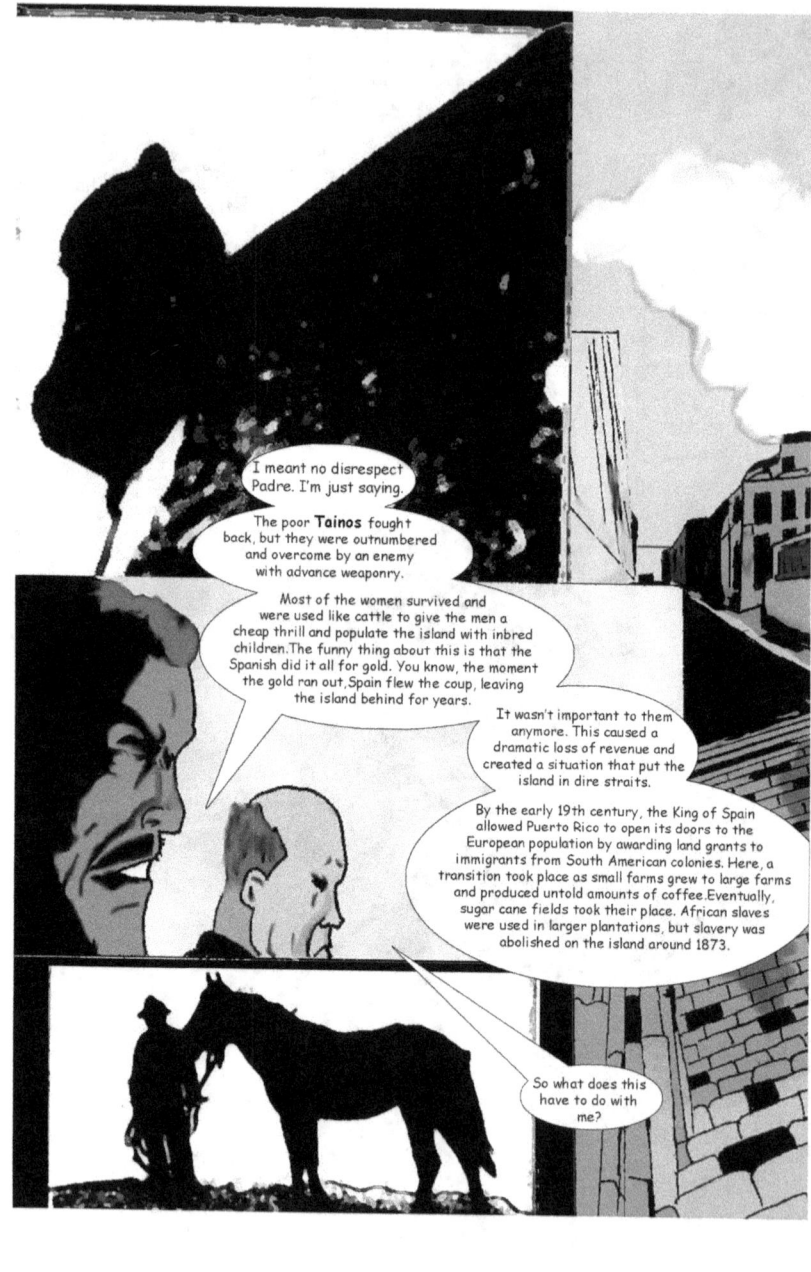

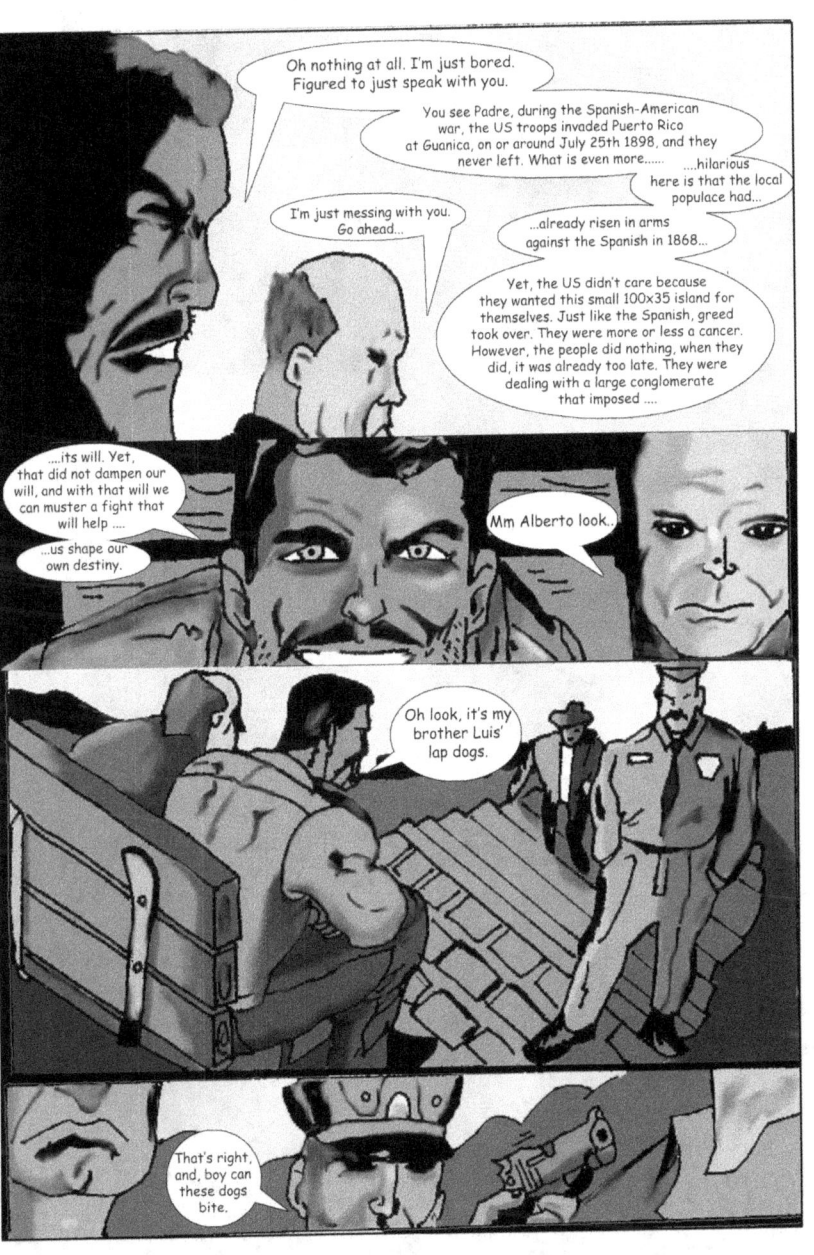

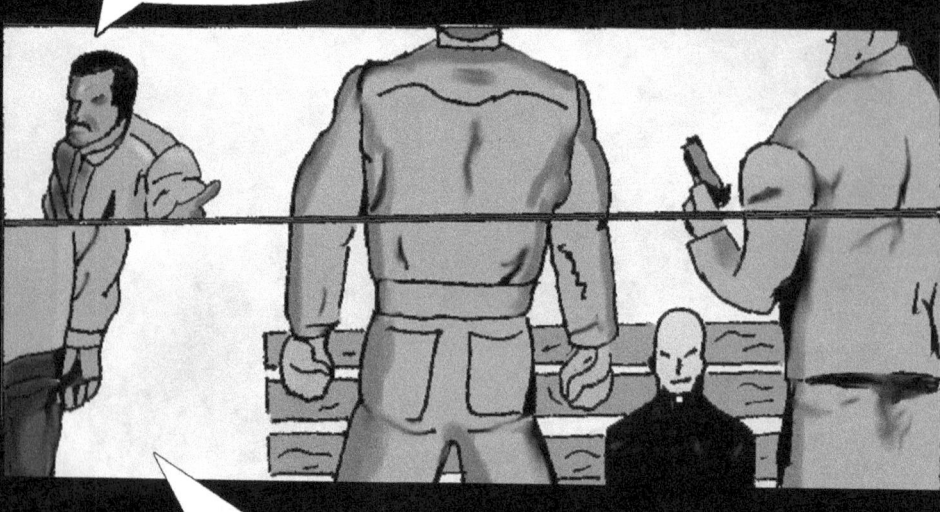

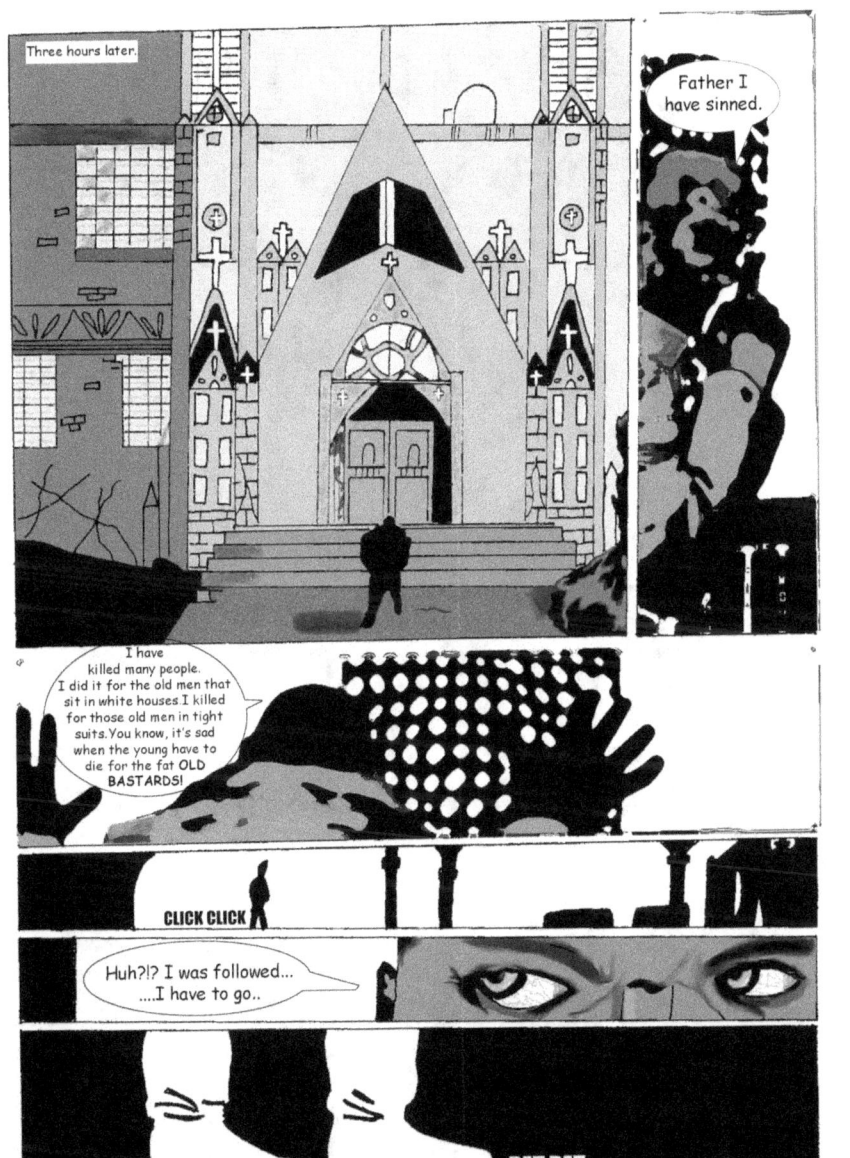

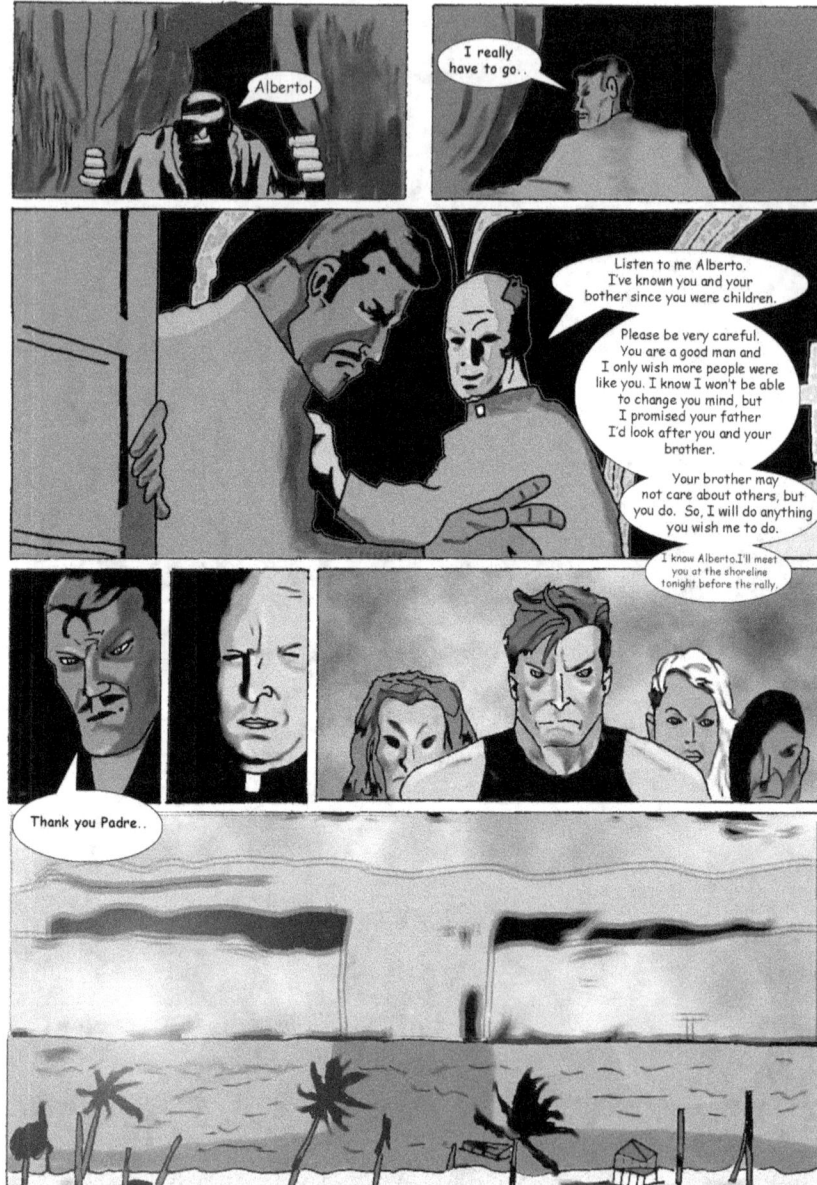

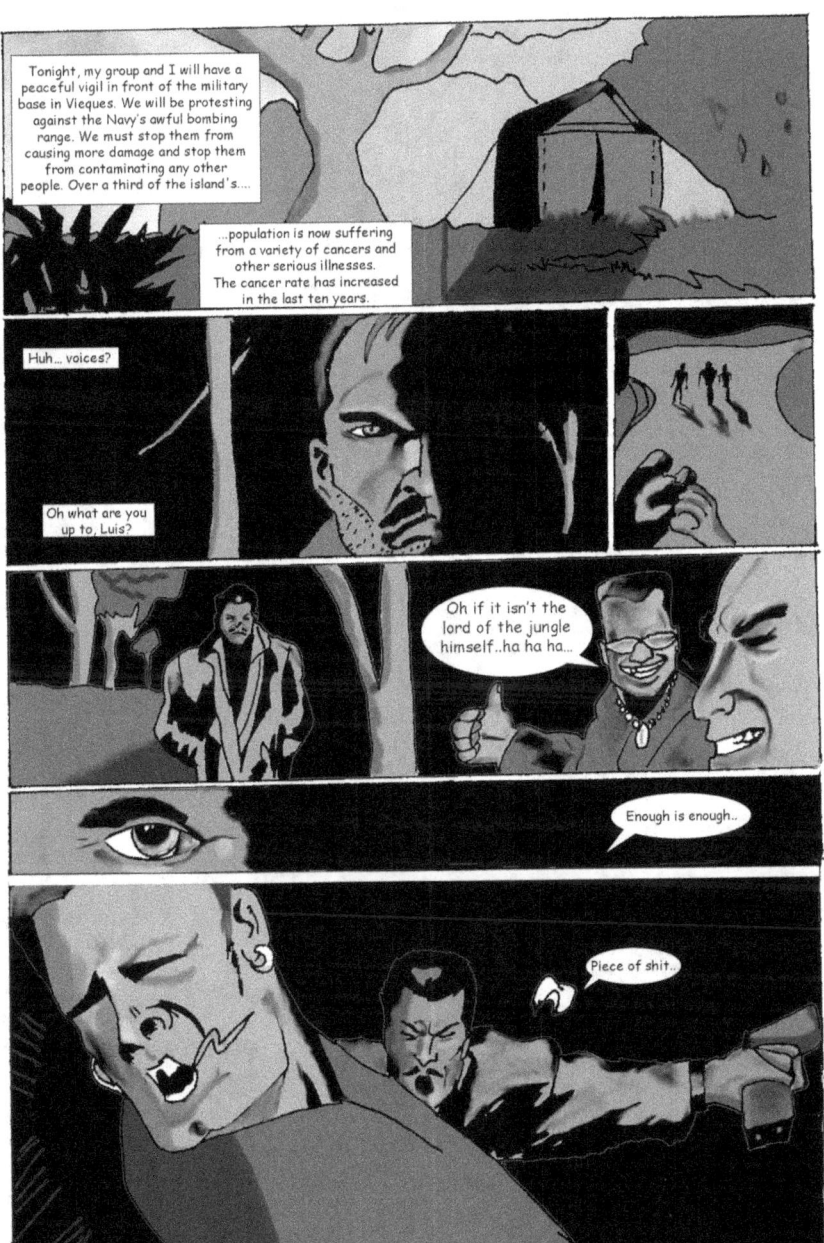

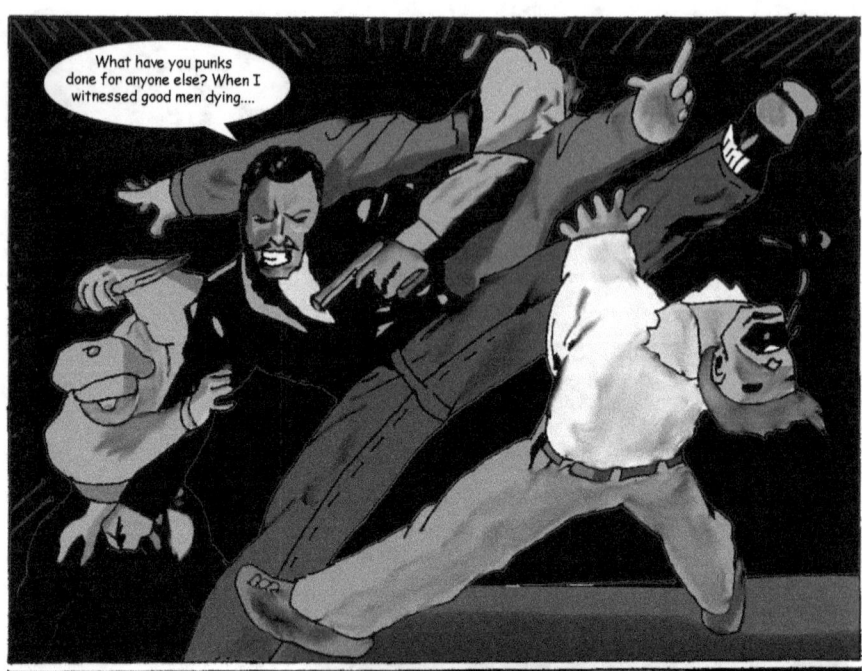

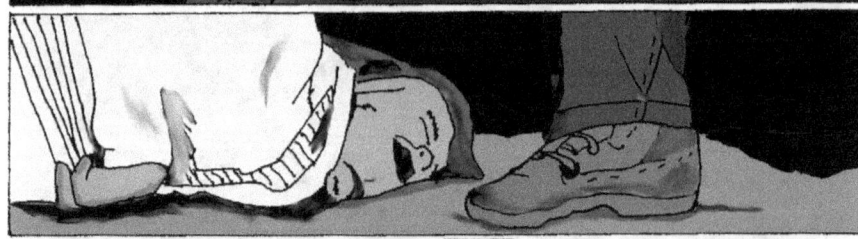

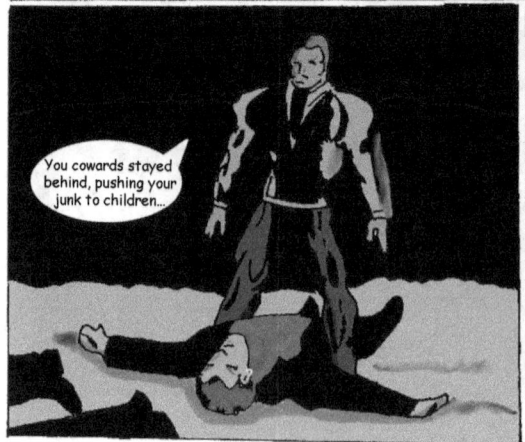

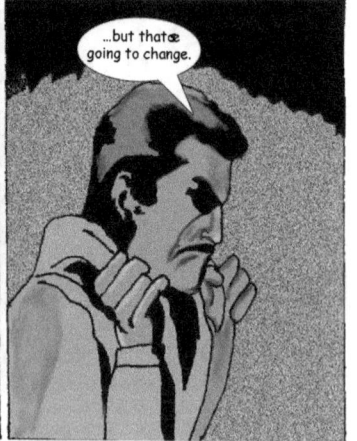

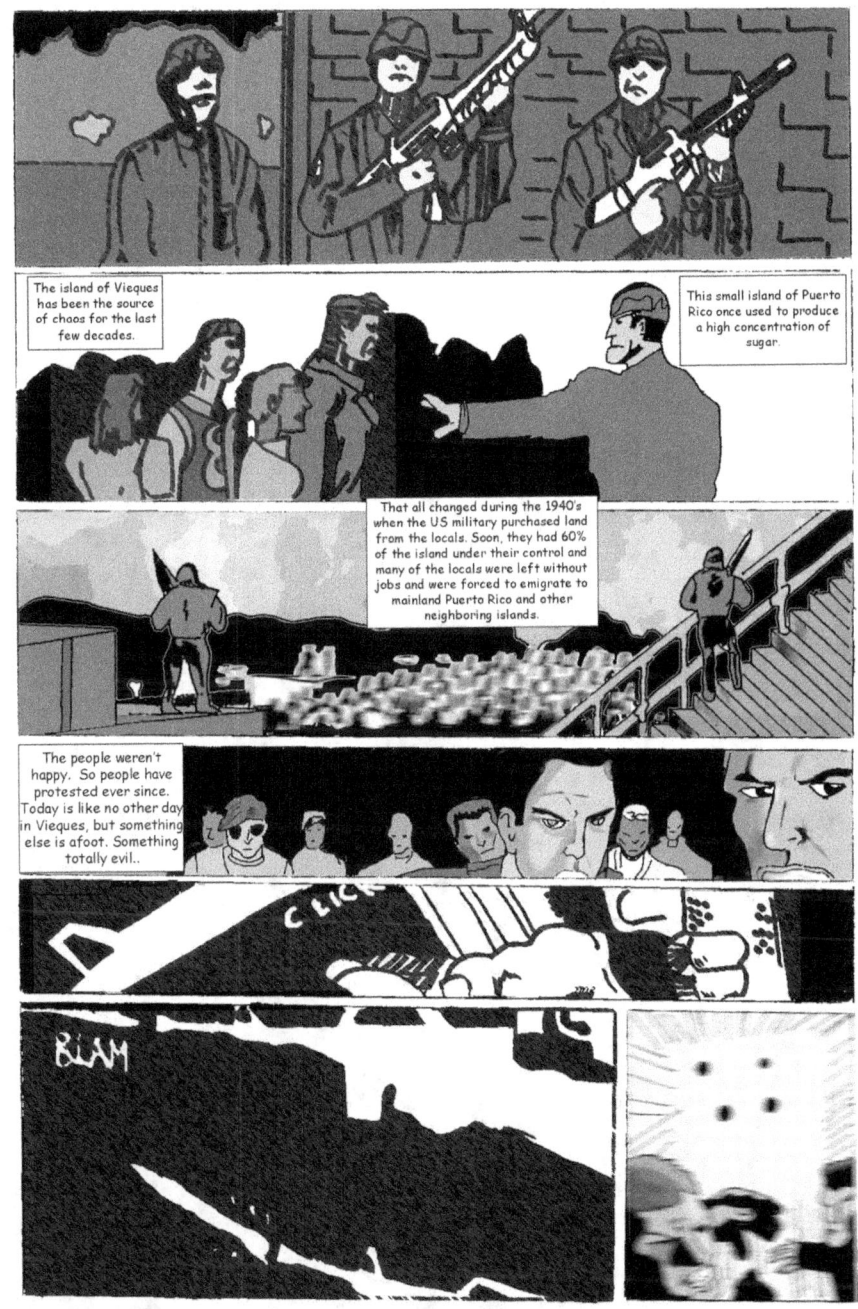

The island of Vieques has been the source of chaos for the last few decades.

This small island of Puerto Rico once used to produce a high concentration of sugar.

That all changed during the 1940's when the US military purchased land from the locals. Soon, they had 60% of the island under their control and many of the locals were left without jobs and were forced to emigrate to mainland Puerto Rico and other neighboring islands.

The people weren't happy. So people have protested ever since. Today is like no other day in Vieques, but something else is afoot. Something totally evil..

CLICK

BLAM

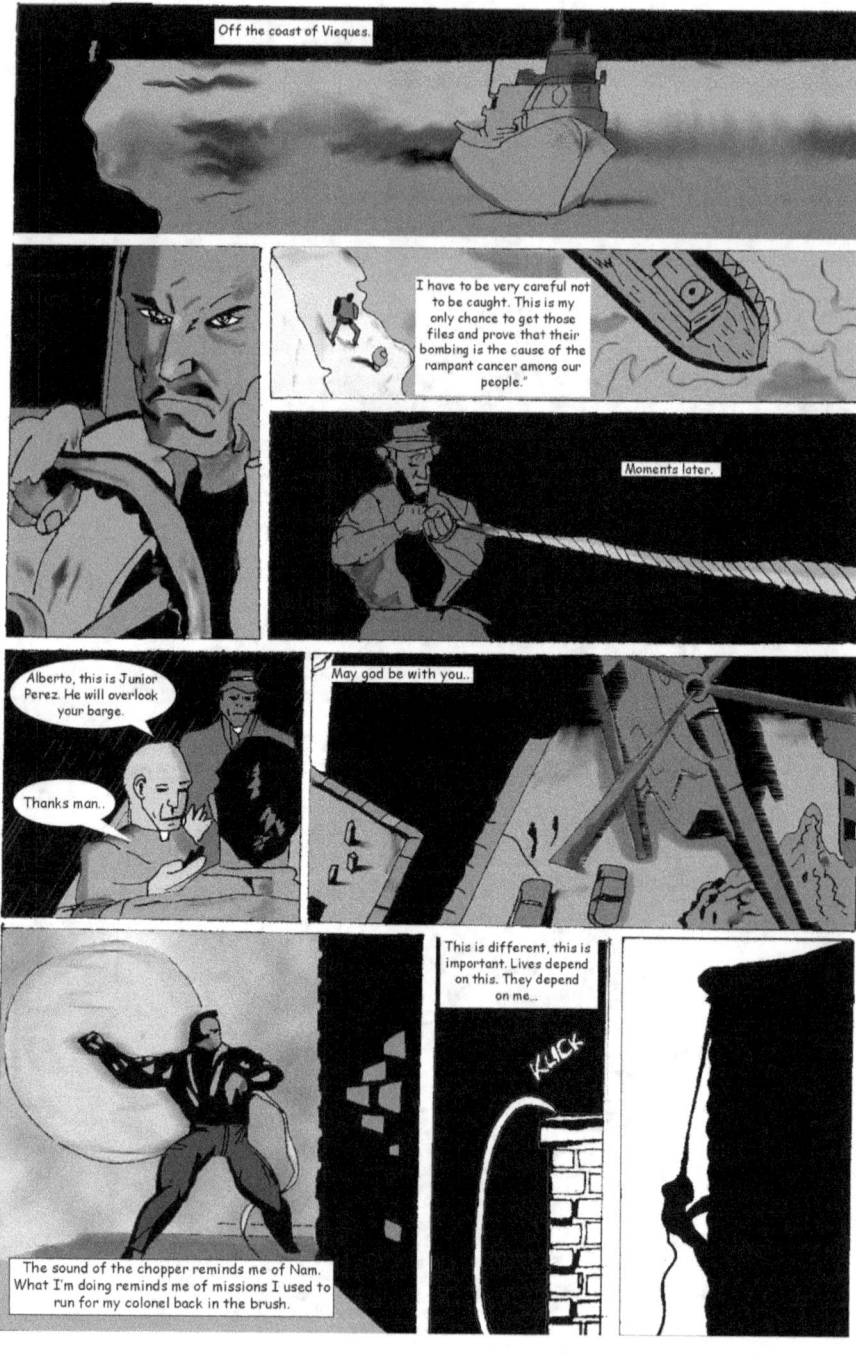

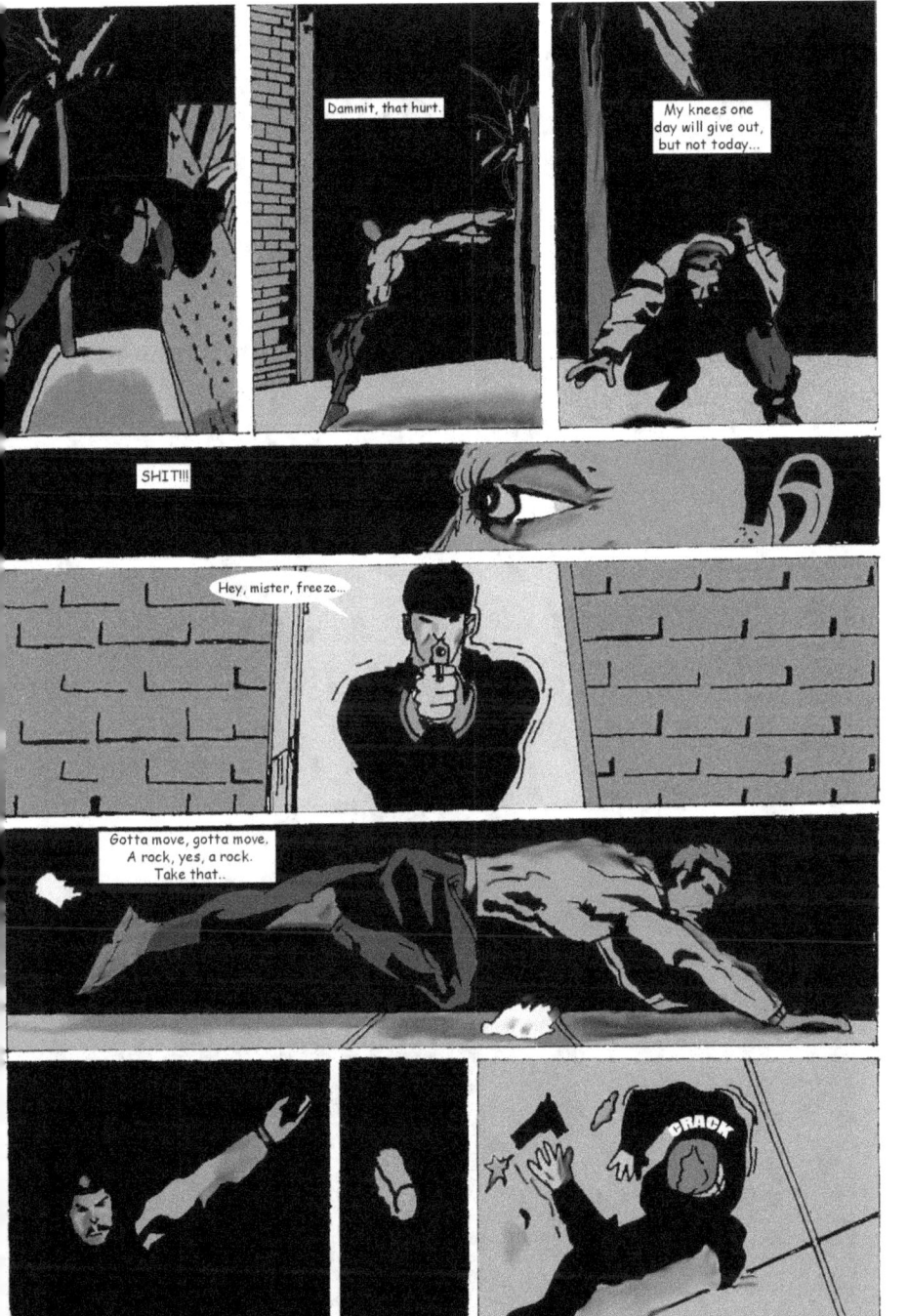

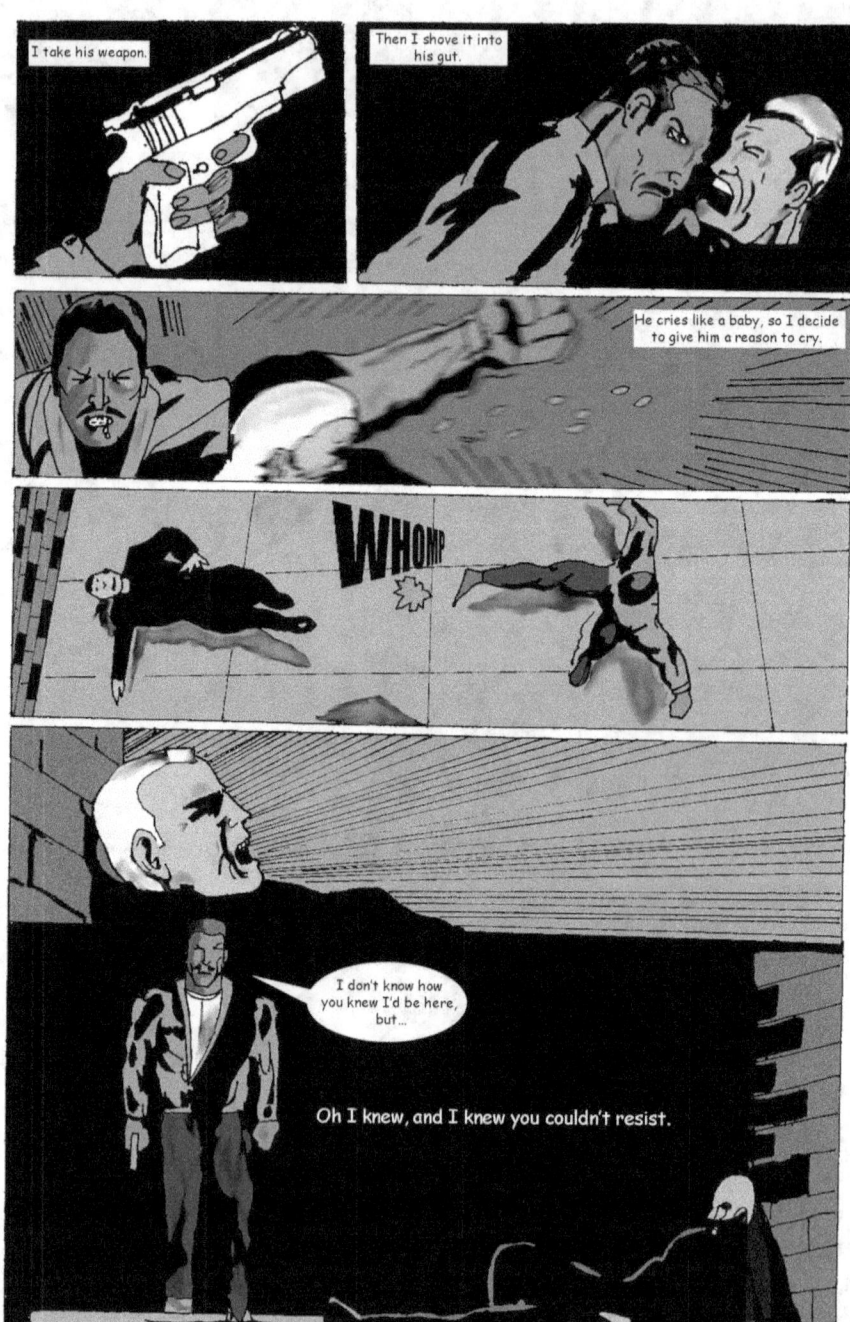

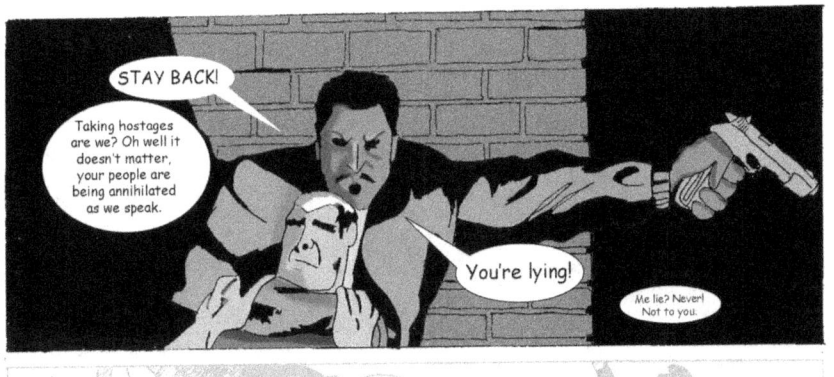

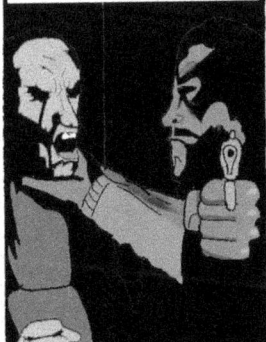

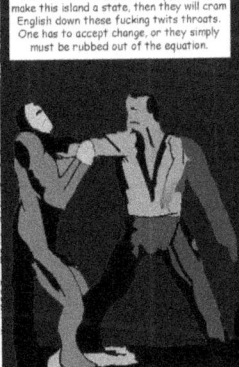

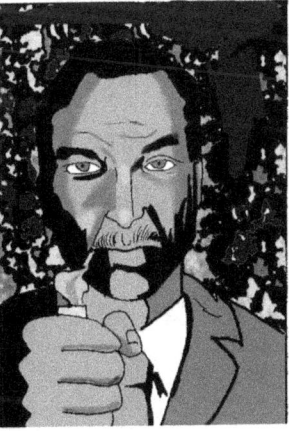

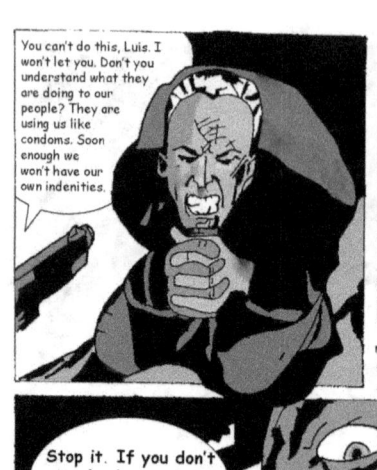

You can't do this, Luis. I won't let you. Don't you understand what they are doing to our people? They are using us like condoms. Soon enough we won't have our own indenities.

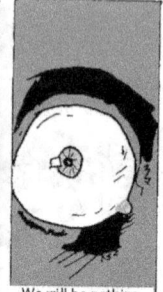

We will be nothing more than oddities in a museum, where people will gawk at us...

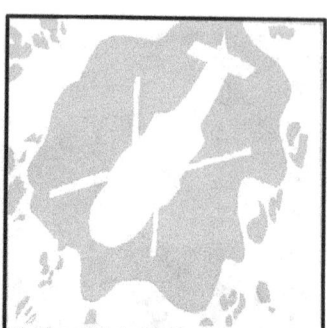

Oh, I know what they're doing. I just don't care. I'm in it for the money and the fame. You and I, brother, must have fallen from different trees.

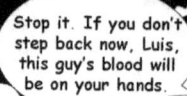

Stop it. If you don't step back now, Luis, this guy's blood will be on your hands.

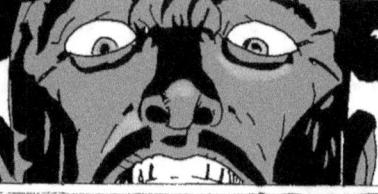

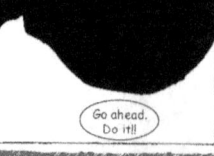

Go ahead. Do it!!

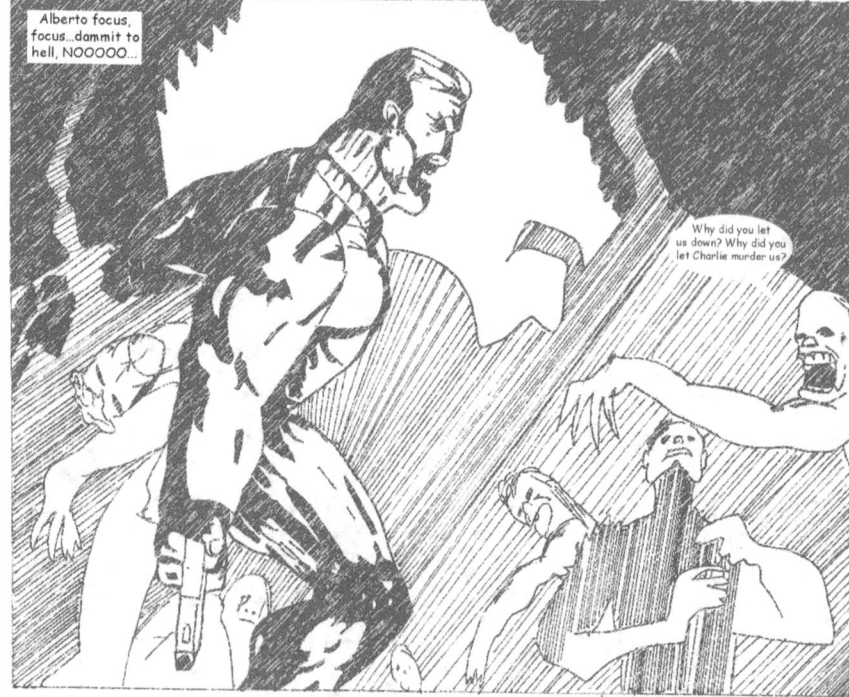

Alberto focus, focus...dammit to hell, NOOOOO...

Why did you let us down? Why did you let Charlie murder us?

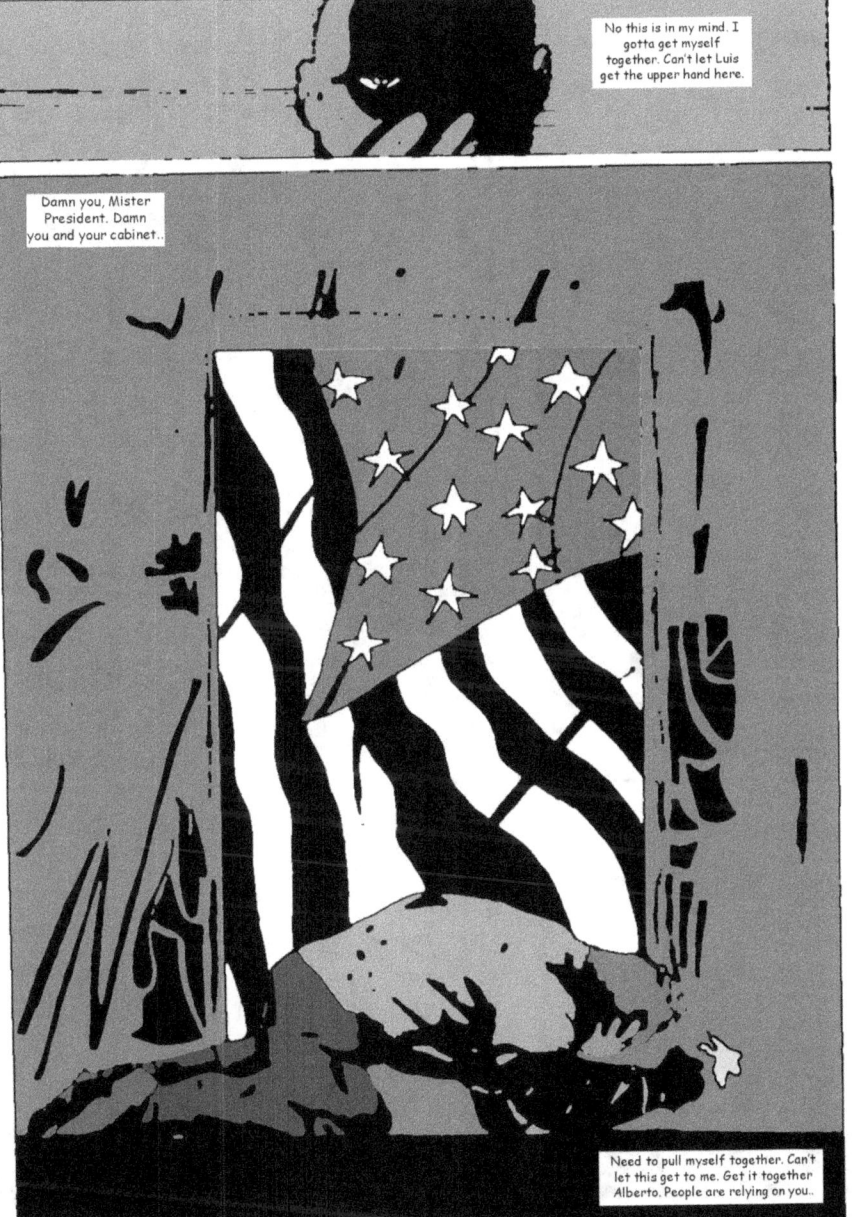

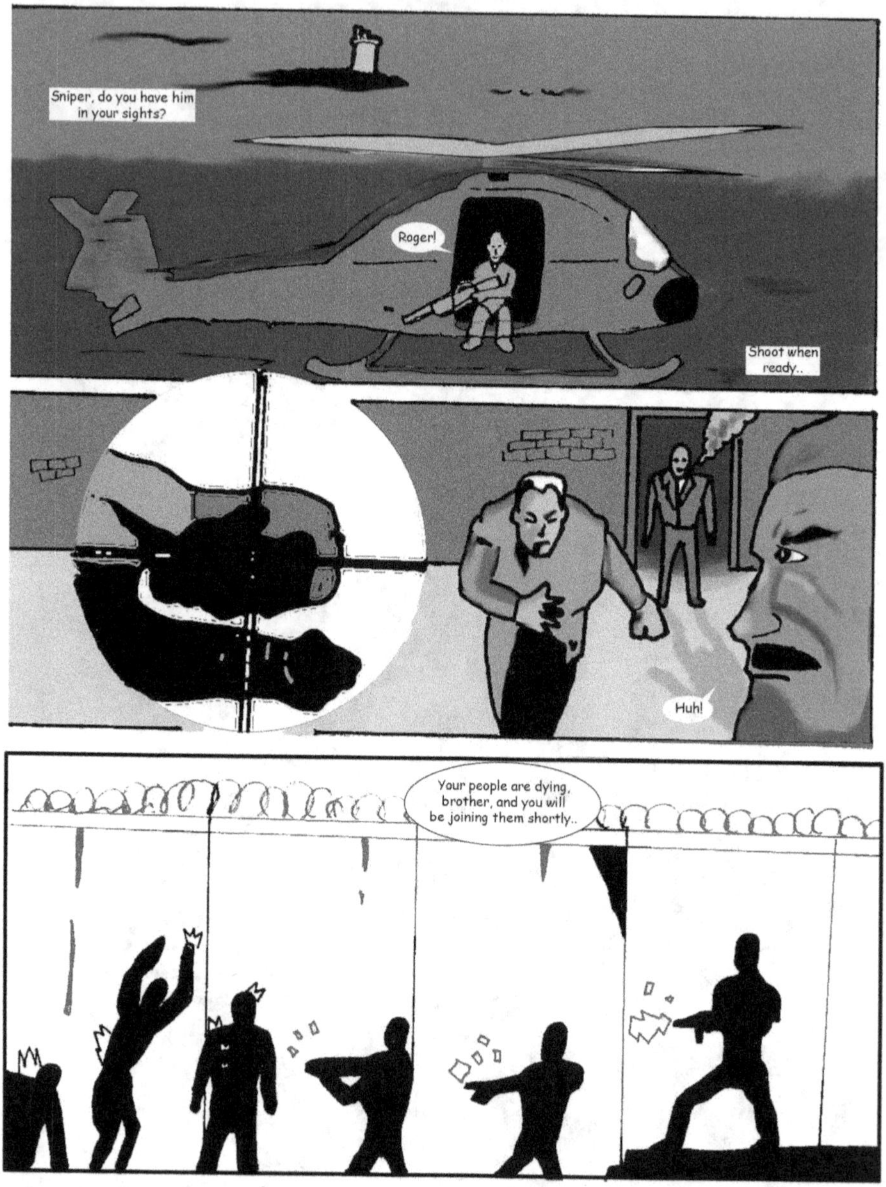

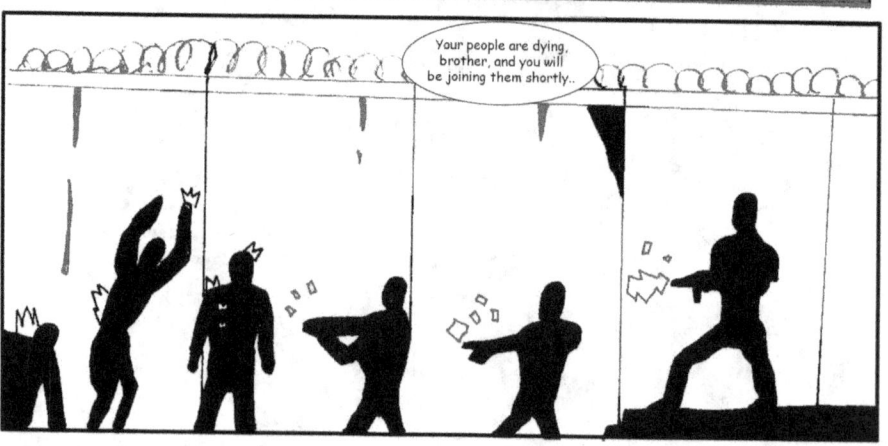

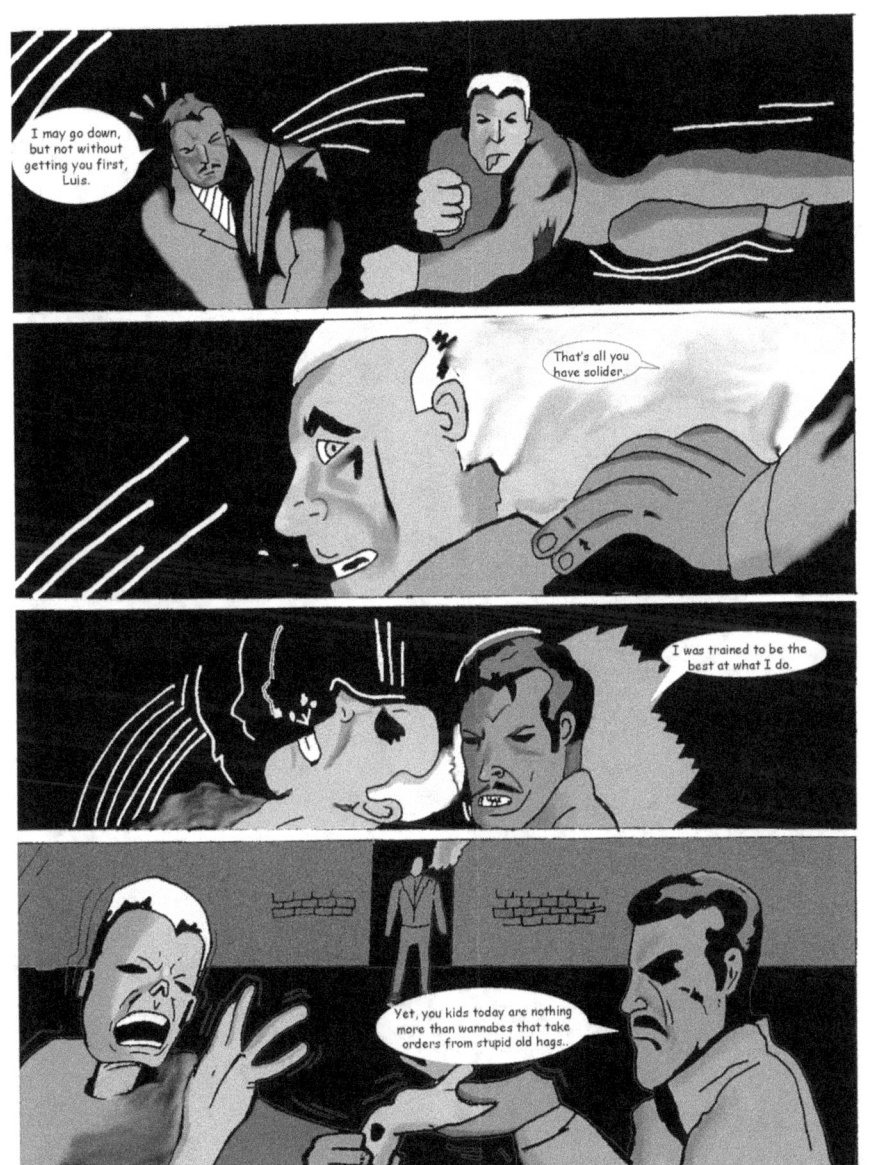

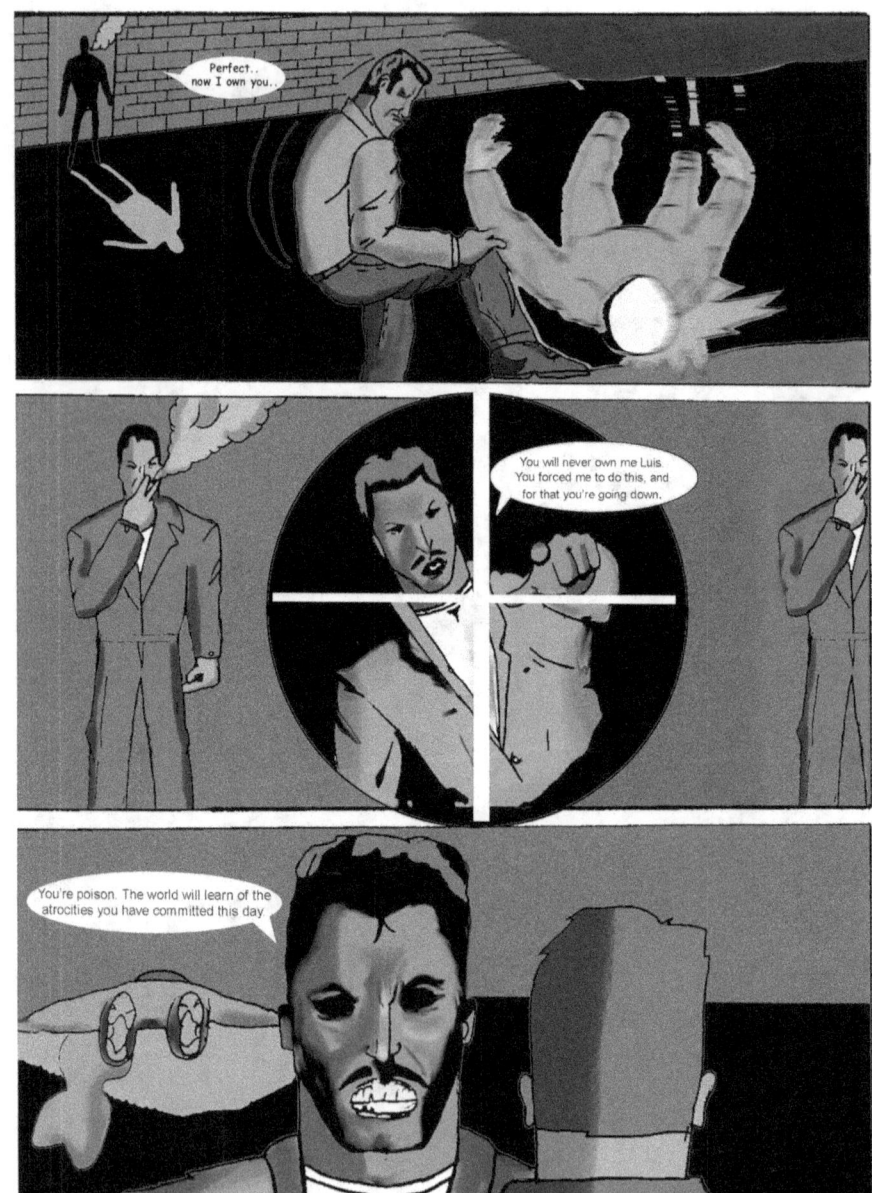

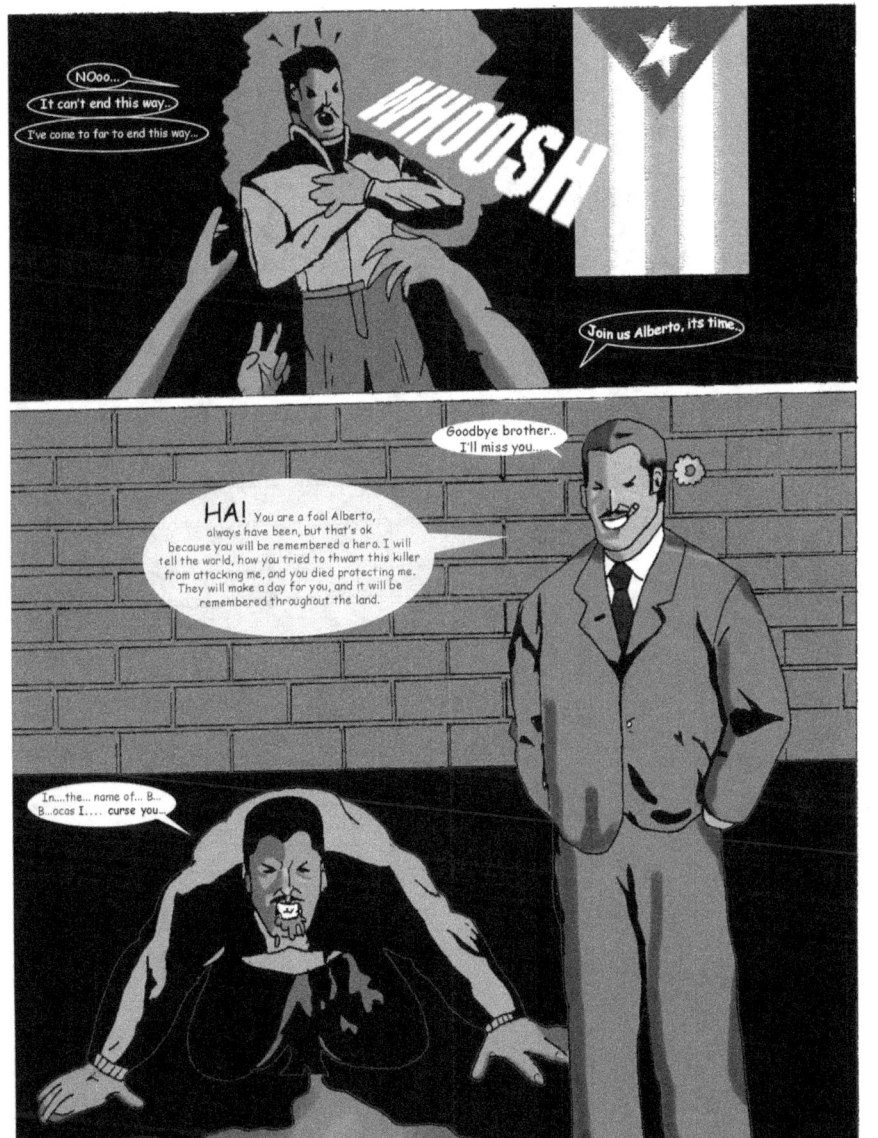

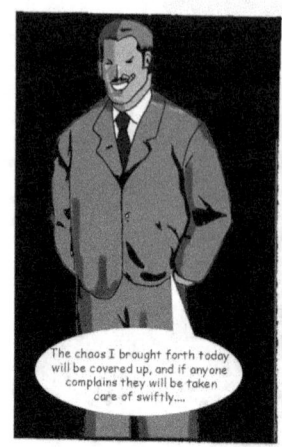

The chaos I brought forth today will be covered up, and if anyone complains they will be taken care of swiftly....

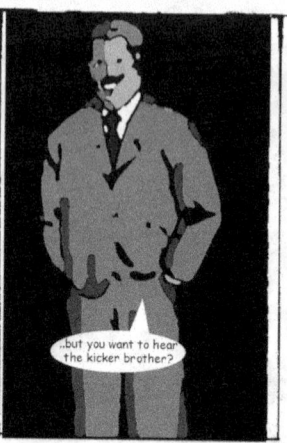

..but you want to hear the kicker brother?

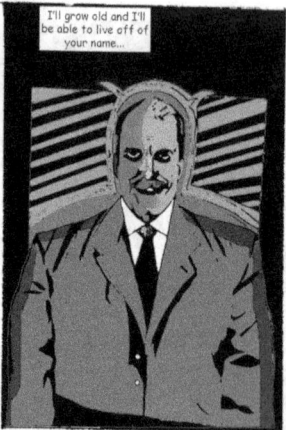

I'll grow old and I'll be able to live off of your name...

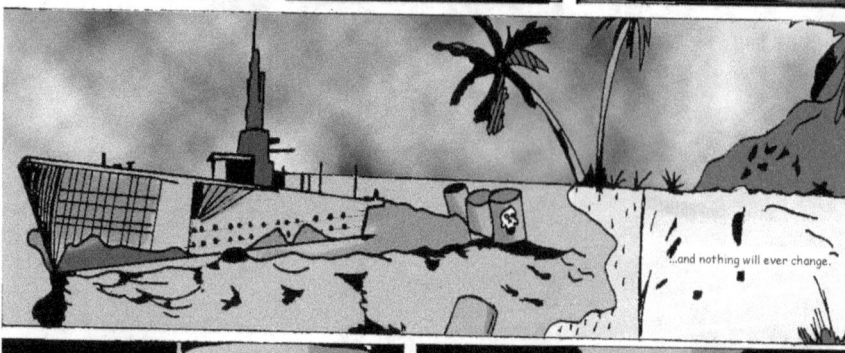

...and nothing will ever change.

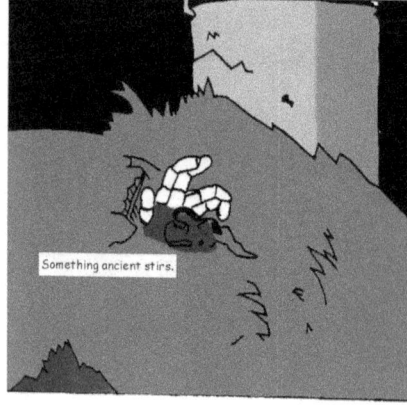

Something ancient stirs.

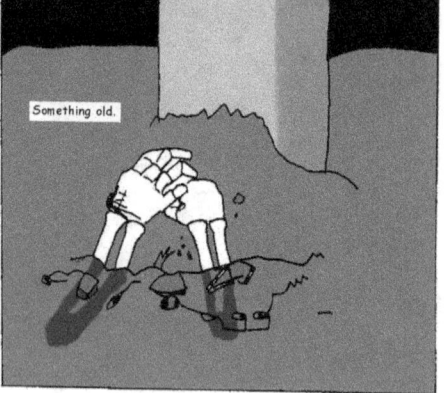

Something old.

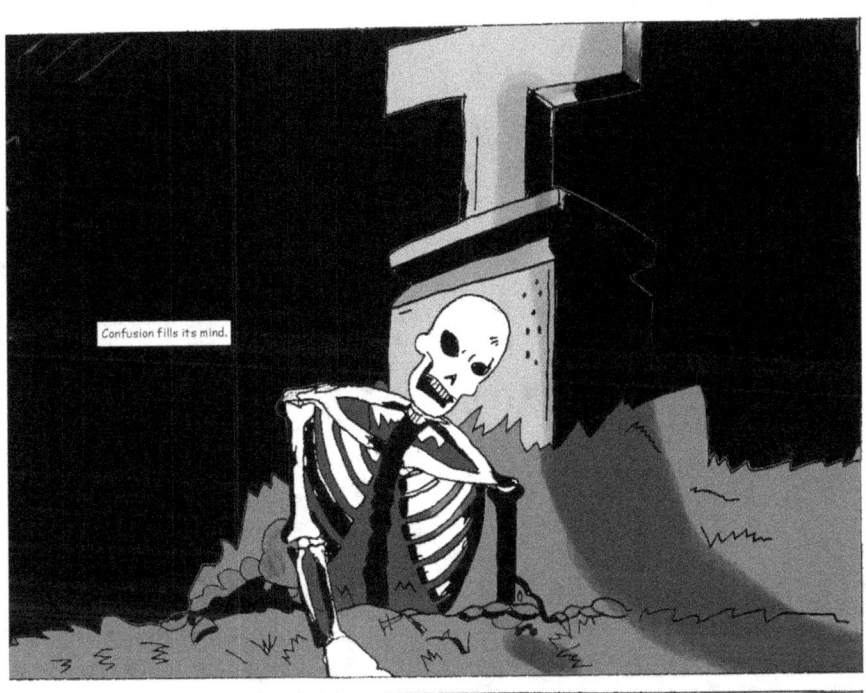

Confusion fills its mind.

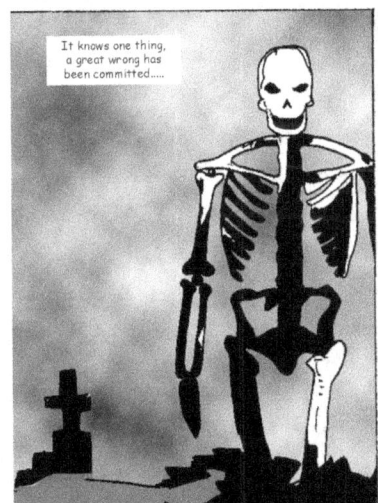

It knows one thing, a great wrong has been committed.....

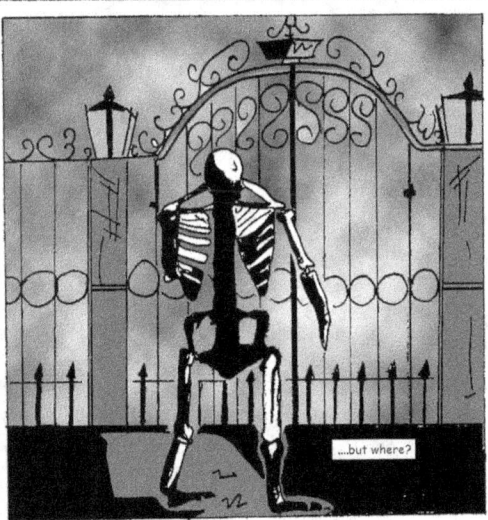

....but where?

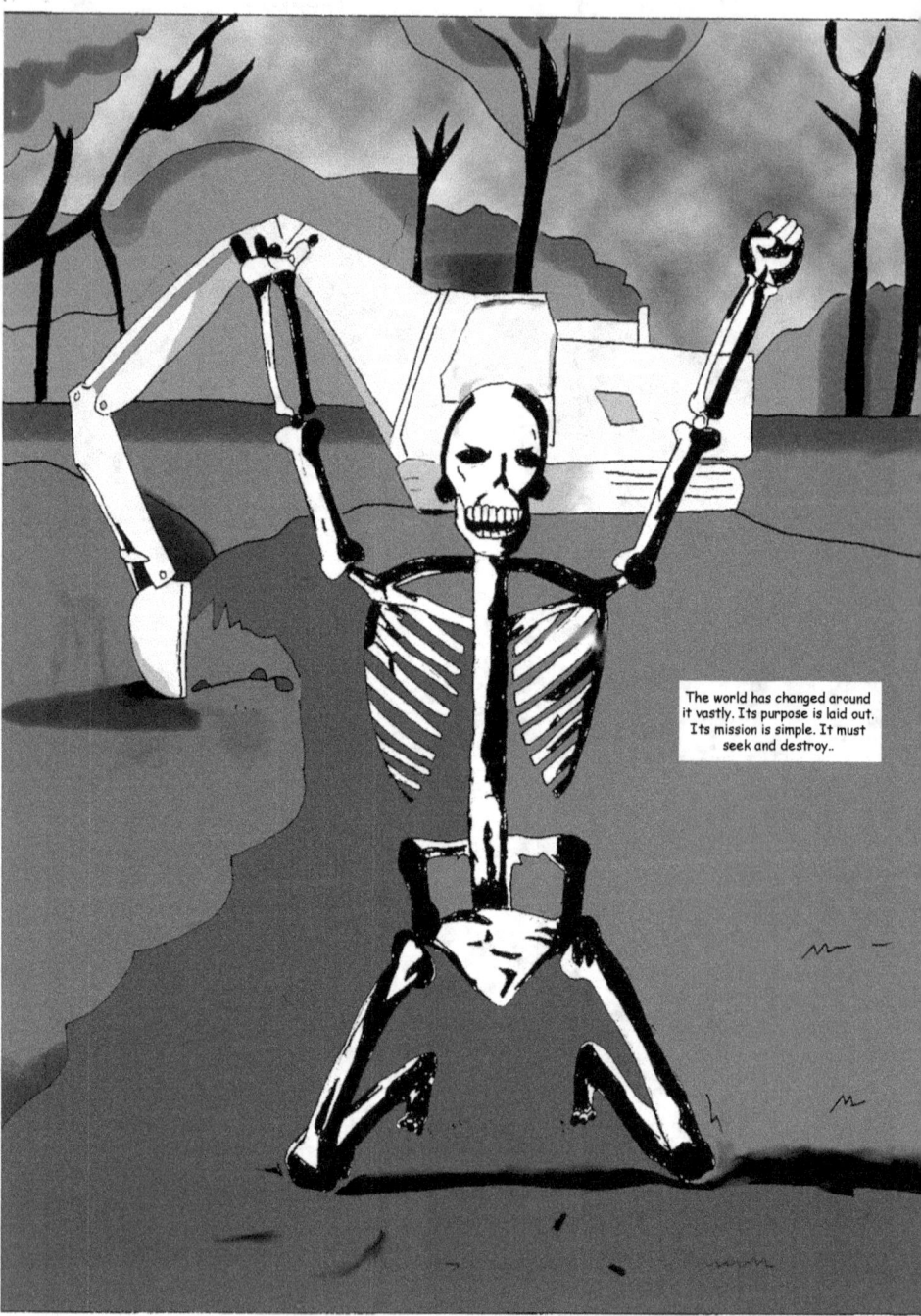

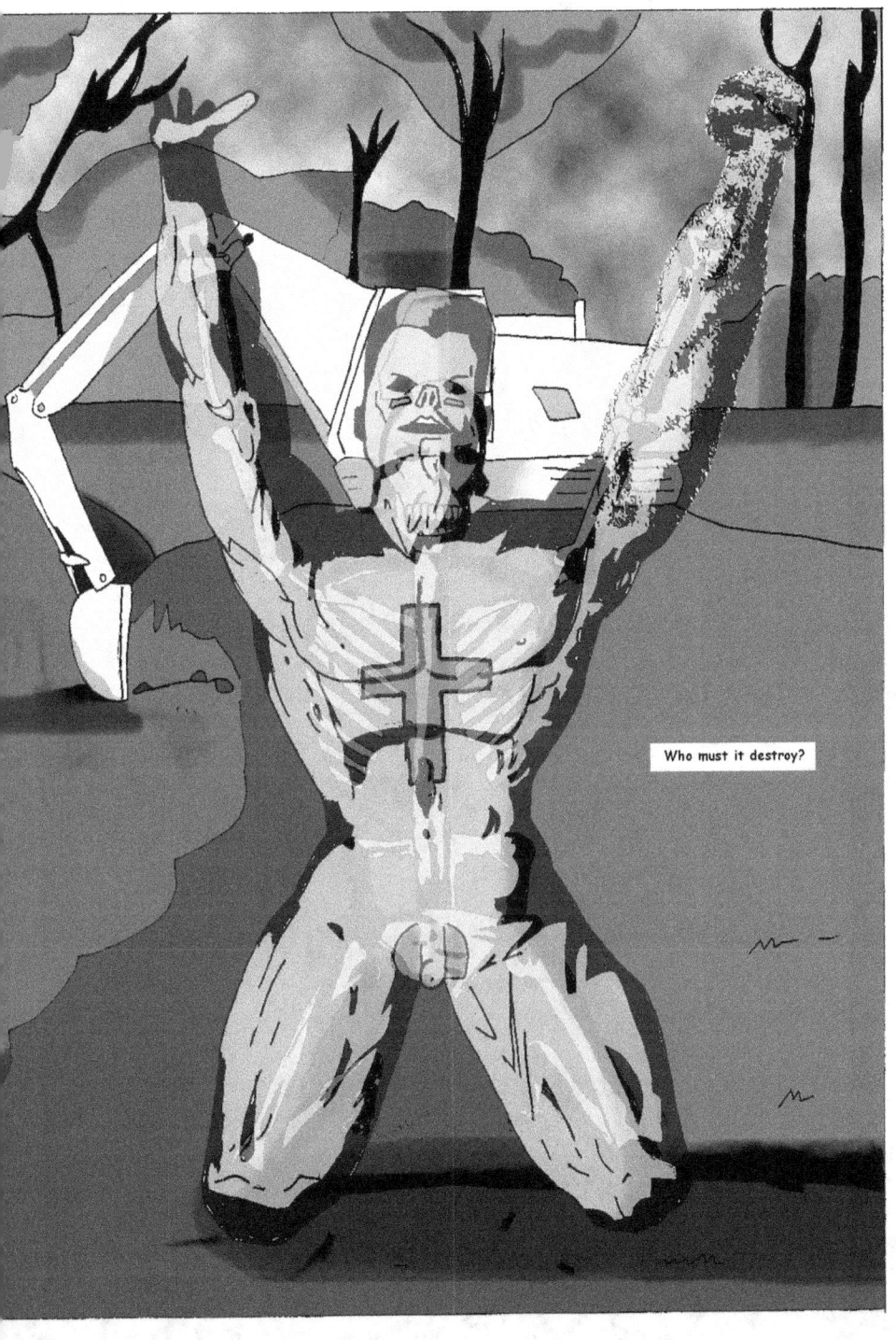

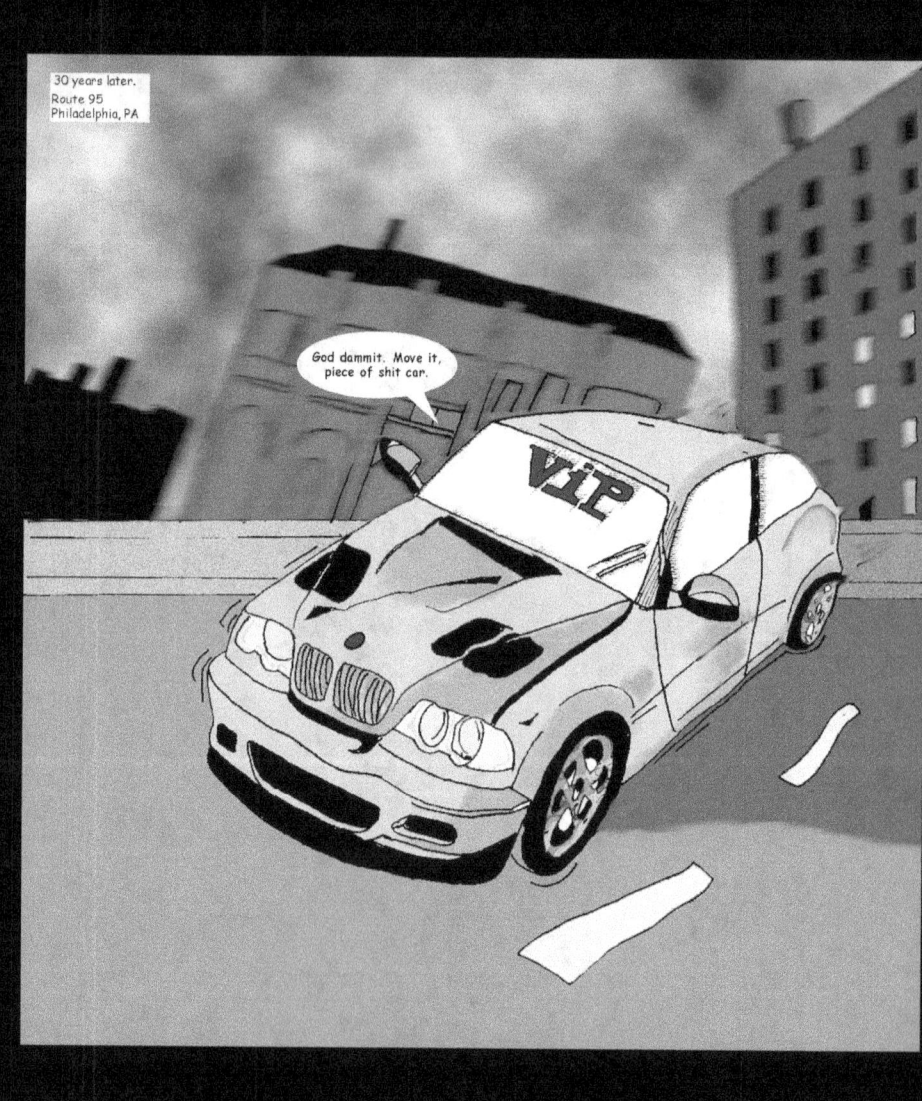

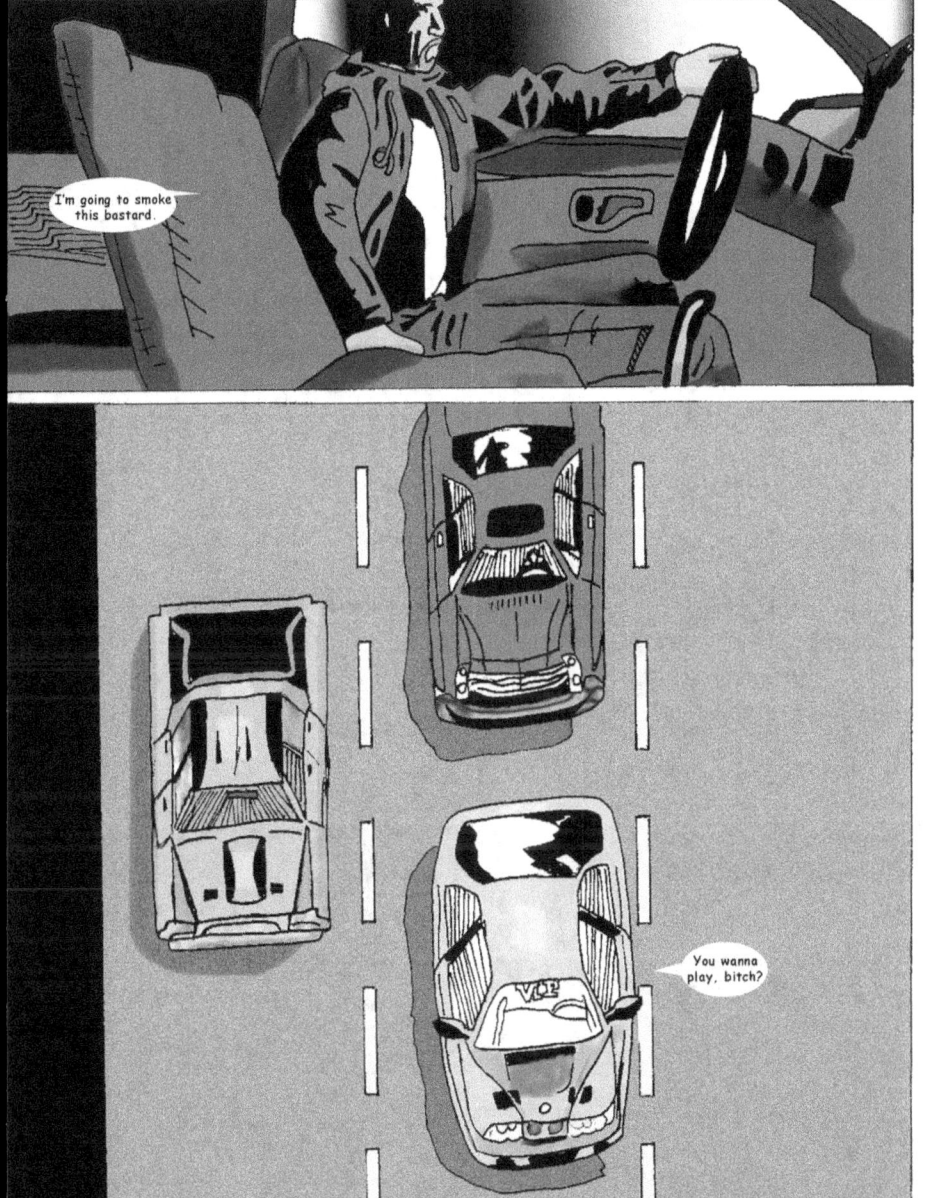

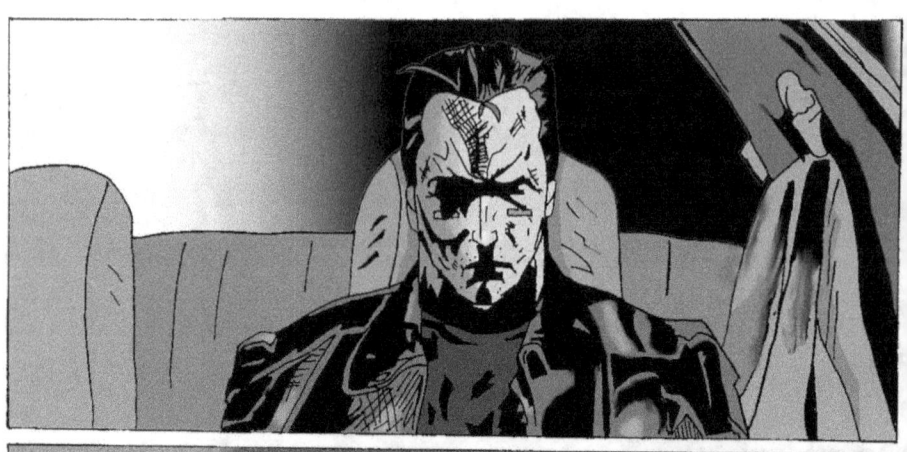

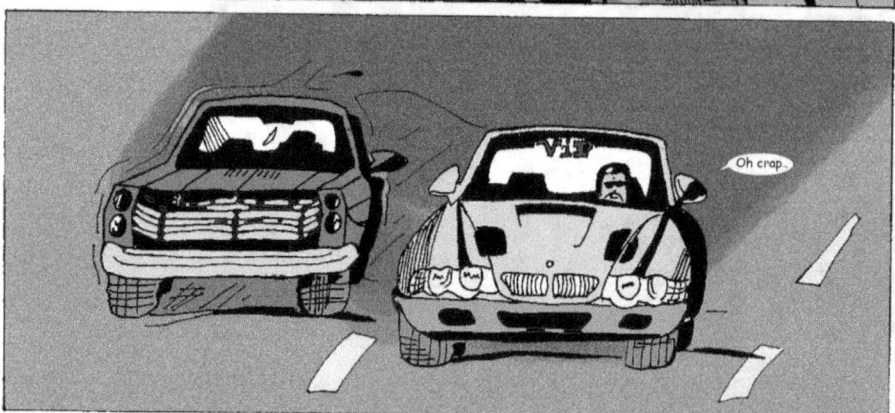

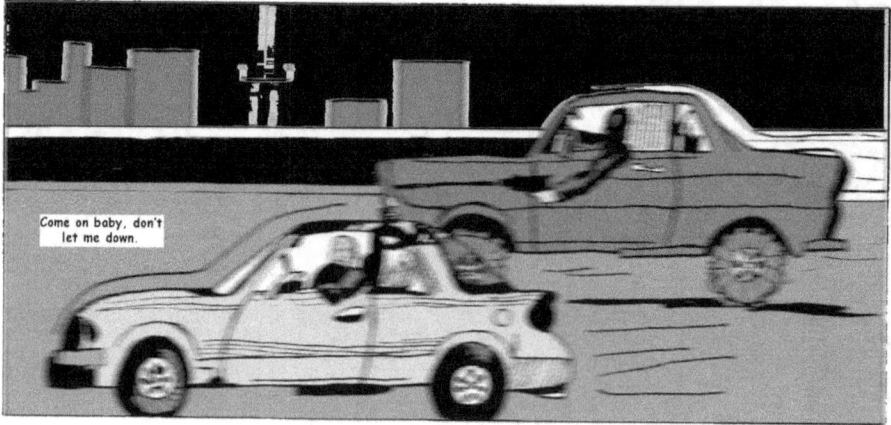

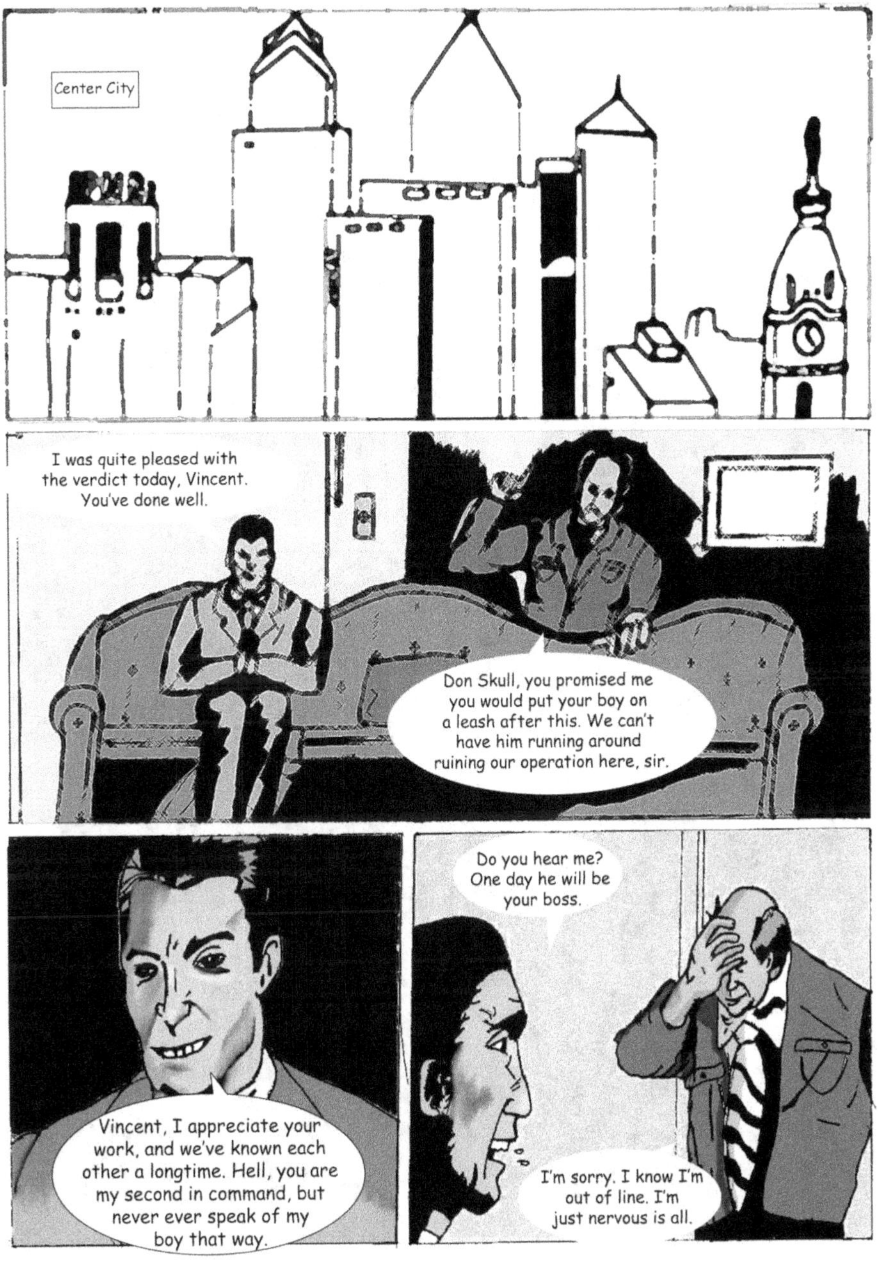

Center City

I was quite pleased with the verdict today, Vincent. You've done well.

Don Skull, you promised me you would put your boy on a leash after this. We can't have him running around ruining our operation here, sir.

Do you hear me? One day he will be your boss.

Vincent, I appreciate your work, and we've known each other a longtime. Hell, you are my second in command, but never ever speak of my boy that way.

I'm sorry. I know I'm out of line. I'm just nervous is all.

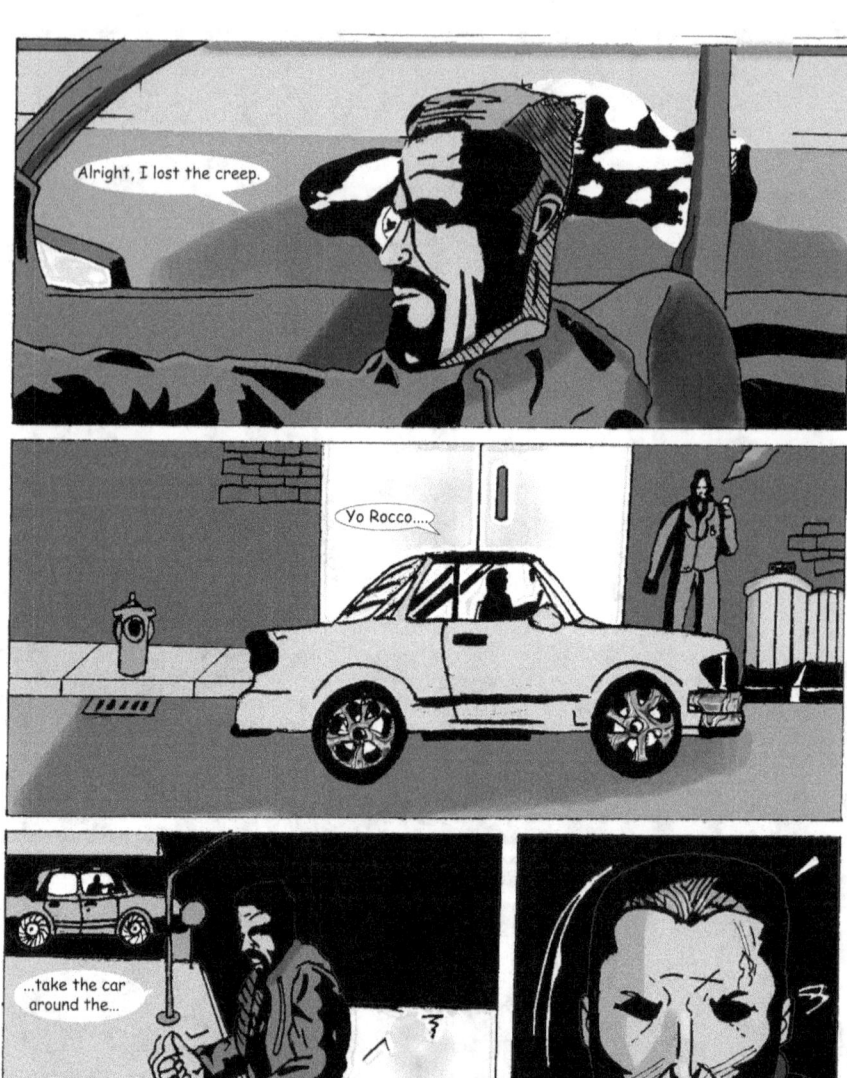

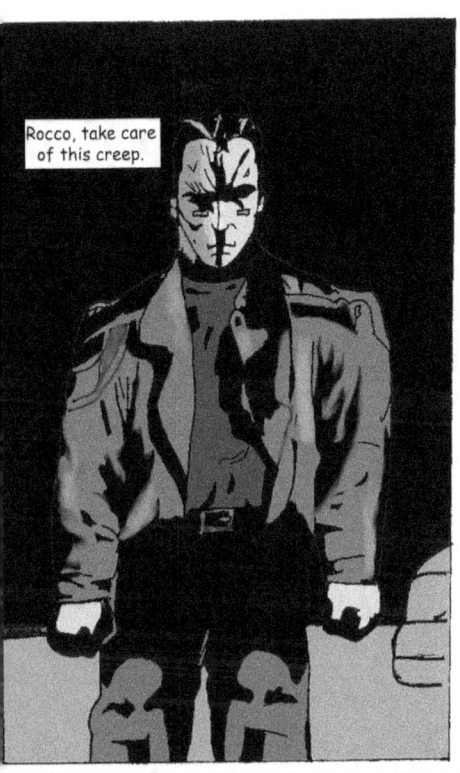

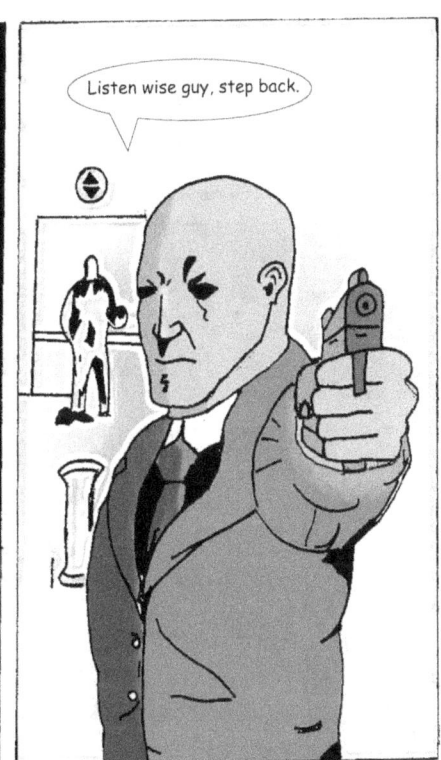

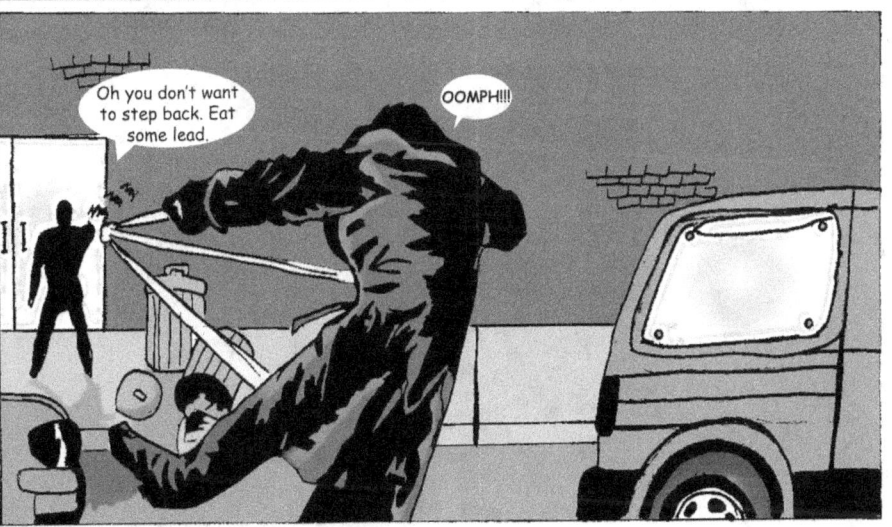

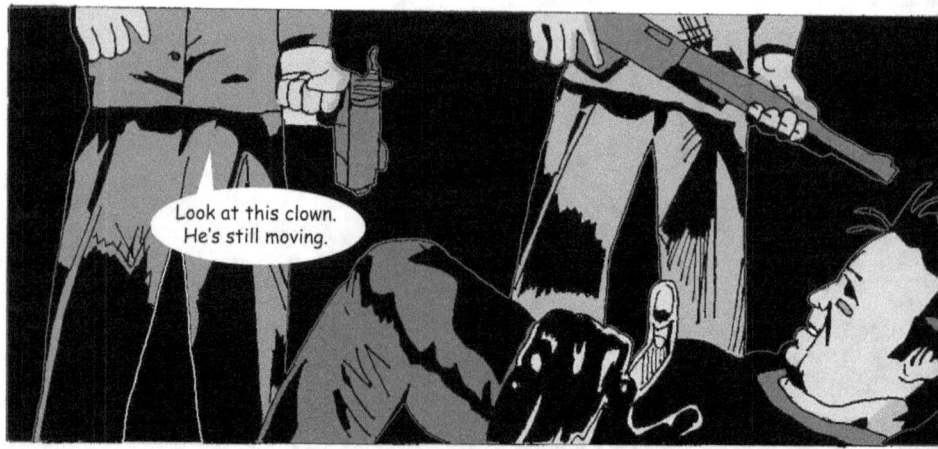

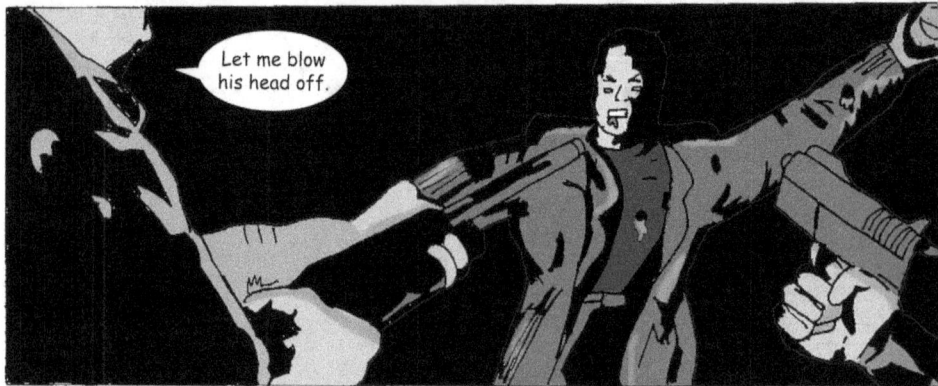

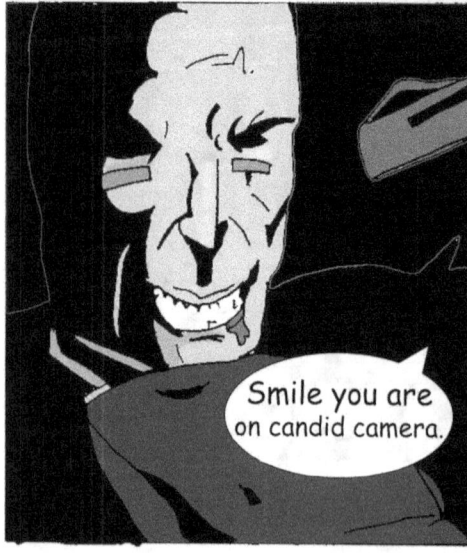

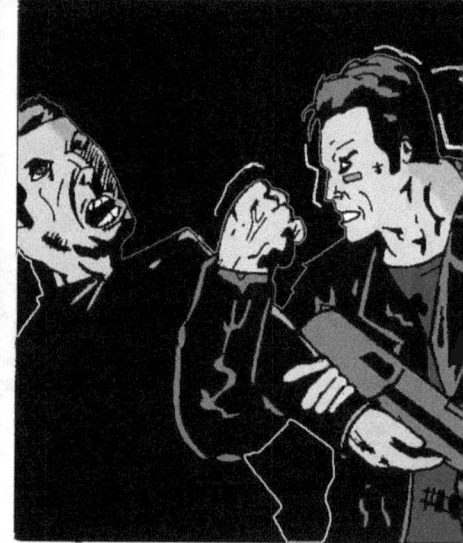

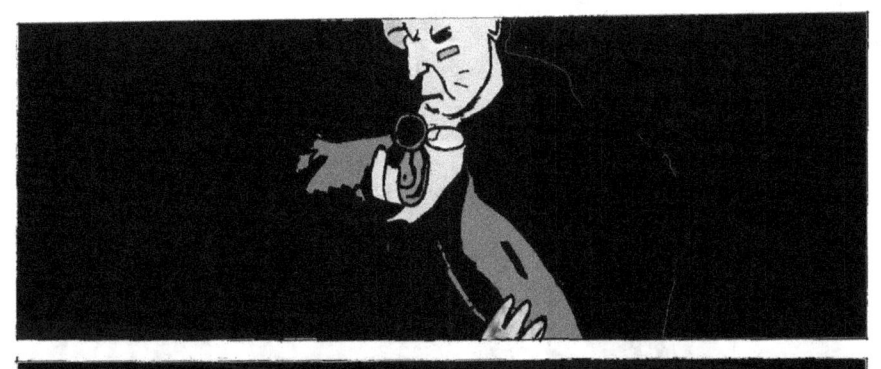

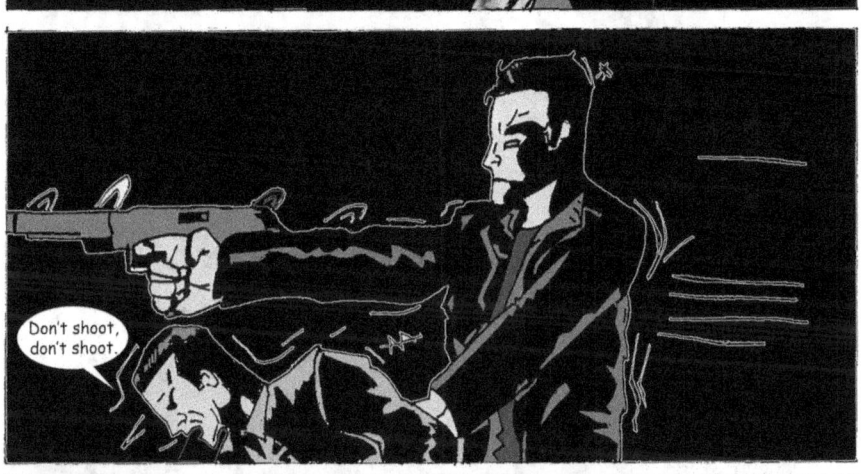

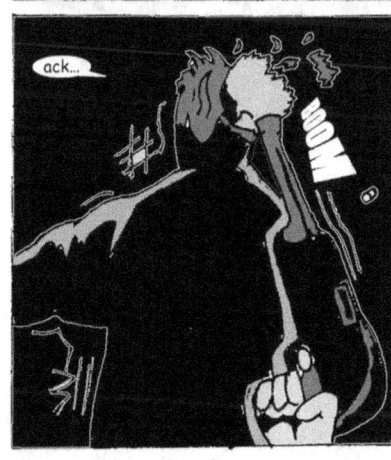

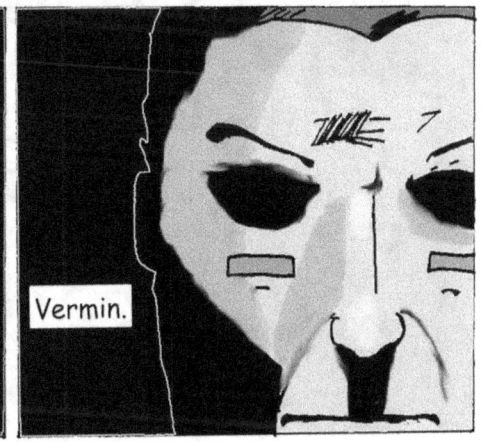

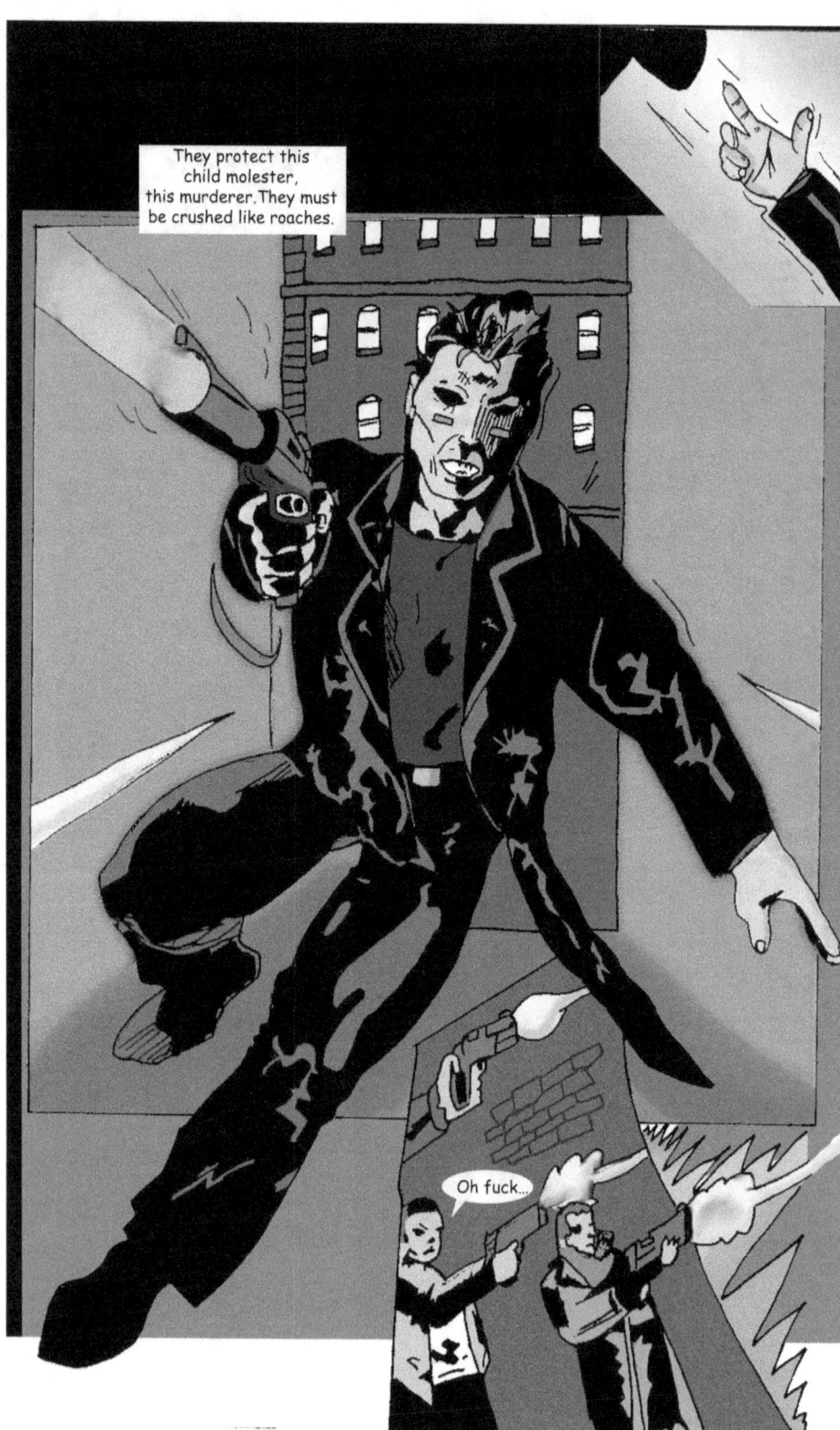

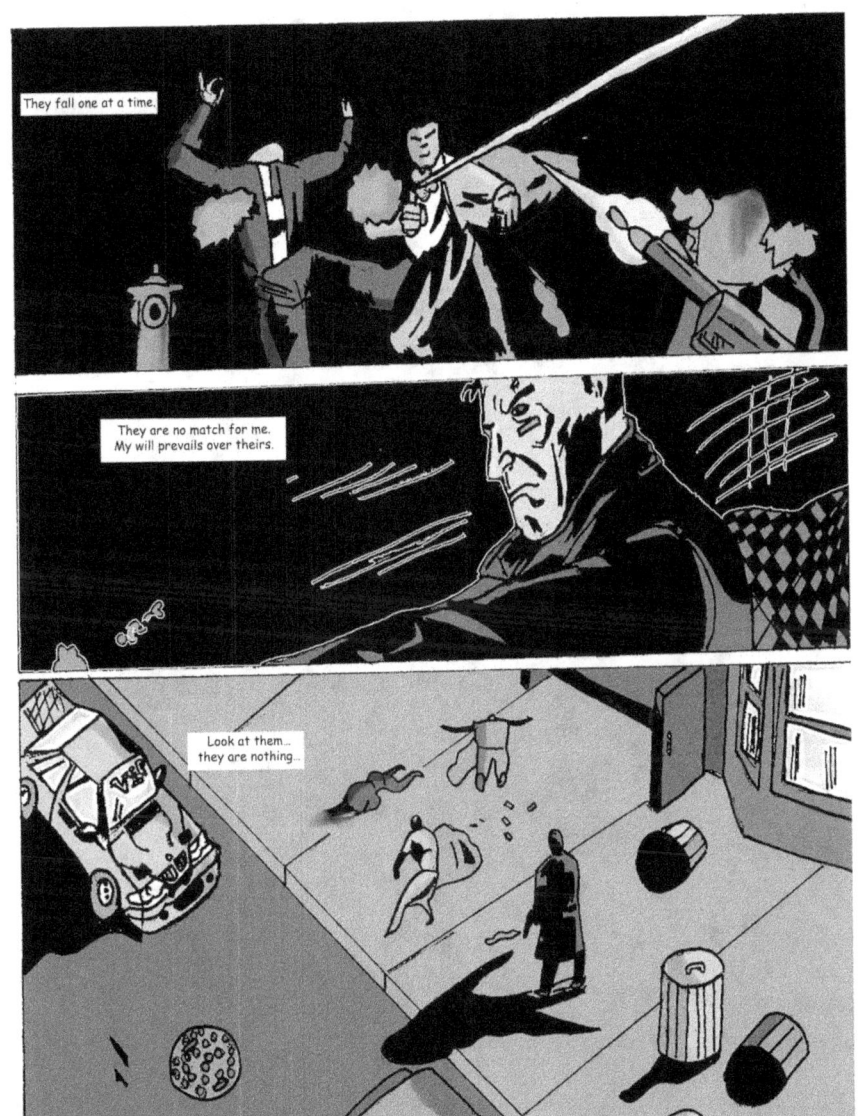

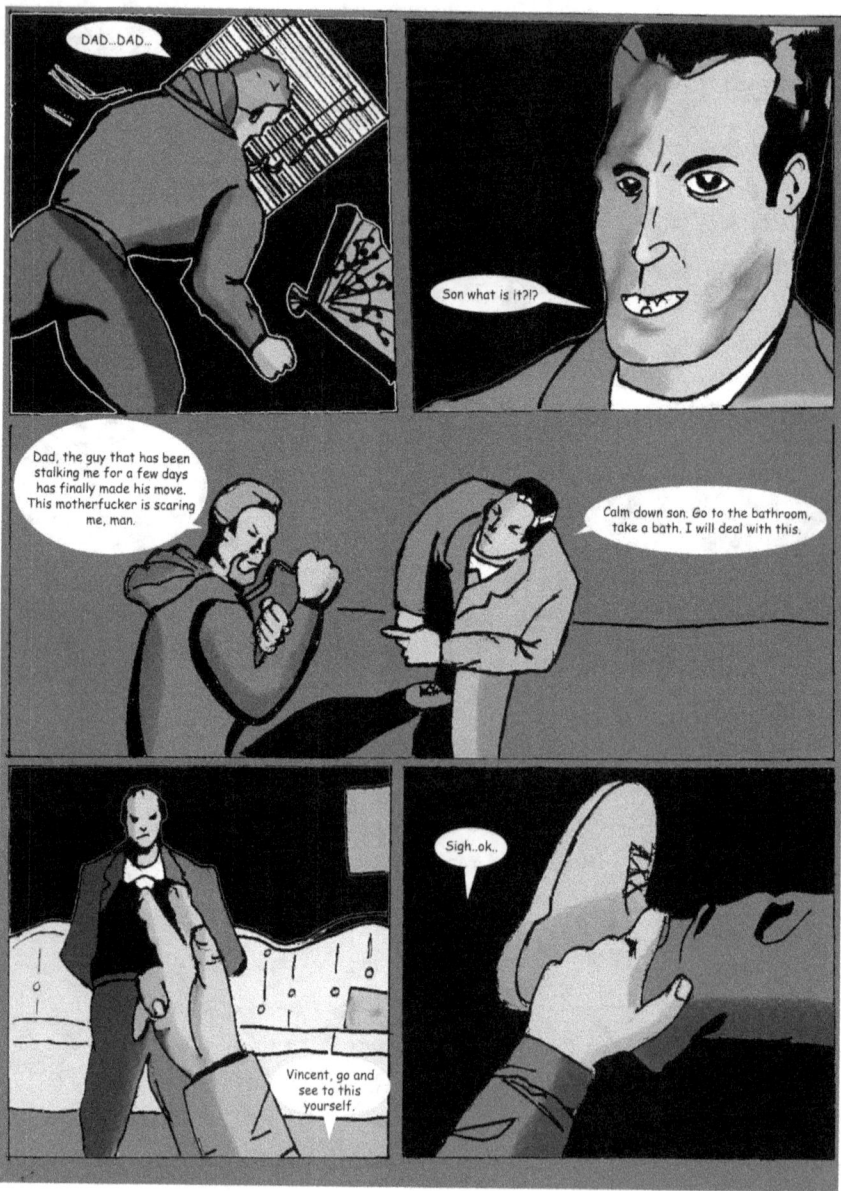

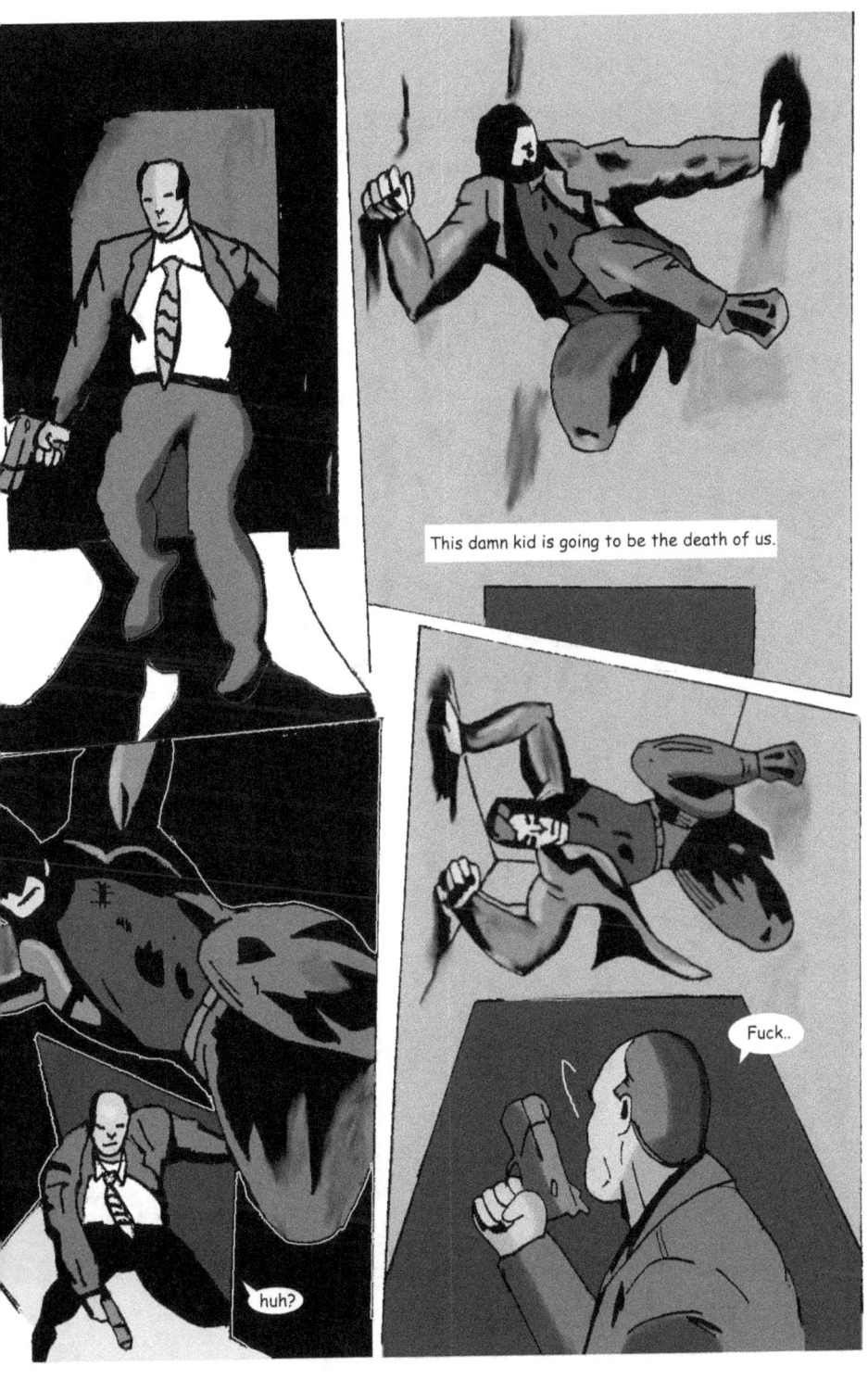

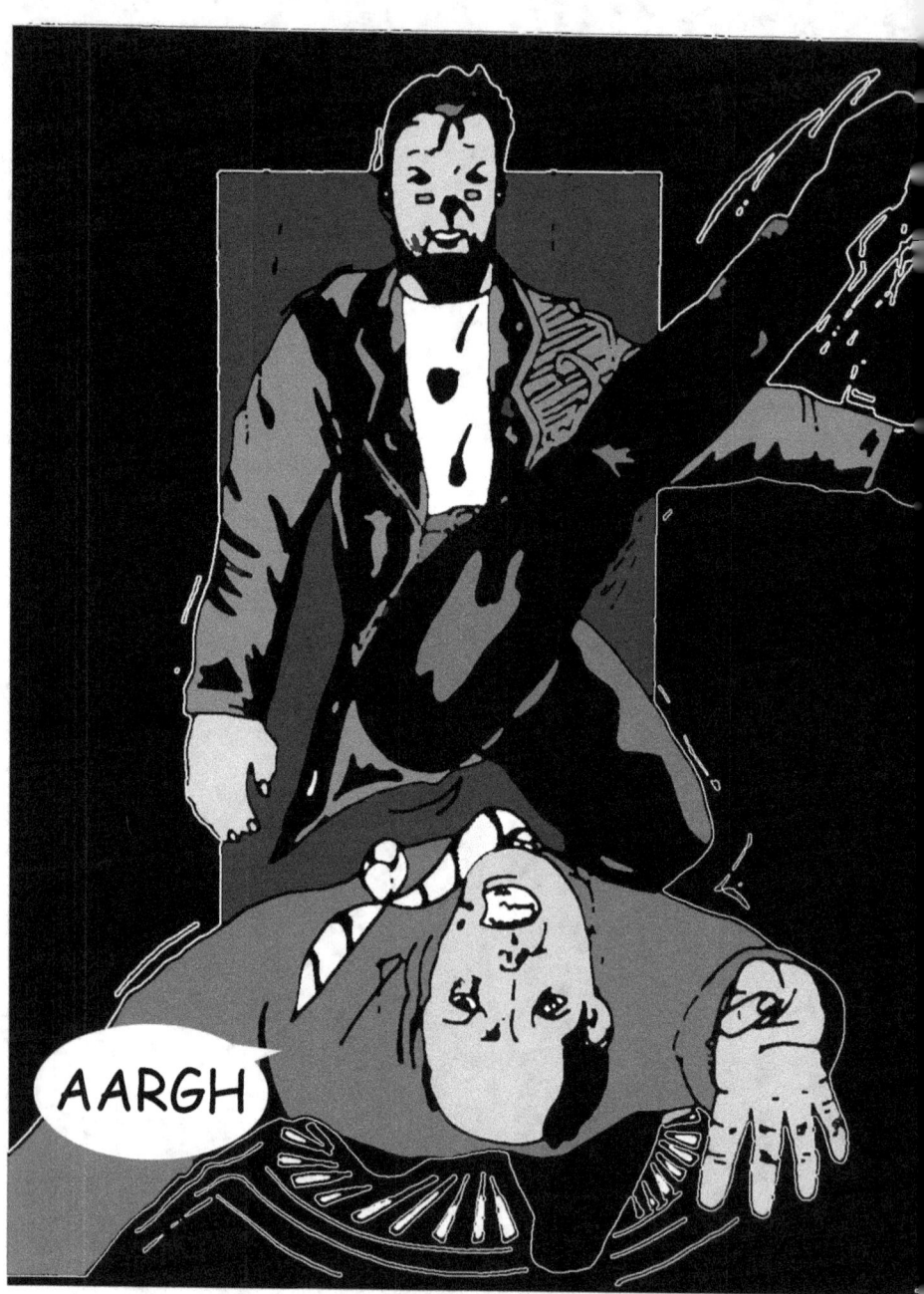

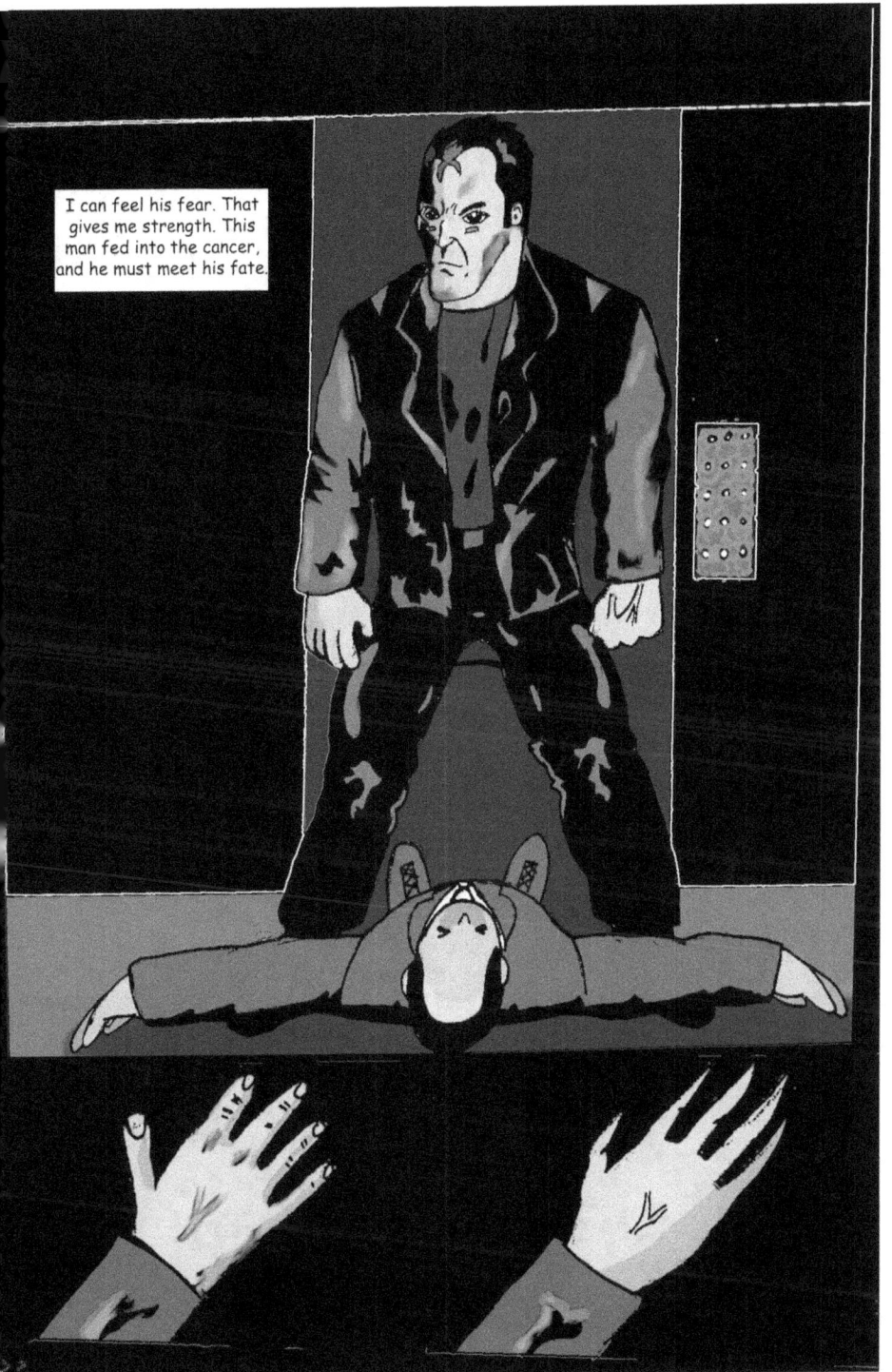

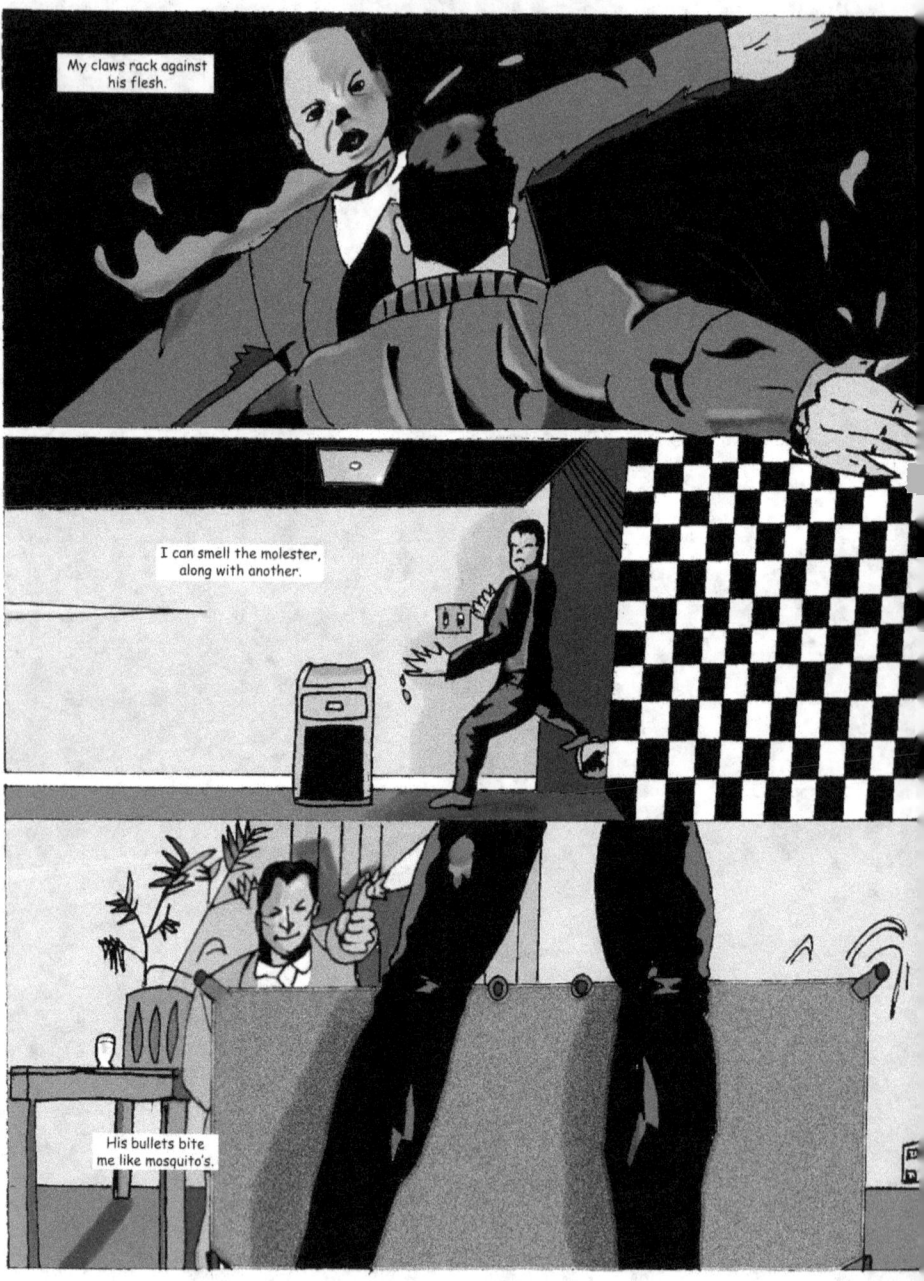

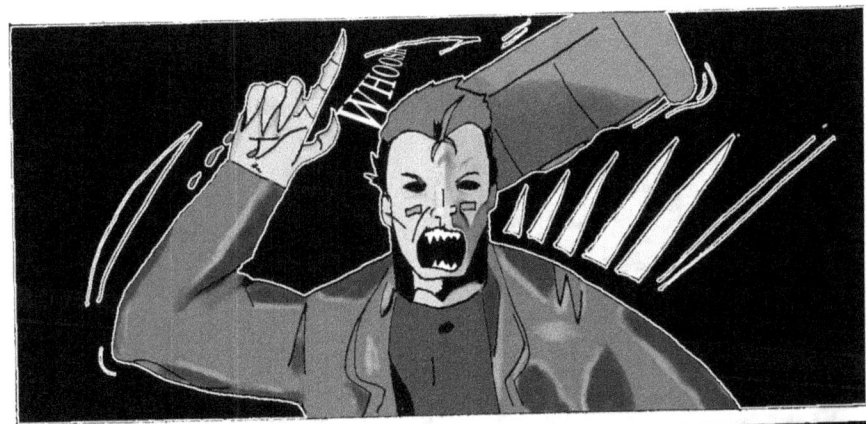

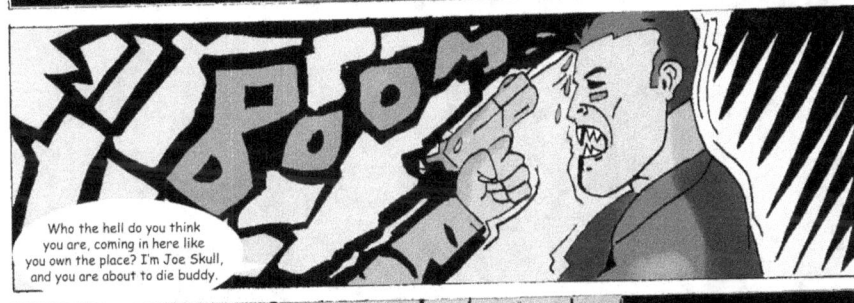

Who the hell do you think you are, coming in here like you own the place? I'm Joe Skull, and you are about to die buddy.

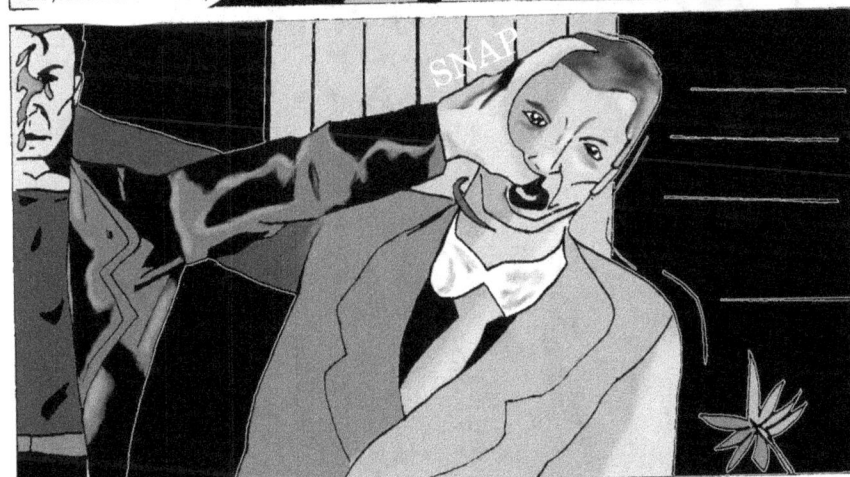

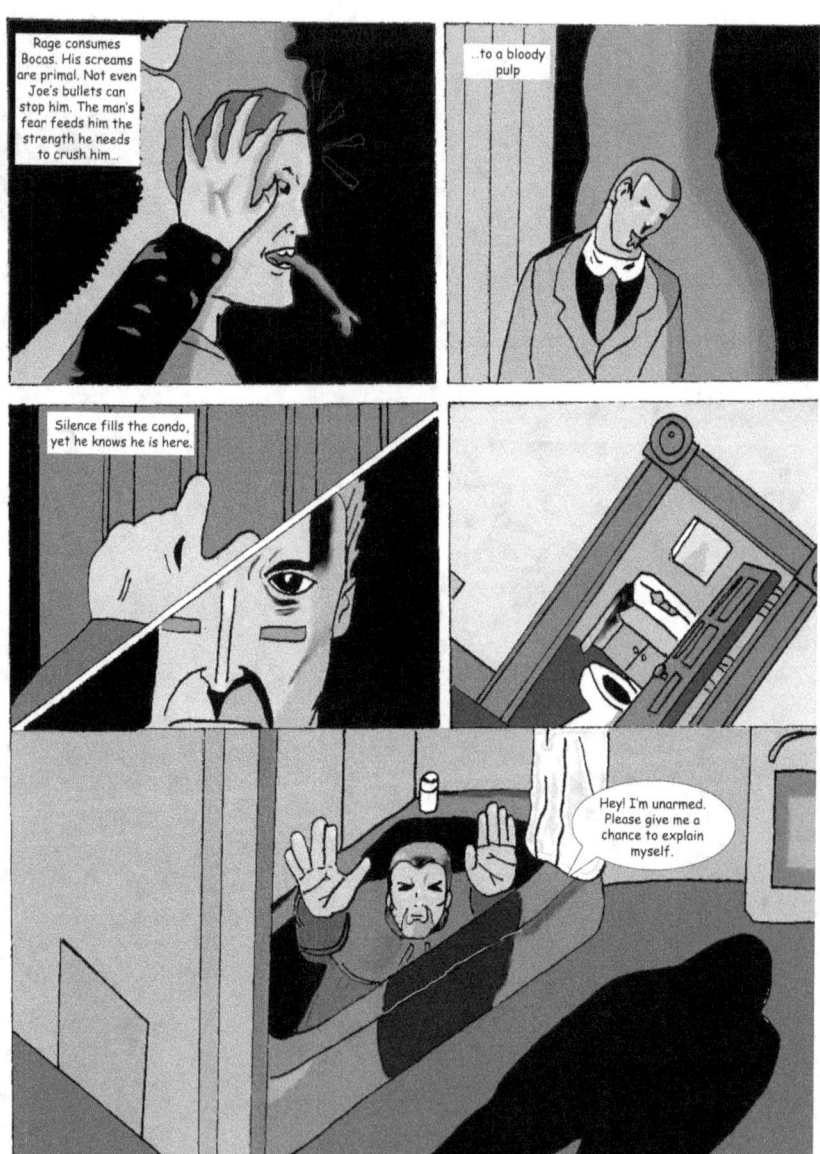

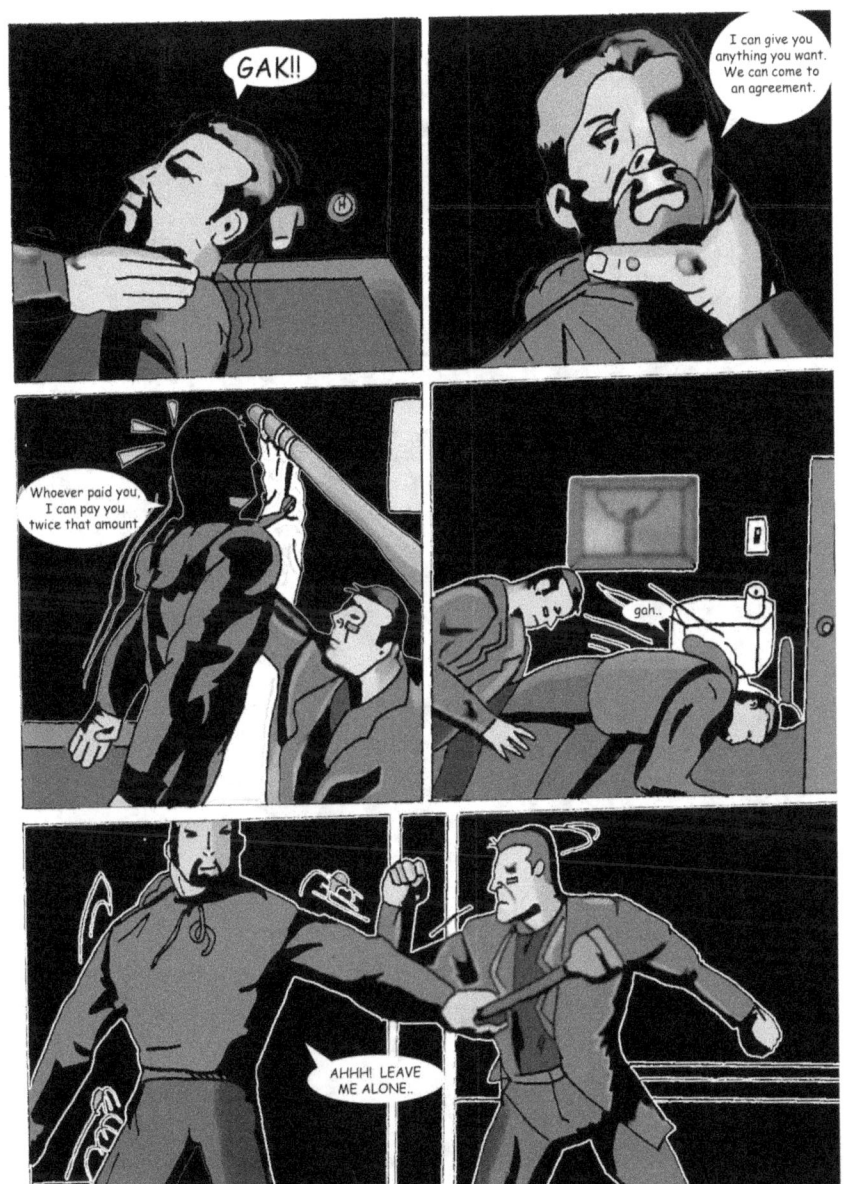

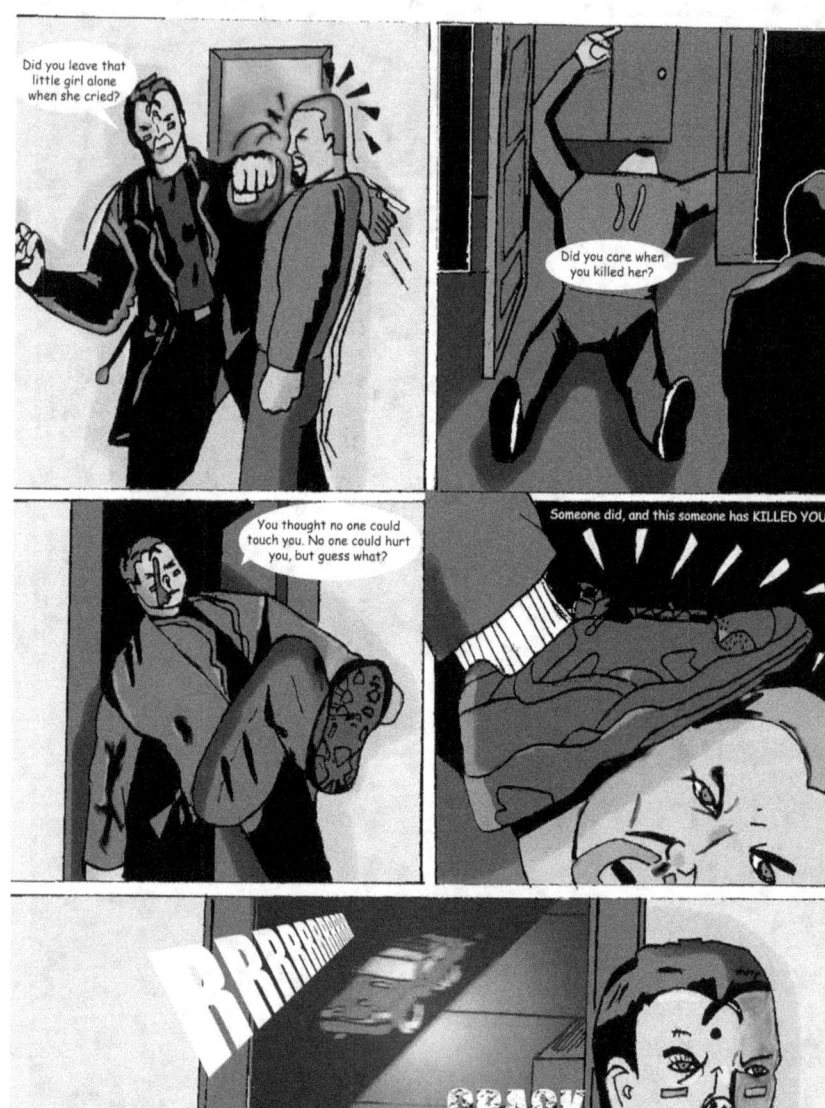

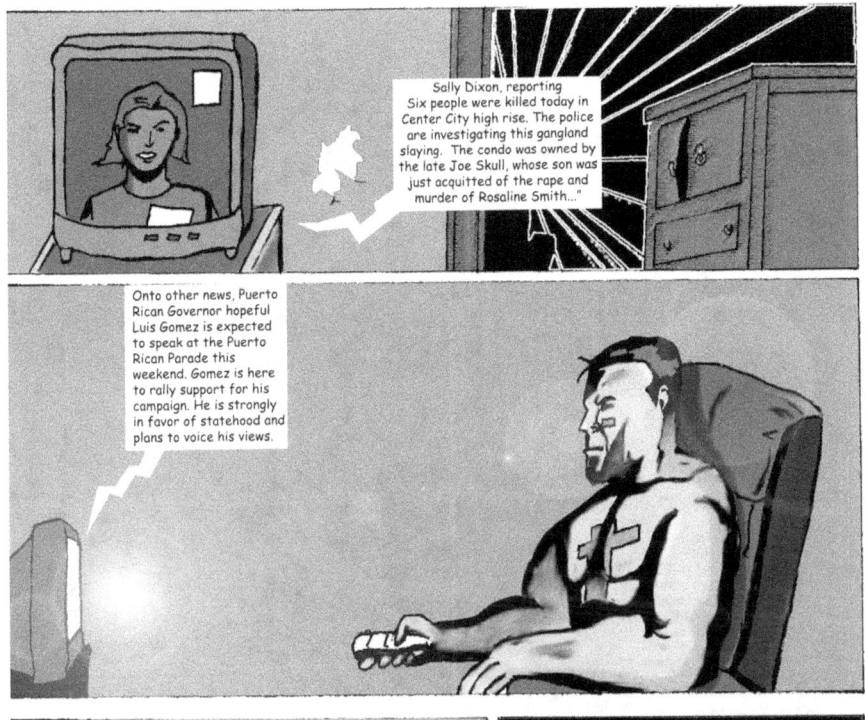

Sally Dixon, reporting Six people were killed today in Center City high rise. The police are investigating this gangland slaying. The condo was owned by the late Joe Skull, whose son was just acquitted of the rape and murder of Rosaline Smith..."

Onto other news, Puerto Rican Governor hopeful Luis Gomez is expected to speak at the Puerto Rican Parade this weekend. Gomez is here to rally support for his campaign. He is strongly in favor of statehood and plans to voice his views.

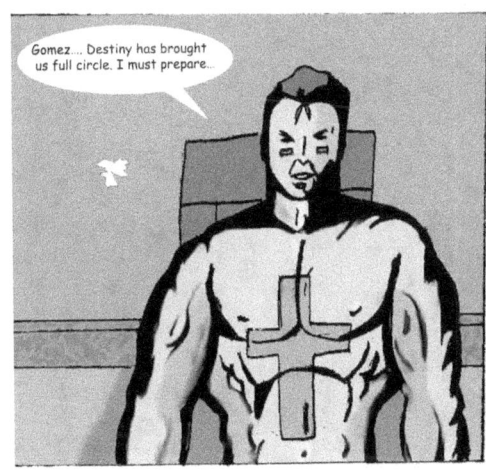

Gomez.... Destiny has brought us full circle. I must prepare...

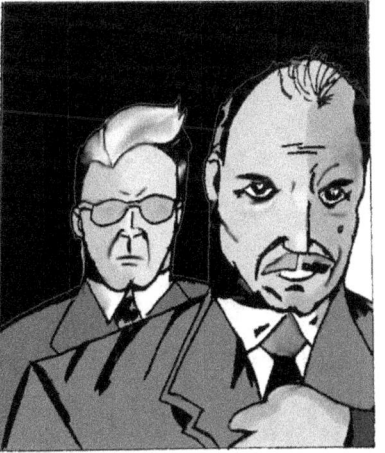

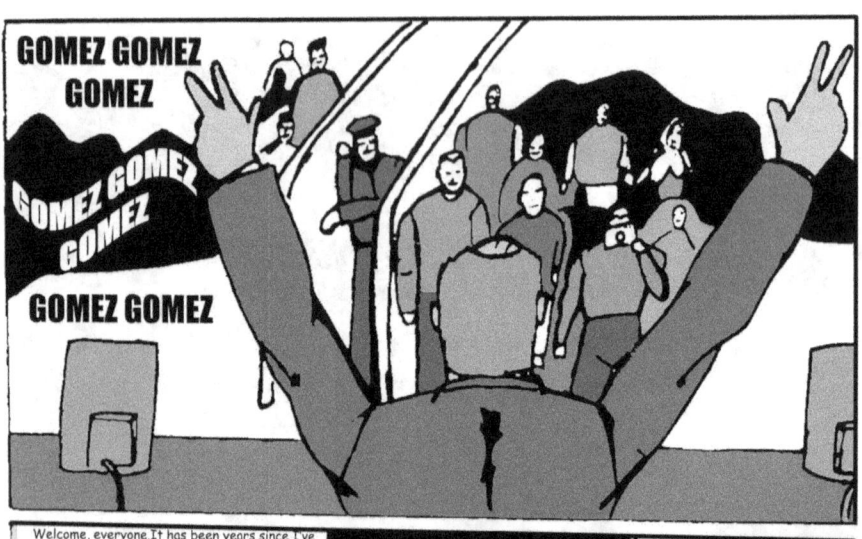

Welcome, everyone. It has been years since I've last come to Philadelphia. Some may wonder why I came. I came because my fellow people are here. I had a vision in which all of you spoke to me. I had to rally you, I had to preach to my fellow people, and tell you that our precious country has remained the same, but we have grown. Some may question why I speak to people about Puerto Rican heritage in the states. A Puerto Rican is a Puerto Rican.

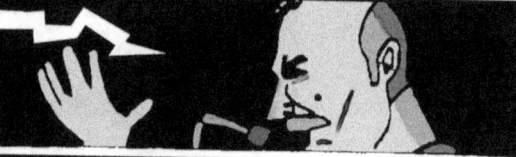

You can change our location, but you can't change our spirit. When we leave that island, we bring our culture...

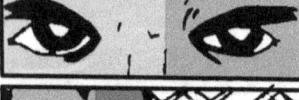

...we bring our customs. We become ambassadors of our island. We become representatives of our people!!

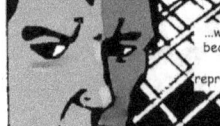

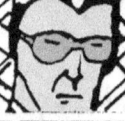

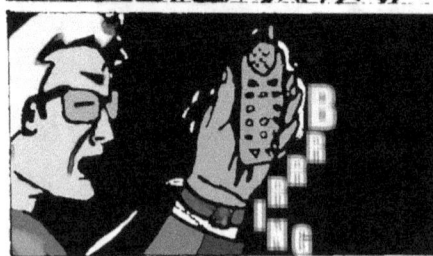

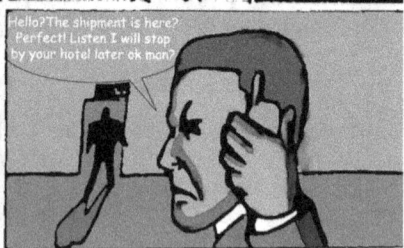

Hello? The shipment is here? Perfect! Listen I will stop by your hotel later ok man?

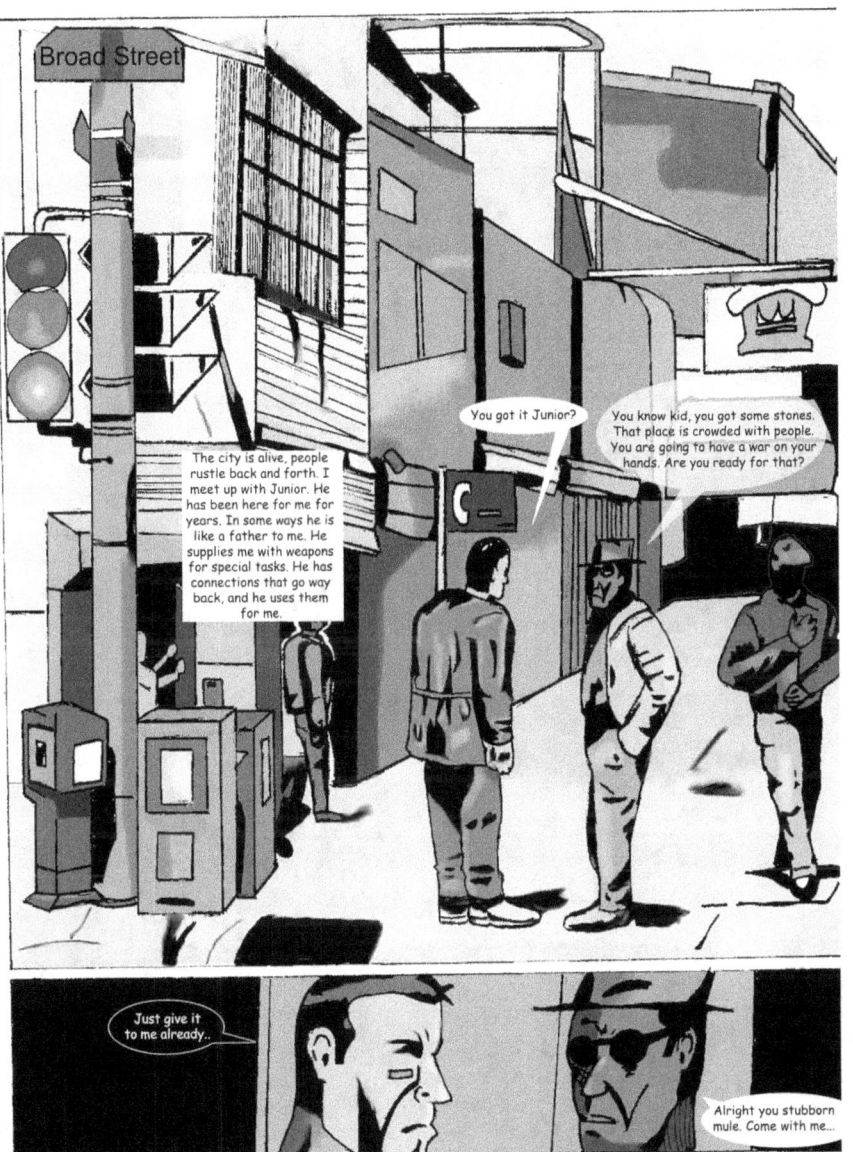

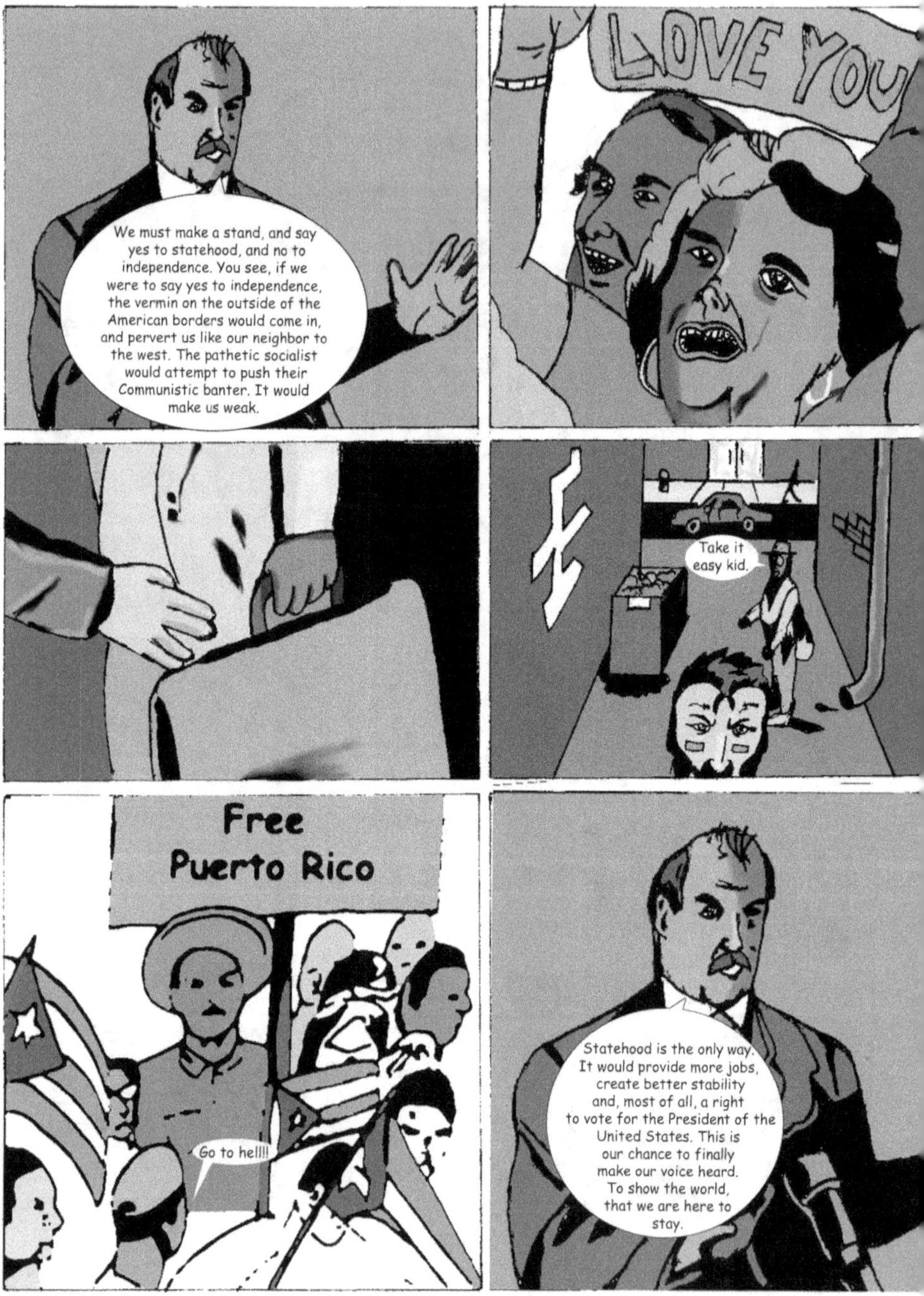

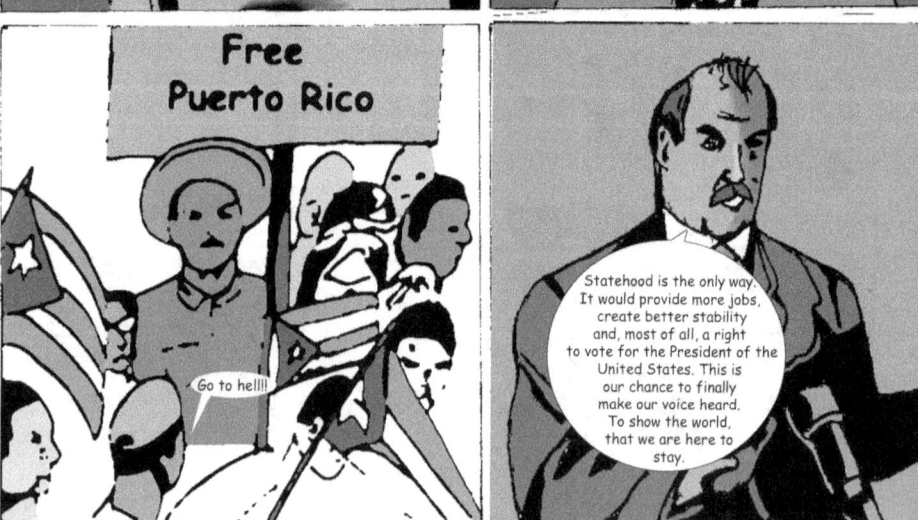

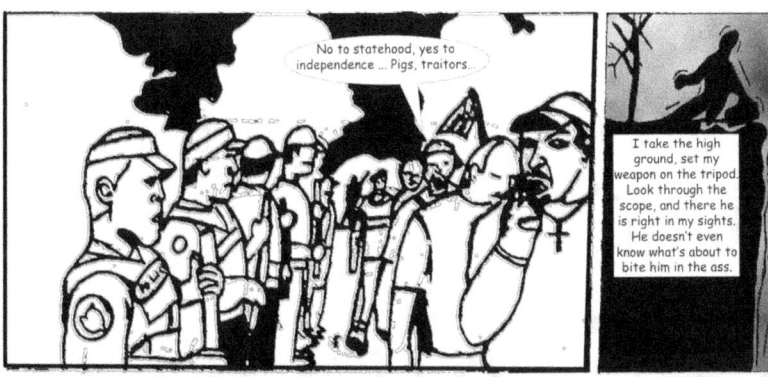

No to statehood, yes to independence ... Pigs, traitors...

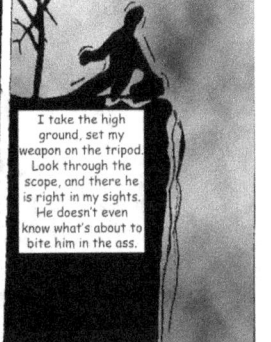

I take the high ground, set my weapon on the tripod. Look through the scope, and there he is right in my sights. He doesn't even know what's about to bite him in the ass.

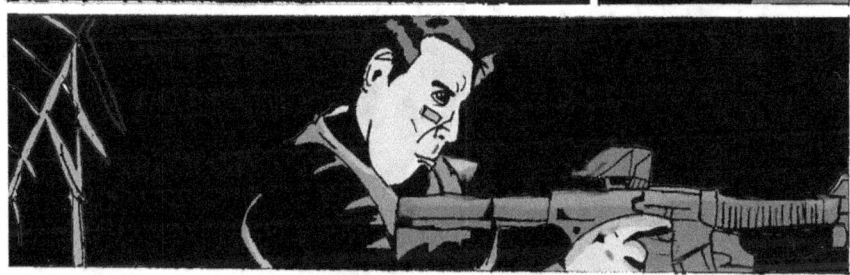

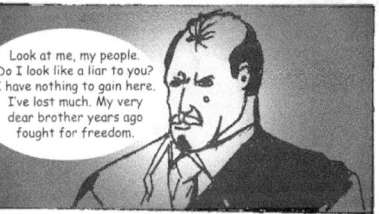

Look at me, my people. Do I look like a liar to you? I have nothing to gain here. I've lost much. My very dear brother years ago fought for freedom.

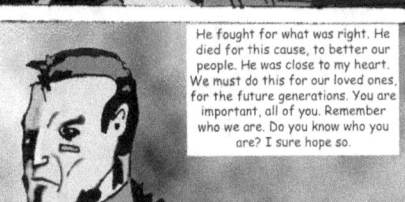

He fought for what was right. He died for this cause, to better our people. He was close to my heart. We must do this for our loved ones, for the future generations. You are important, all of you. Remember who we are. Do you know who you are? I sure hope so.

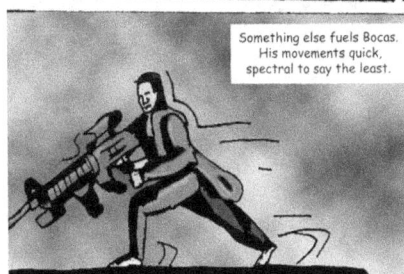

Something else fuels Bocas. His movements quick, spectral to say the least.

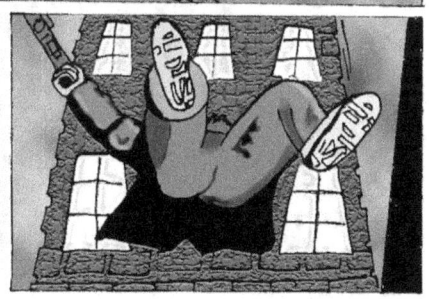

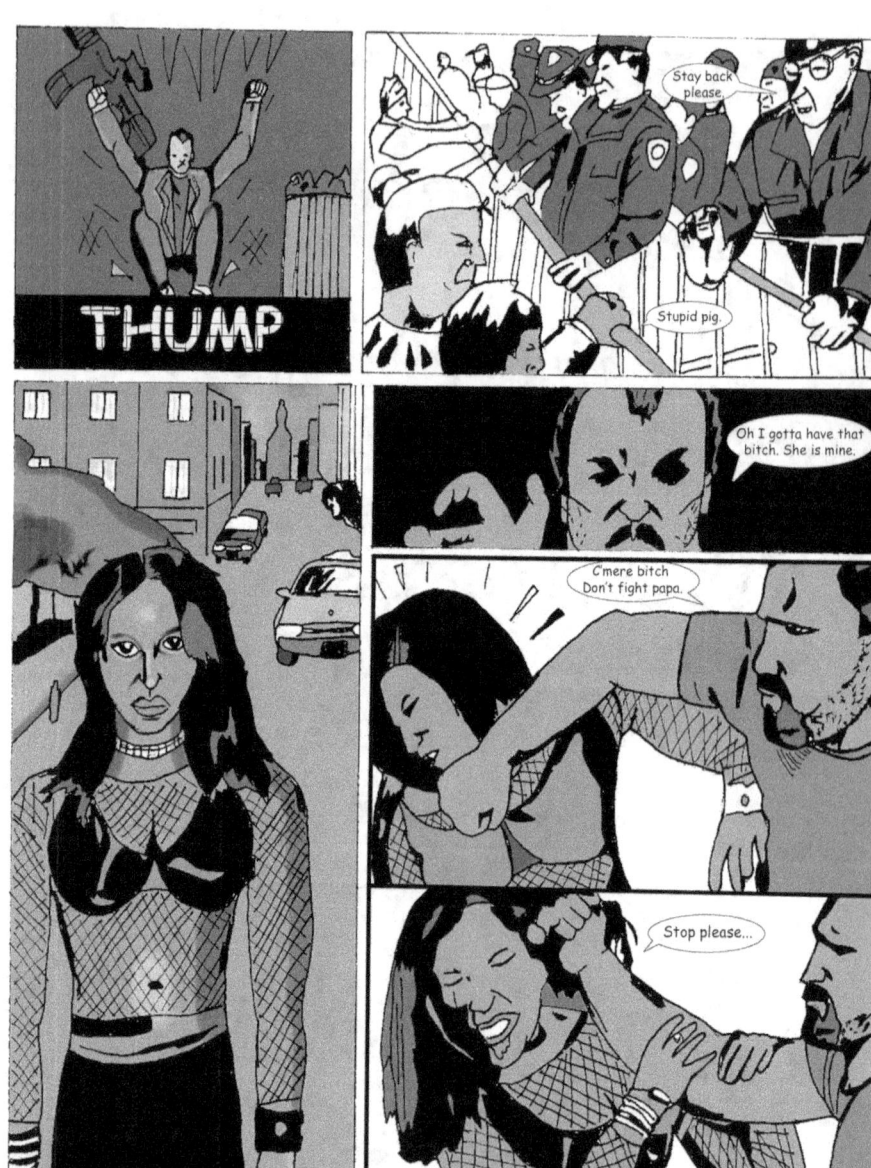

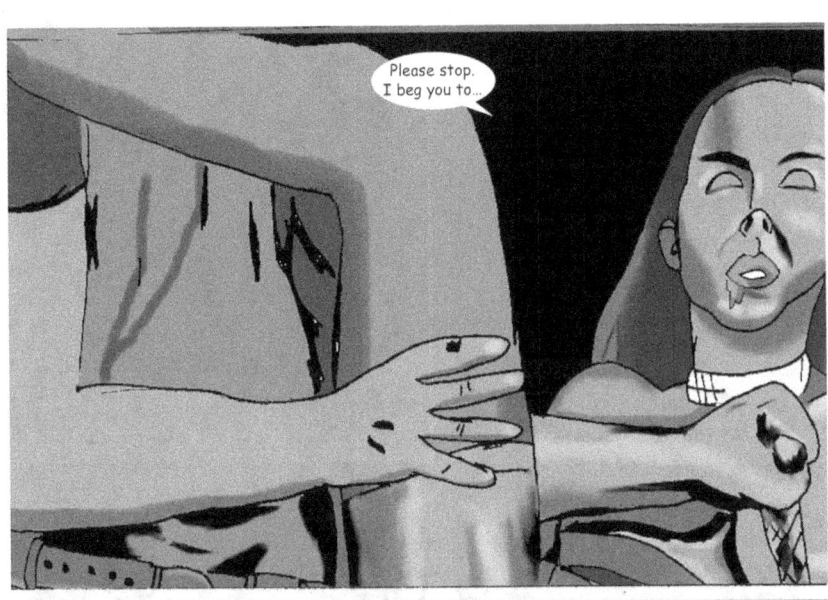

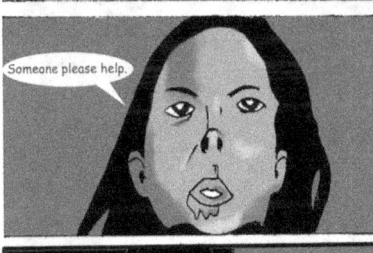

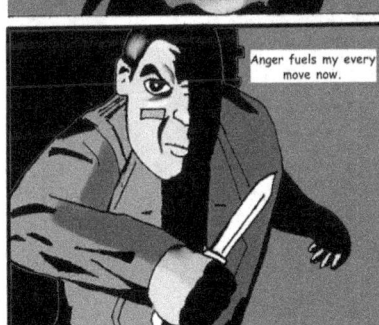

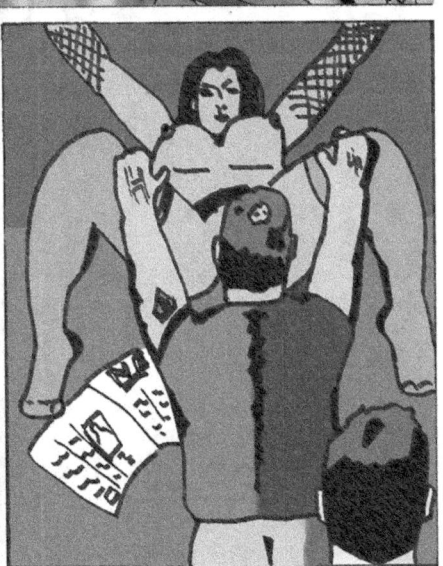

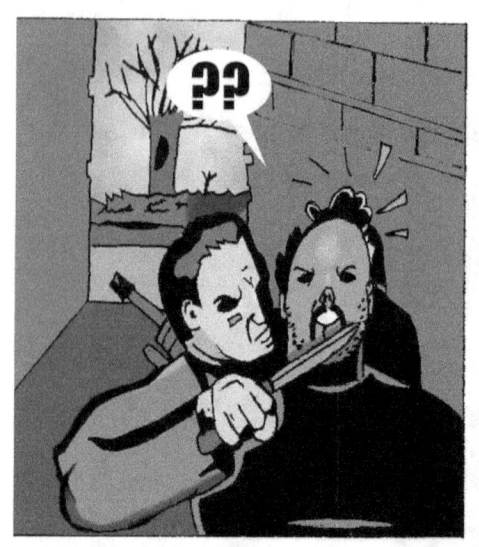
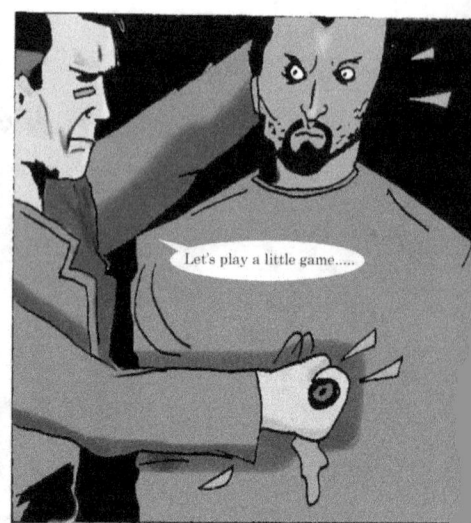
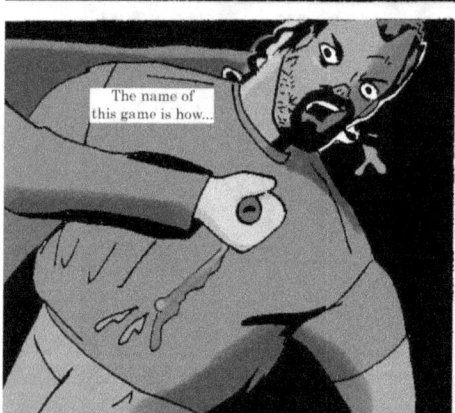
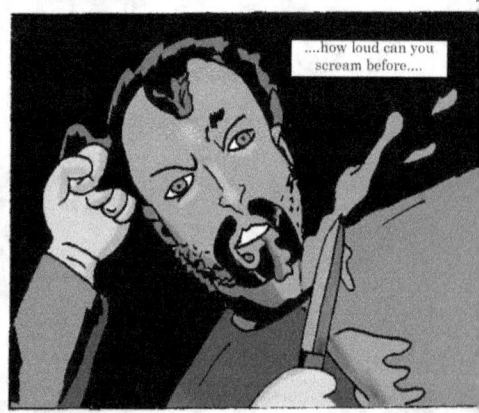
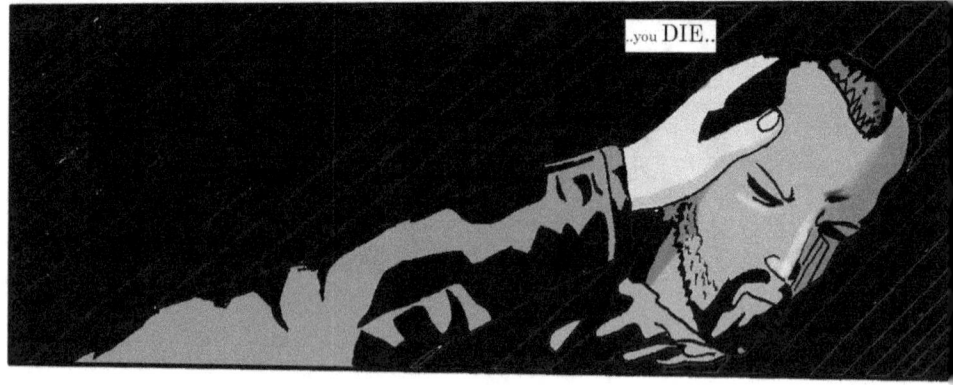

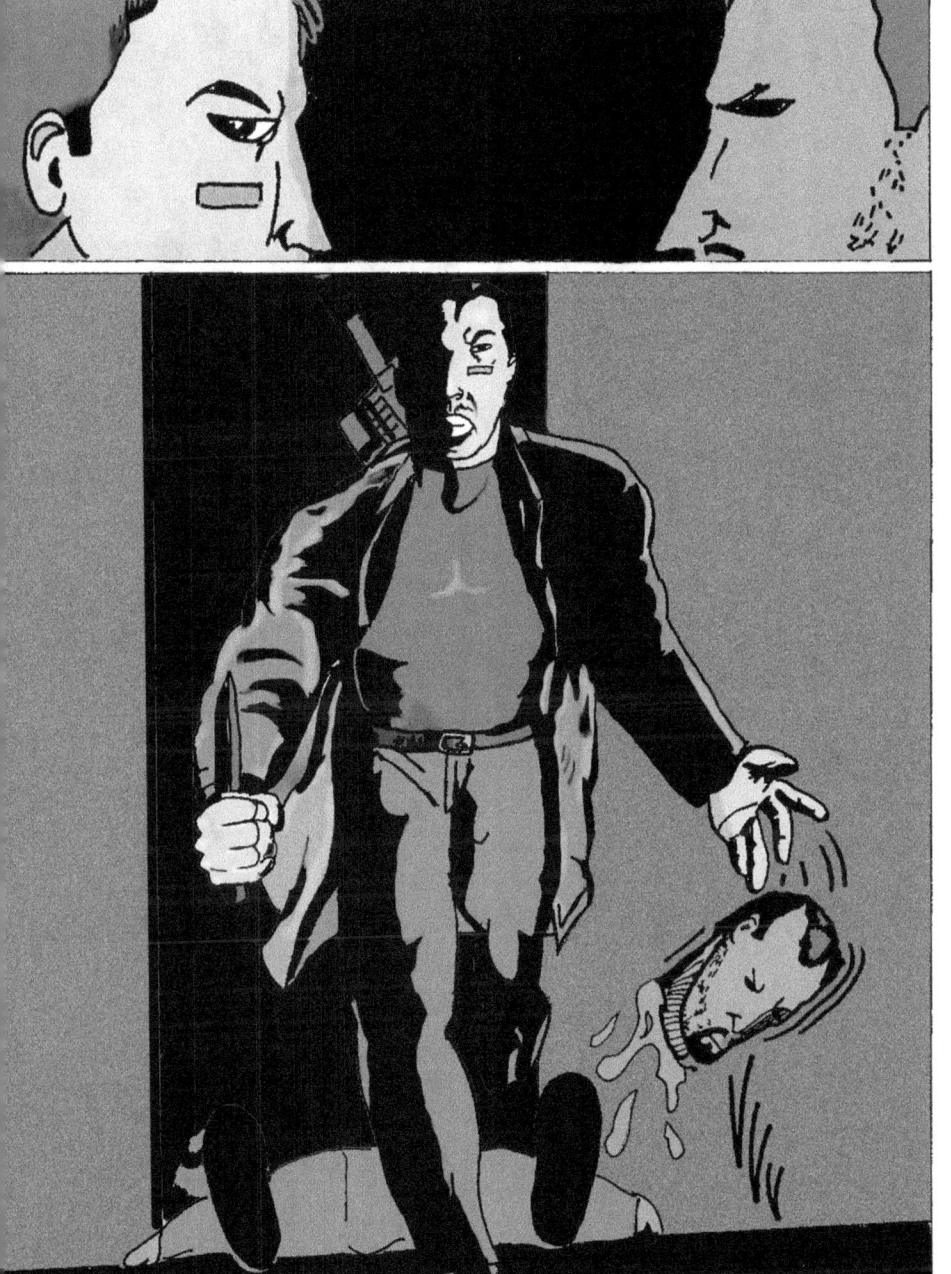

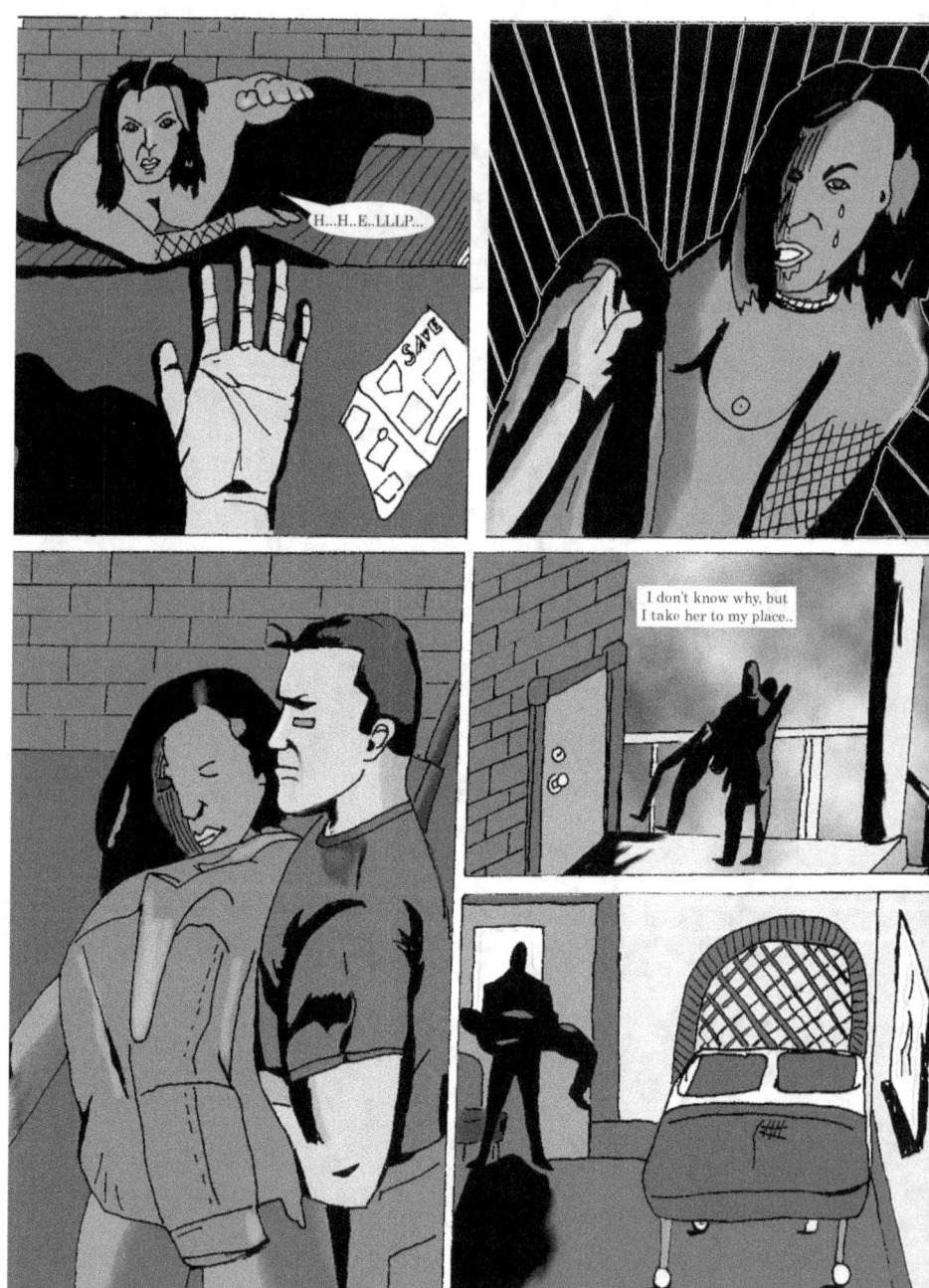

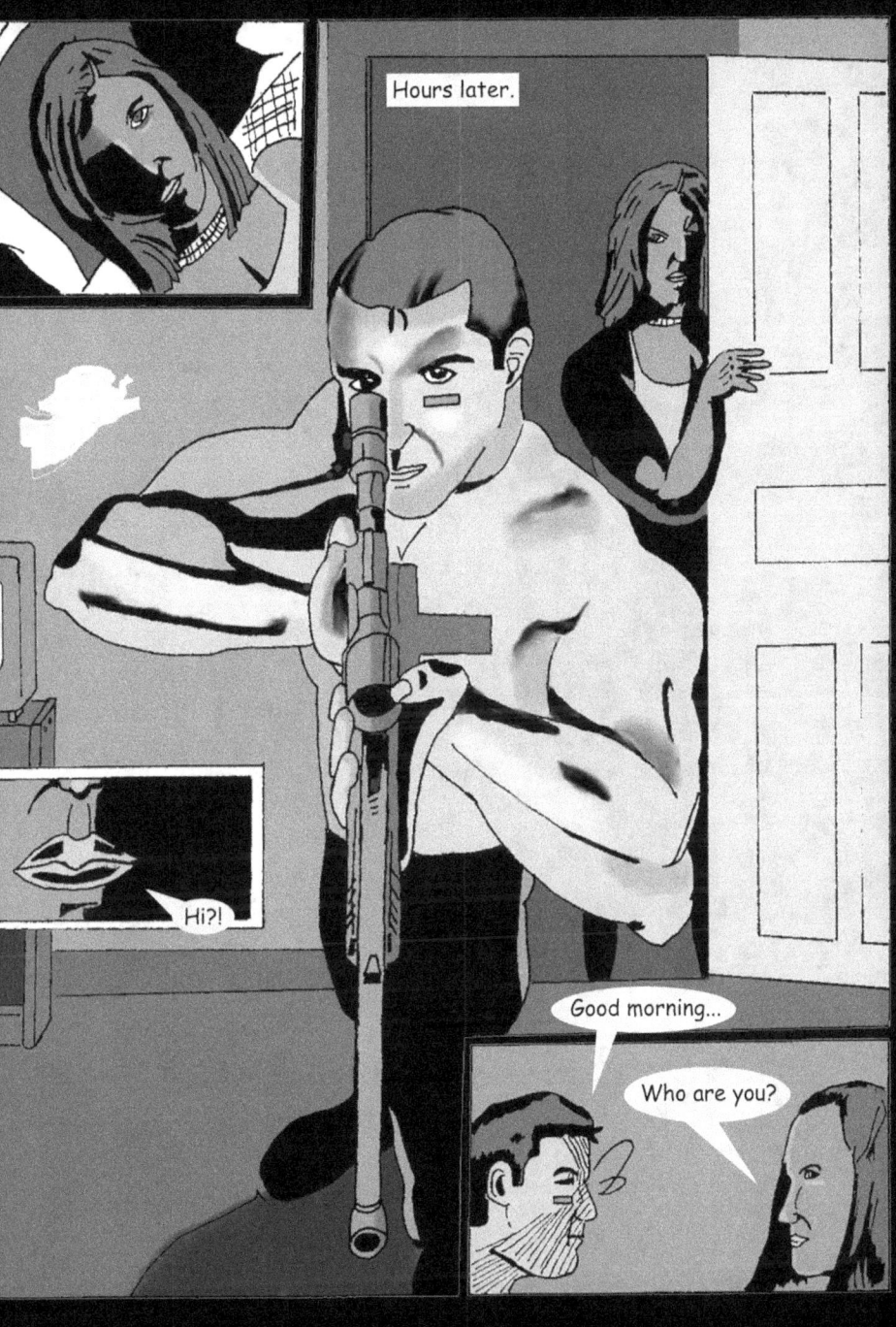

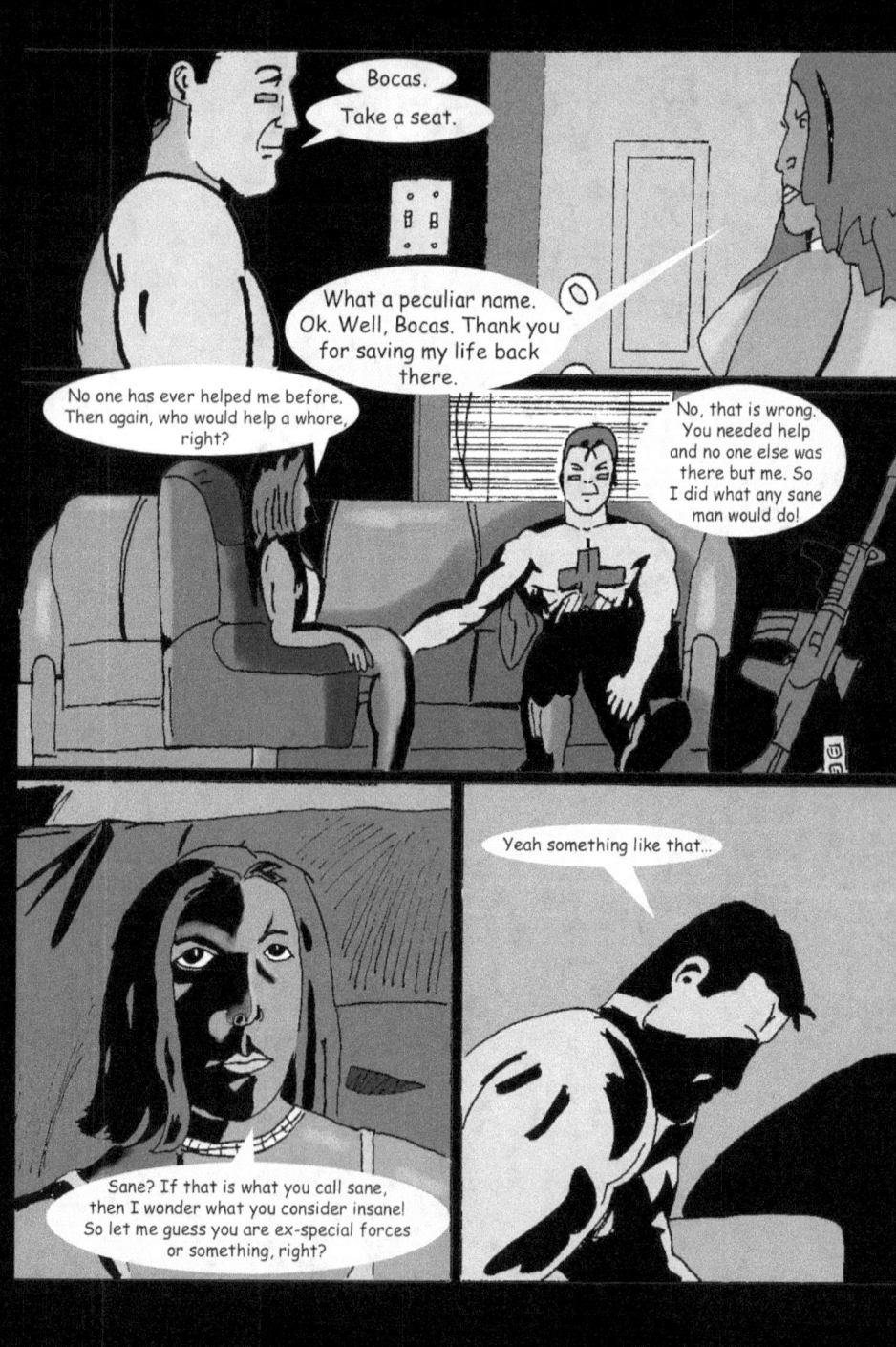

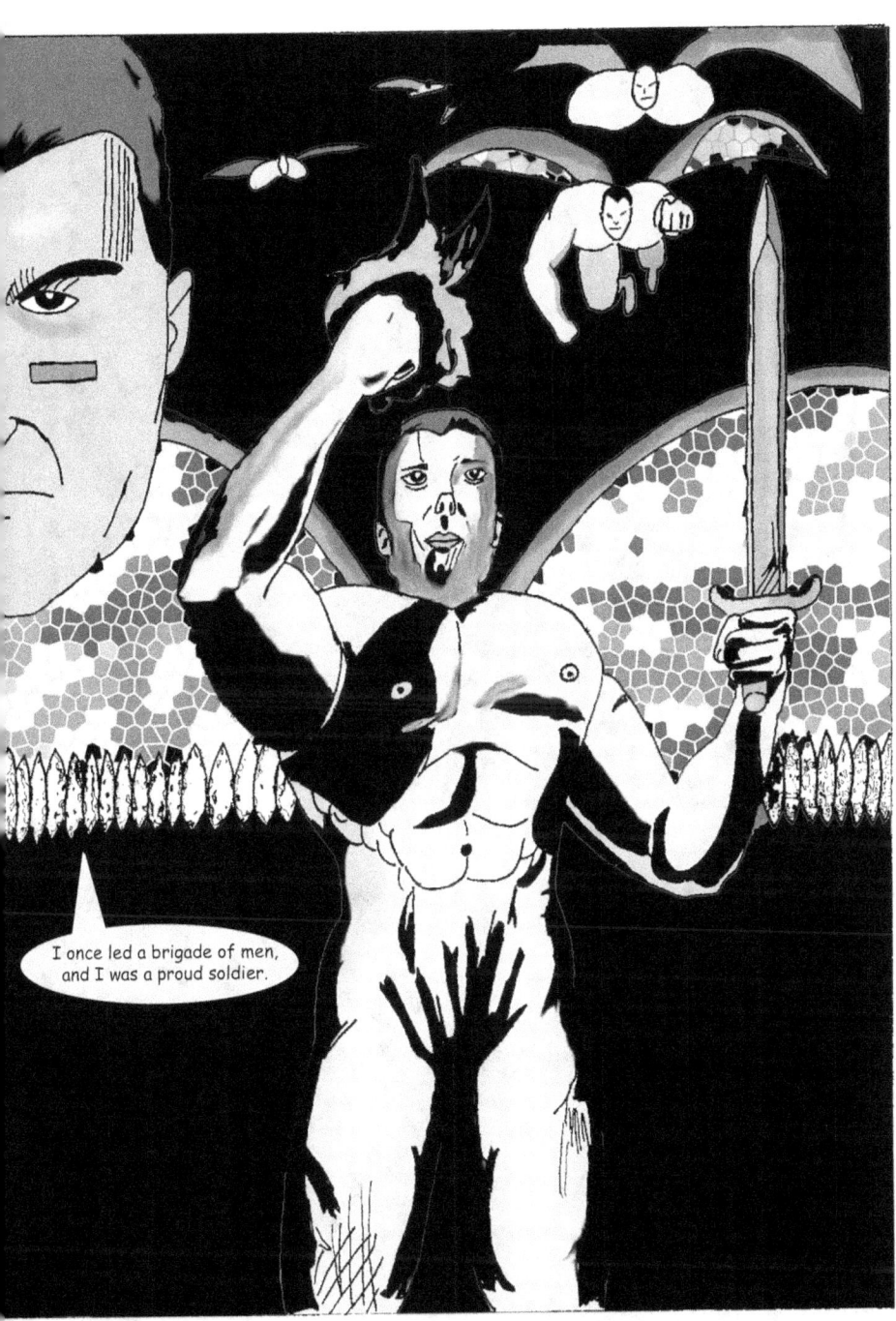

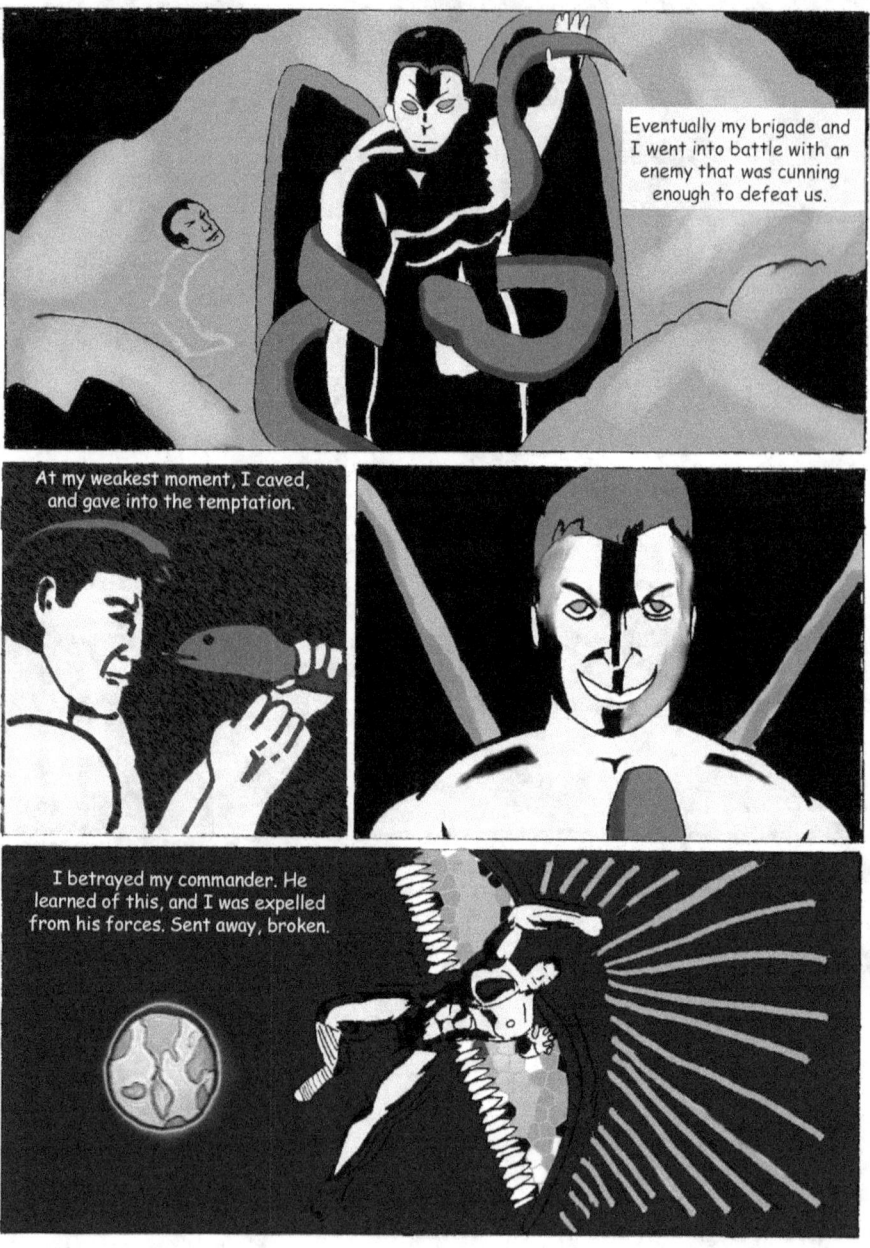

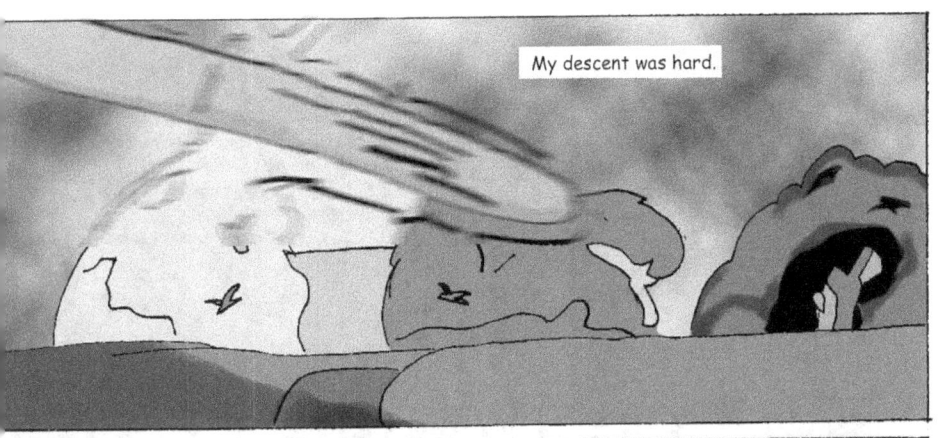

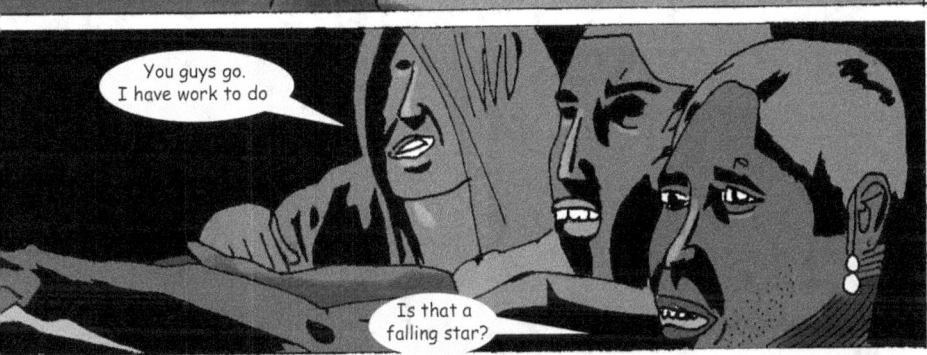

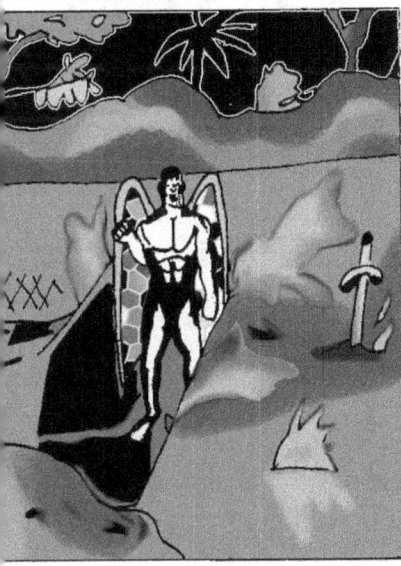

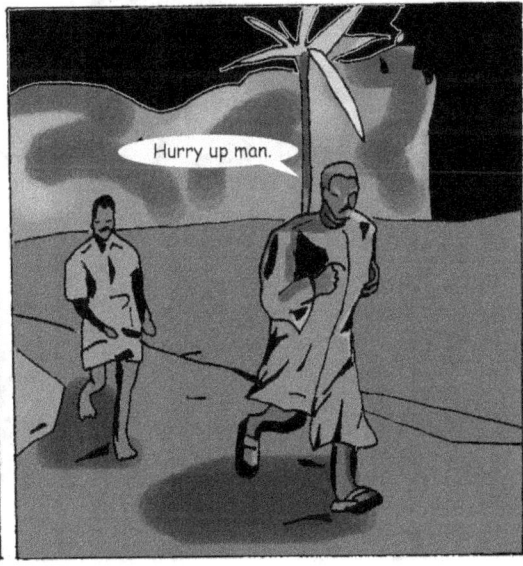

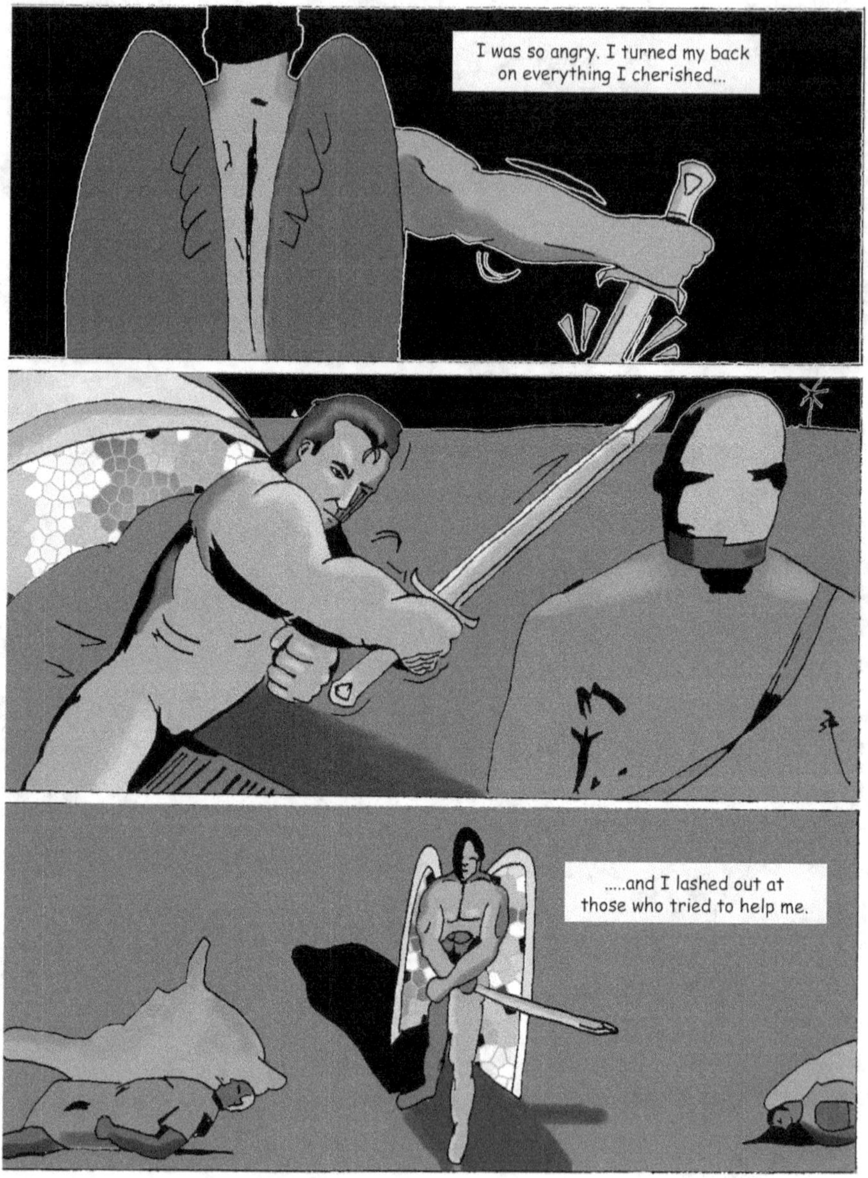

I was so angry. I turned my back on everything I cherished...

.....and I lashed out at those who tried to help me.

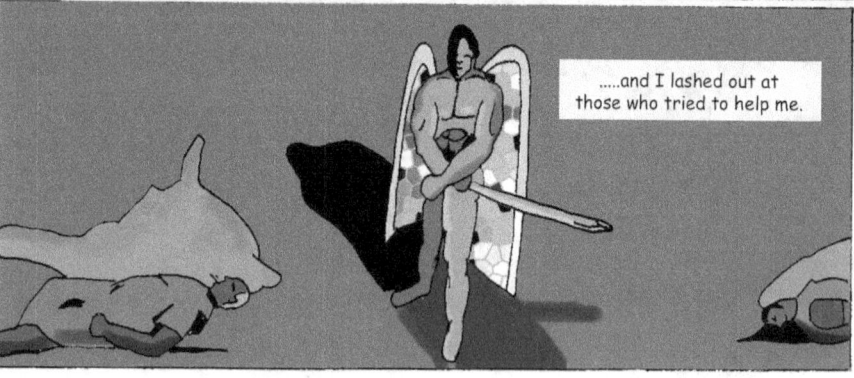

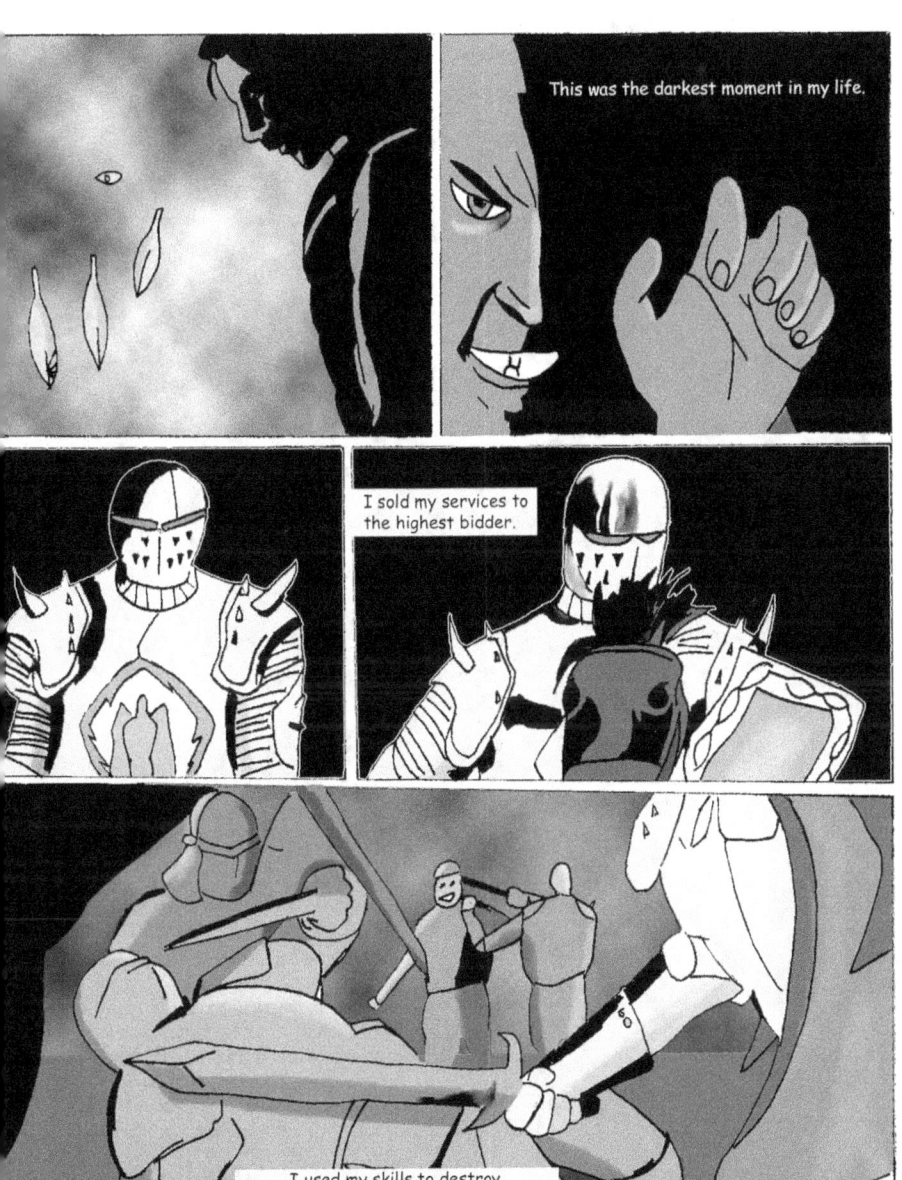

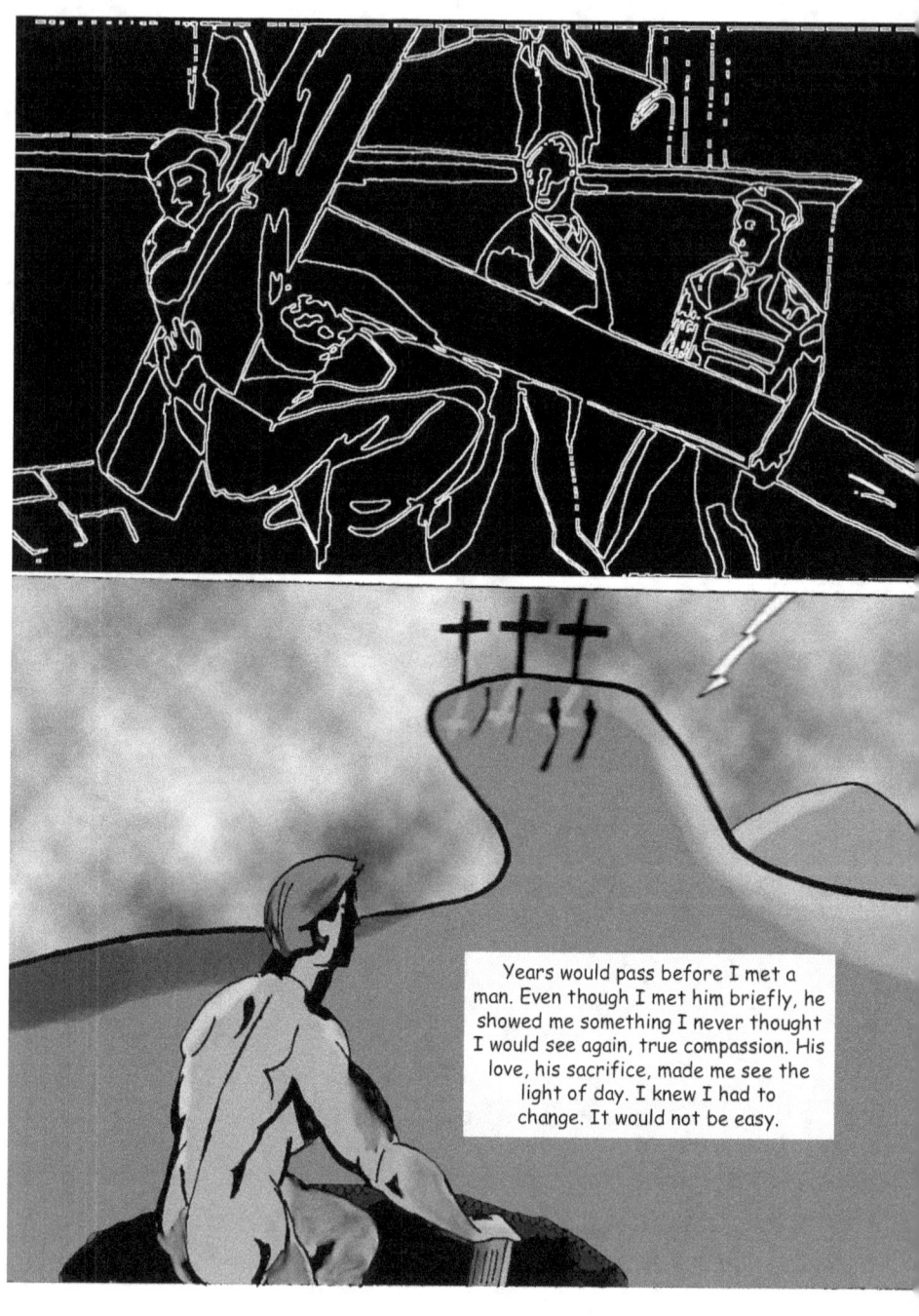

Years would pass before I met a man. Even though I met him briefly, he showed me something I never thought I would see again, true compassion. His love, his sacrifice, made me see the light of day. I knew I had to change. It would not be easy.

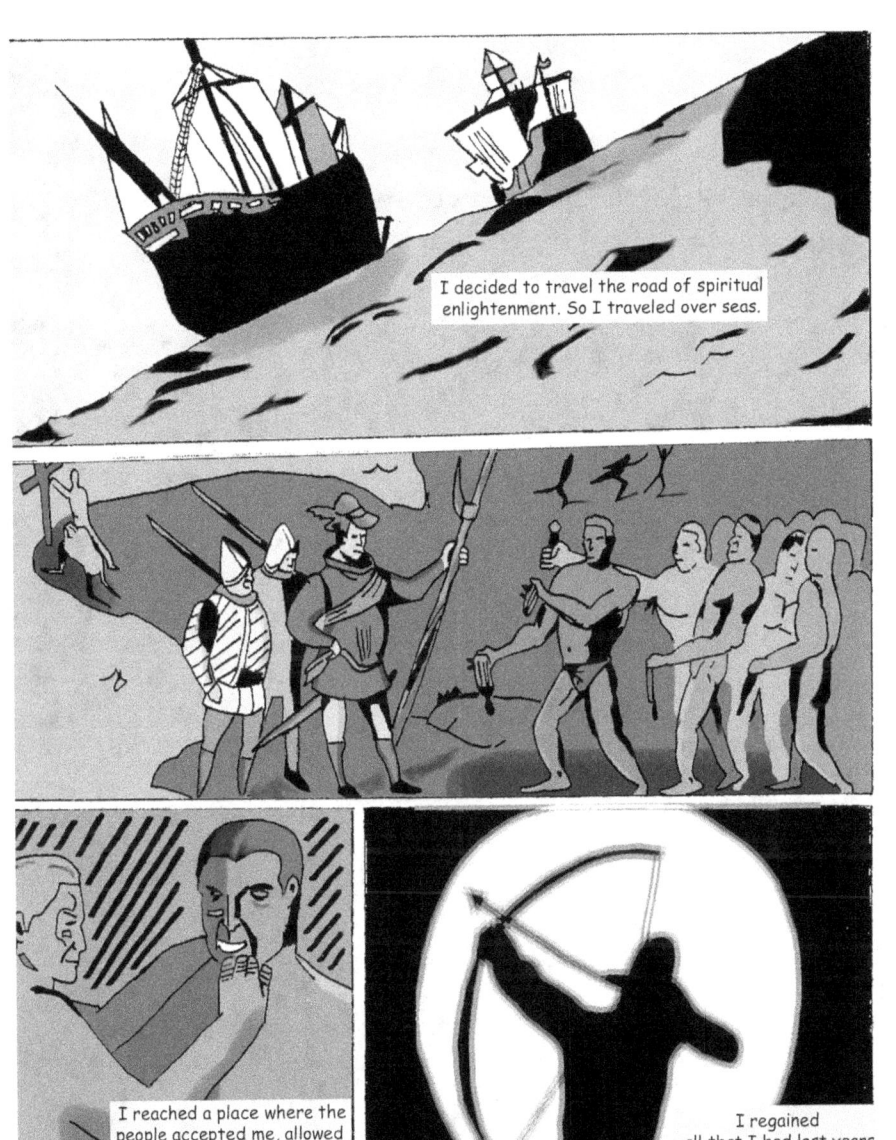

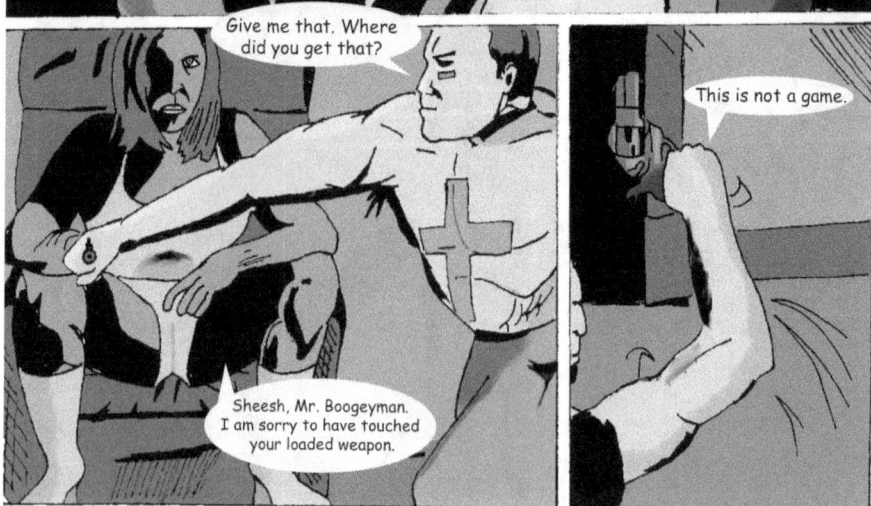

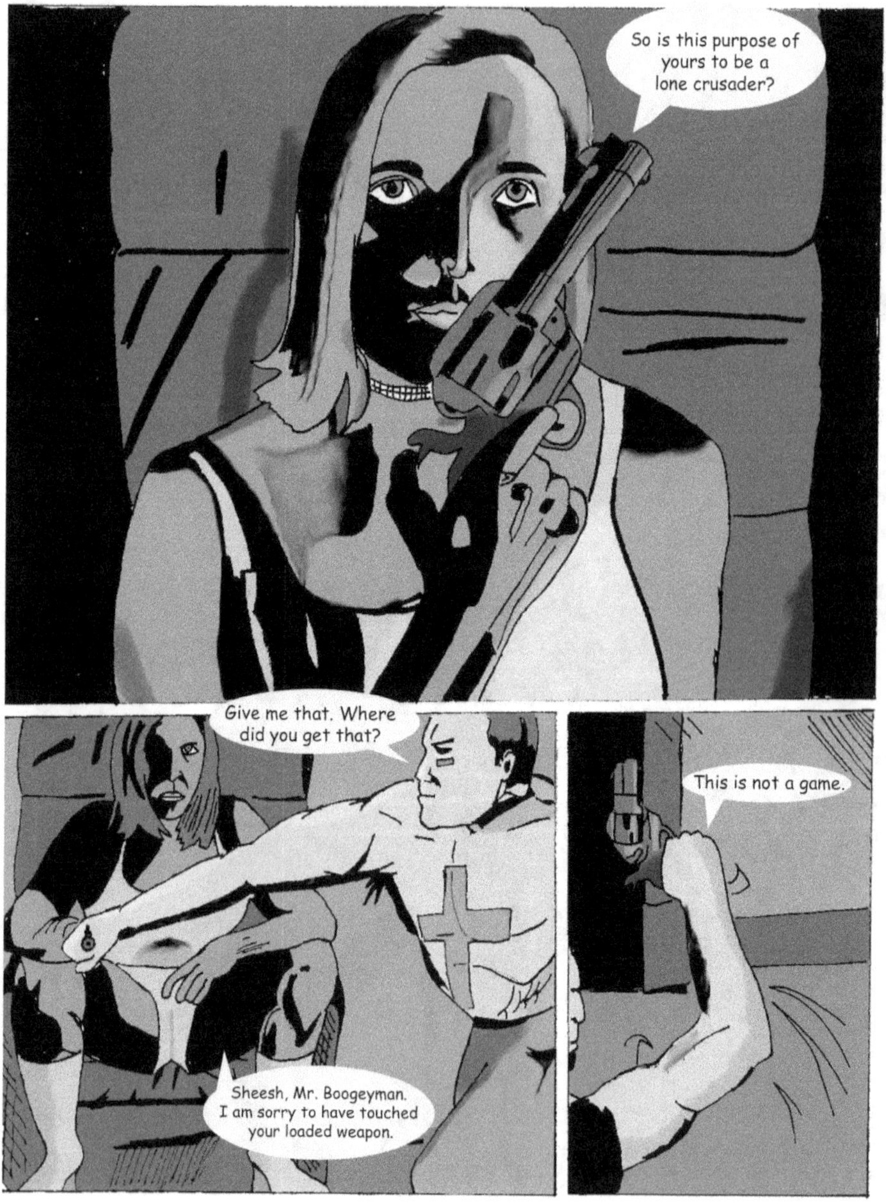

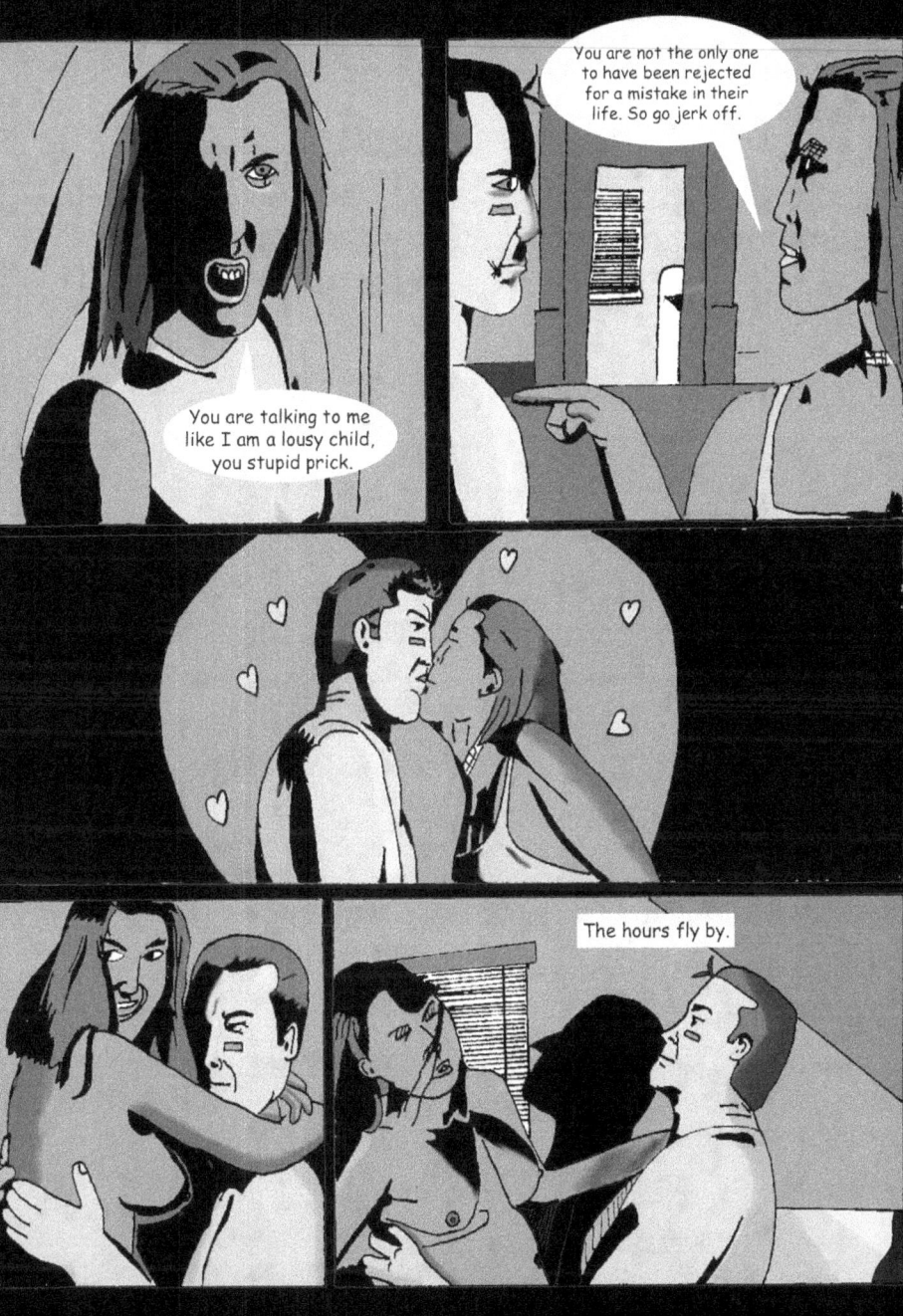

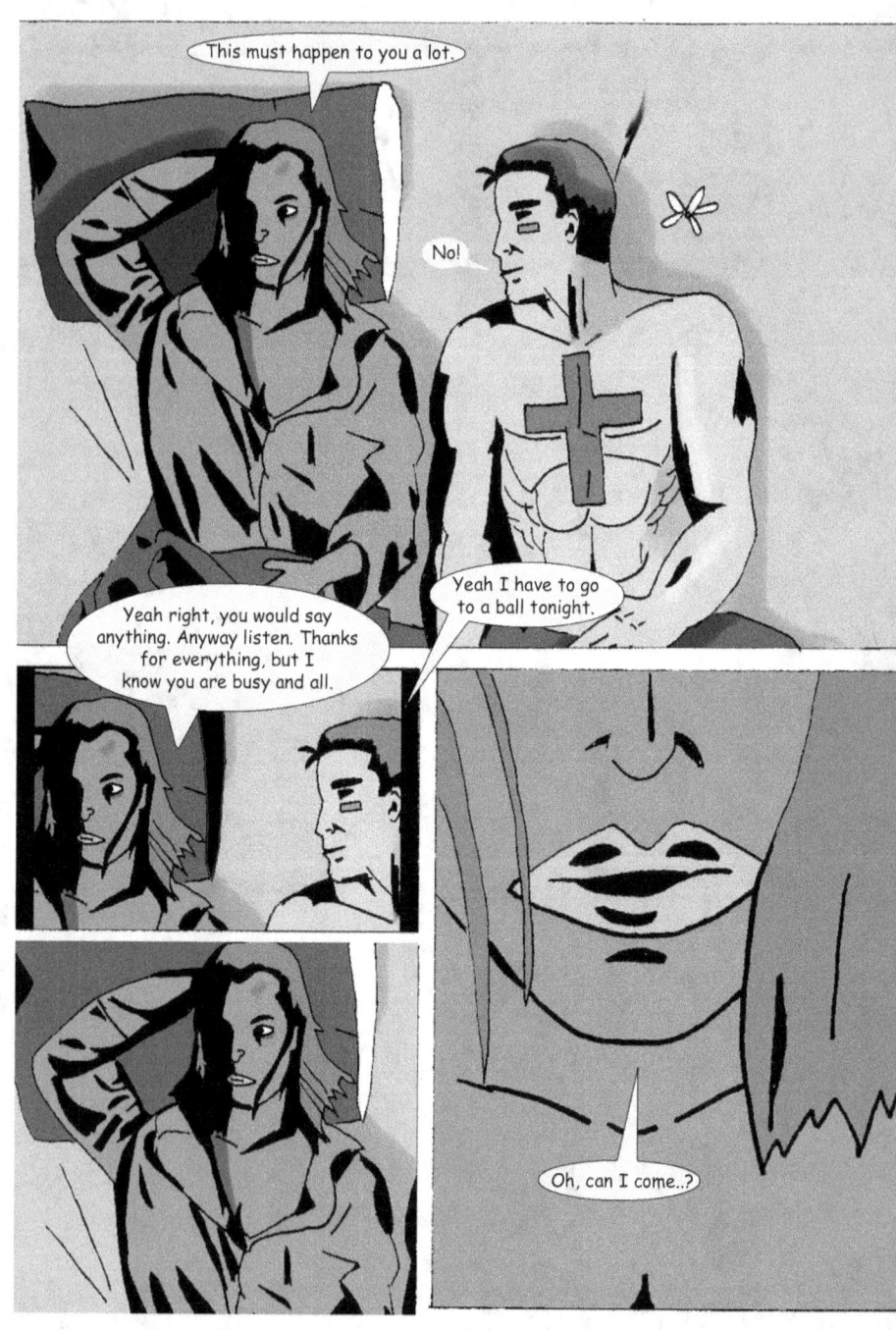

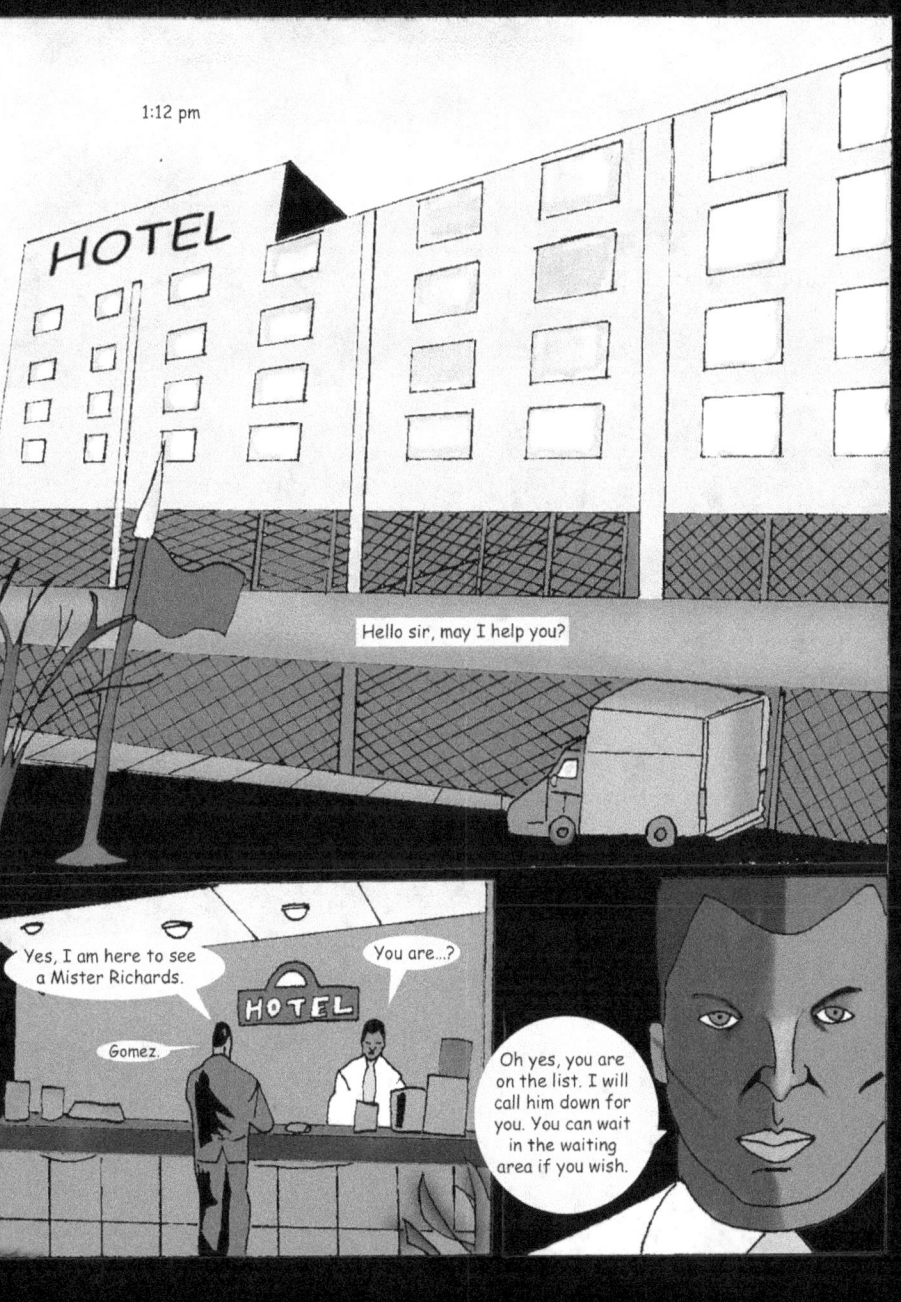

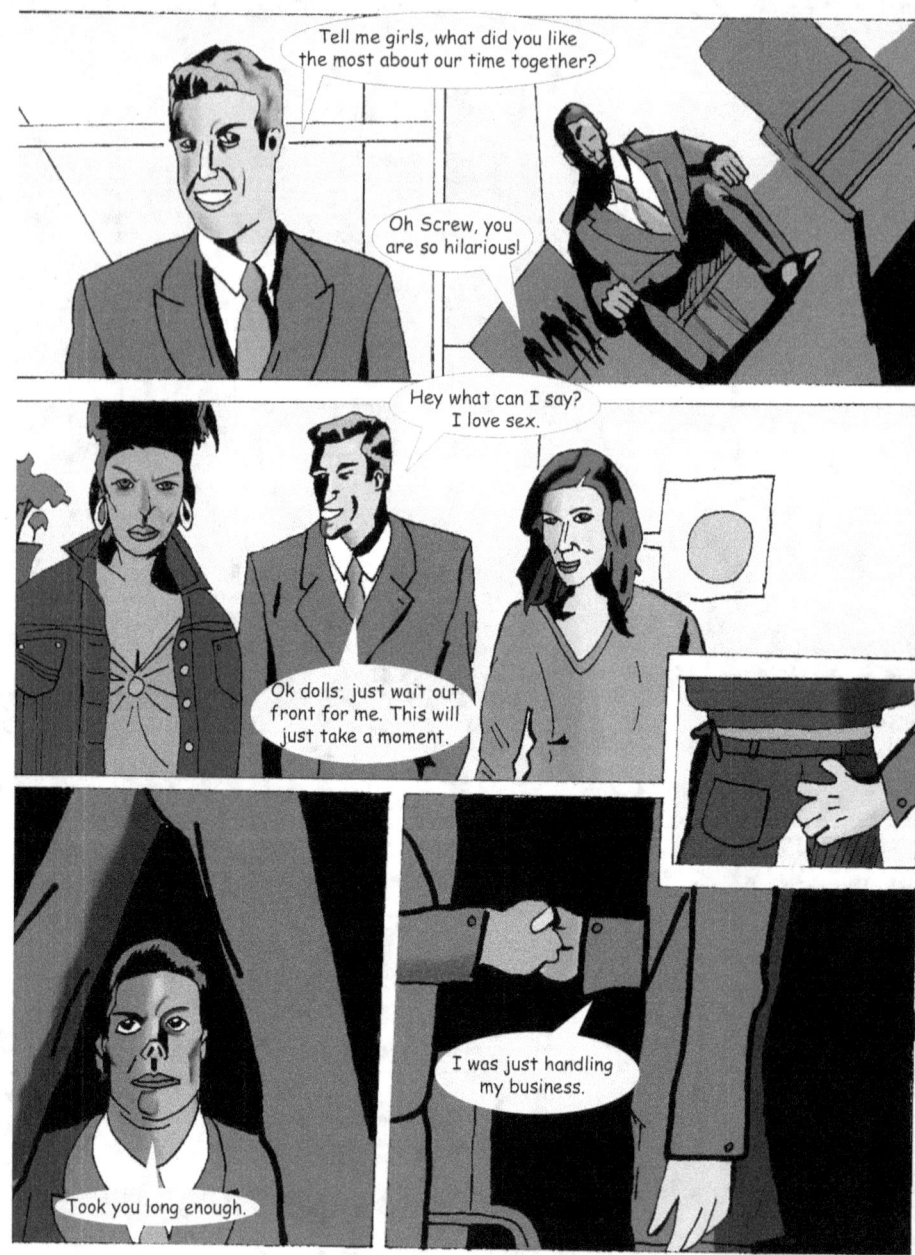

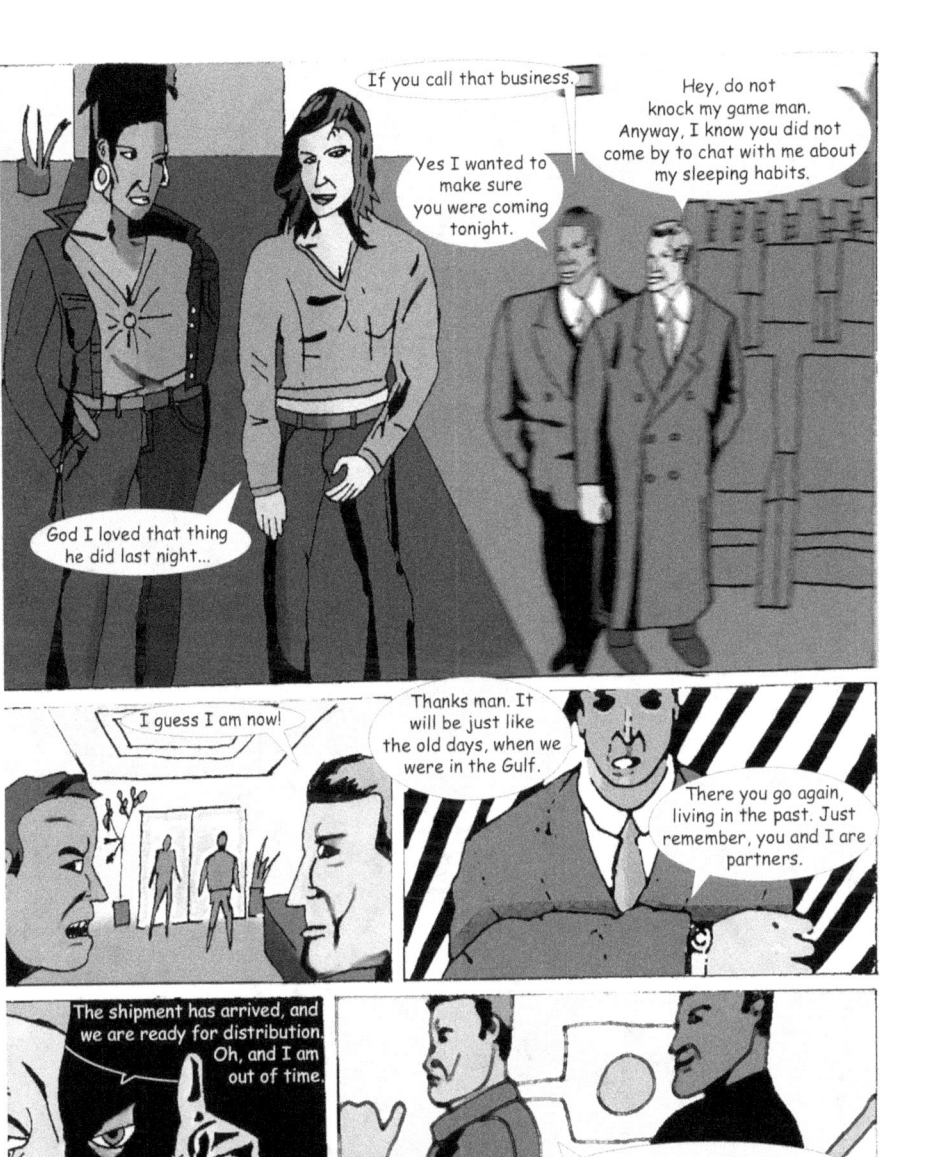

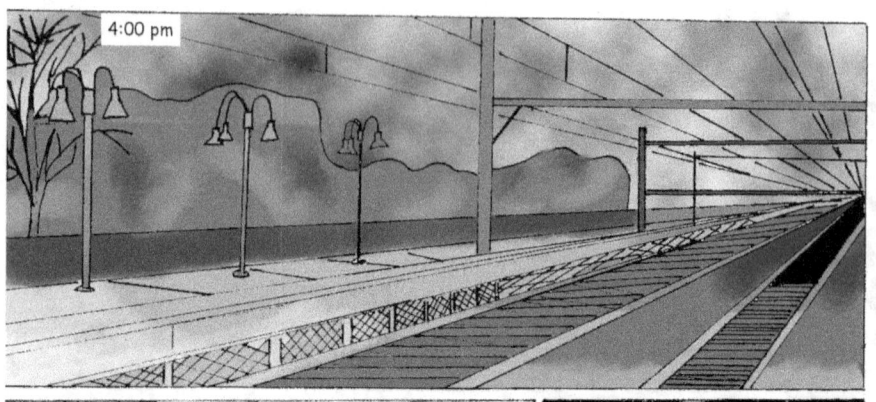

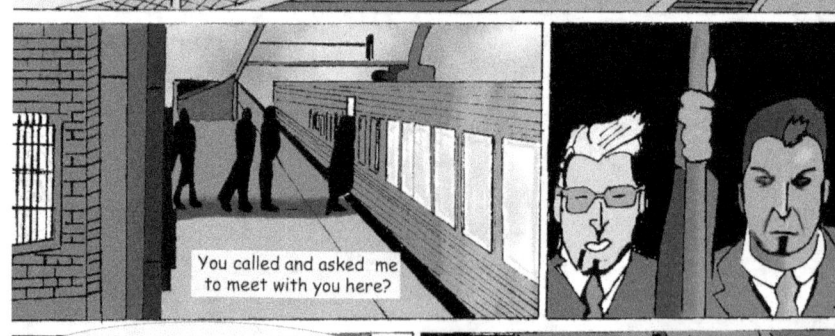

You called and asked me to meet with you here?

Look, Jerry, you know I care about you and your father. I have been a part of your lives for years now.

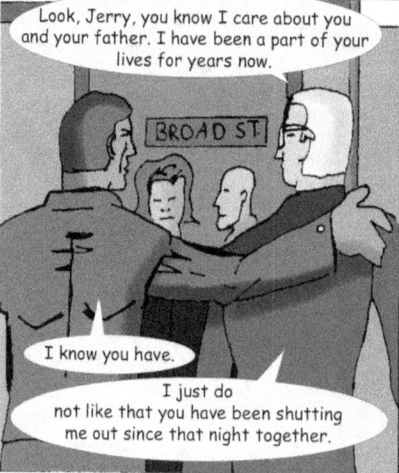

BROAD ST.

I know you have.

I just do not like that you have been shutting me out since that night together.

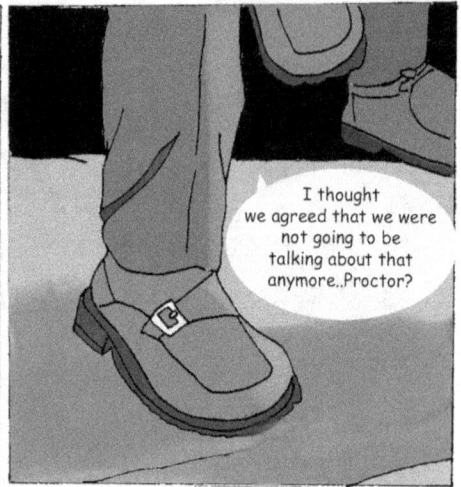

I thought we agreed that we were not going to be talking about that anymore..Proctor?

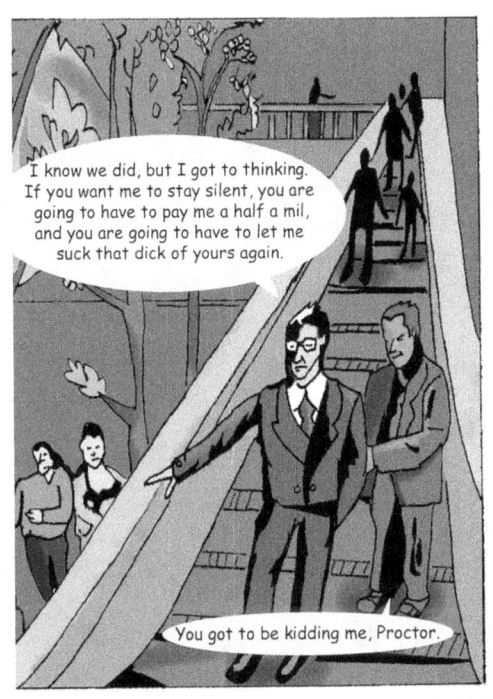

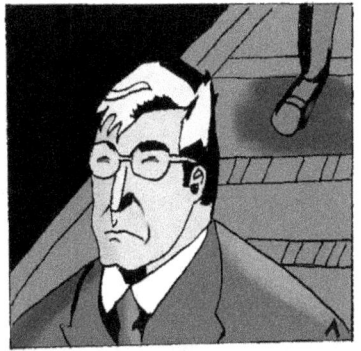

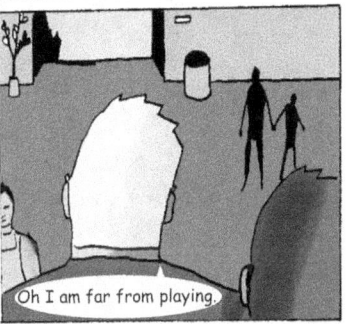

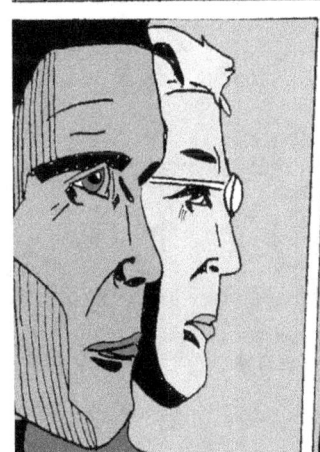

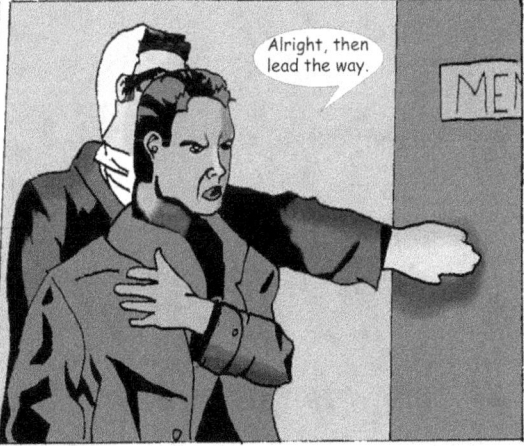

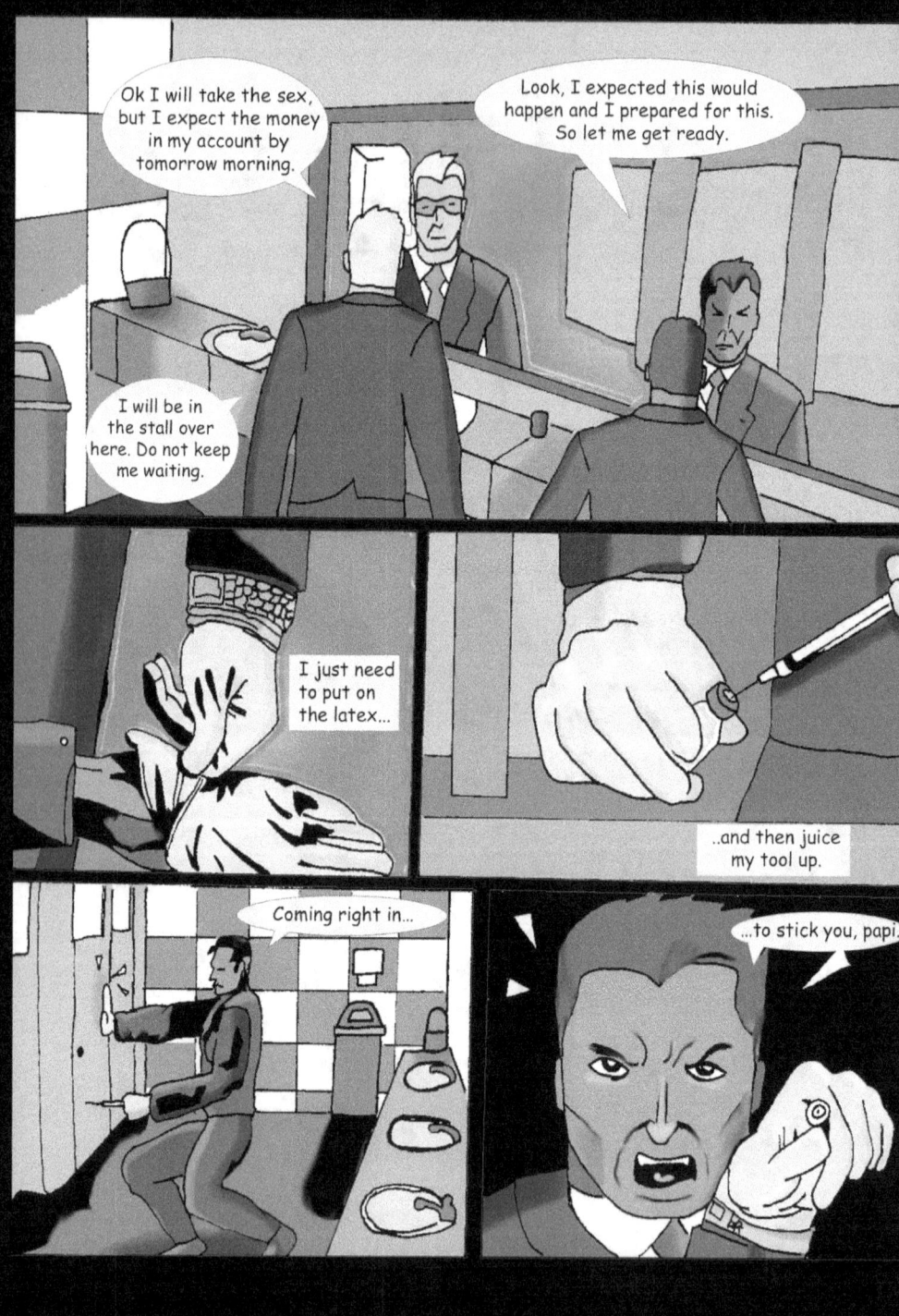

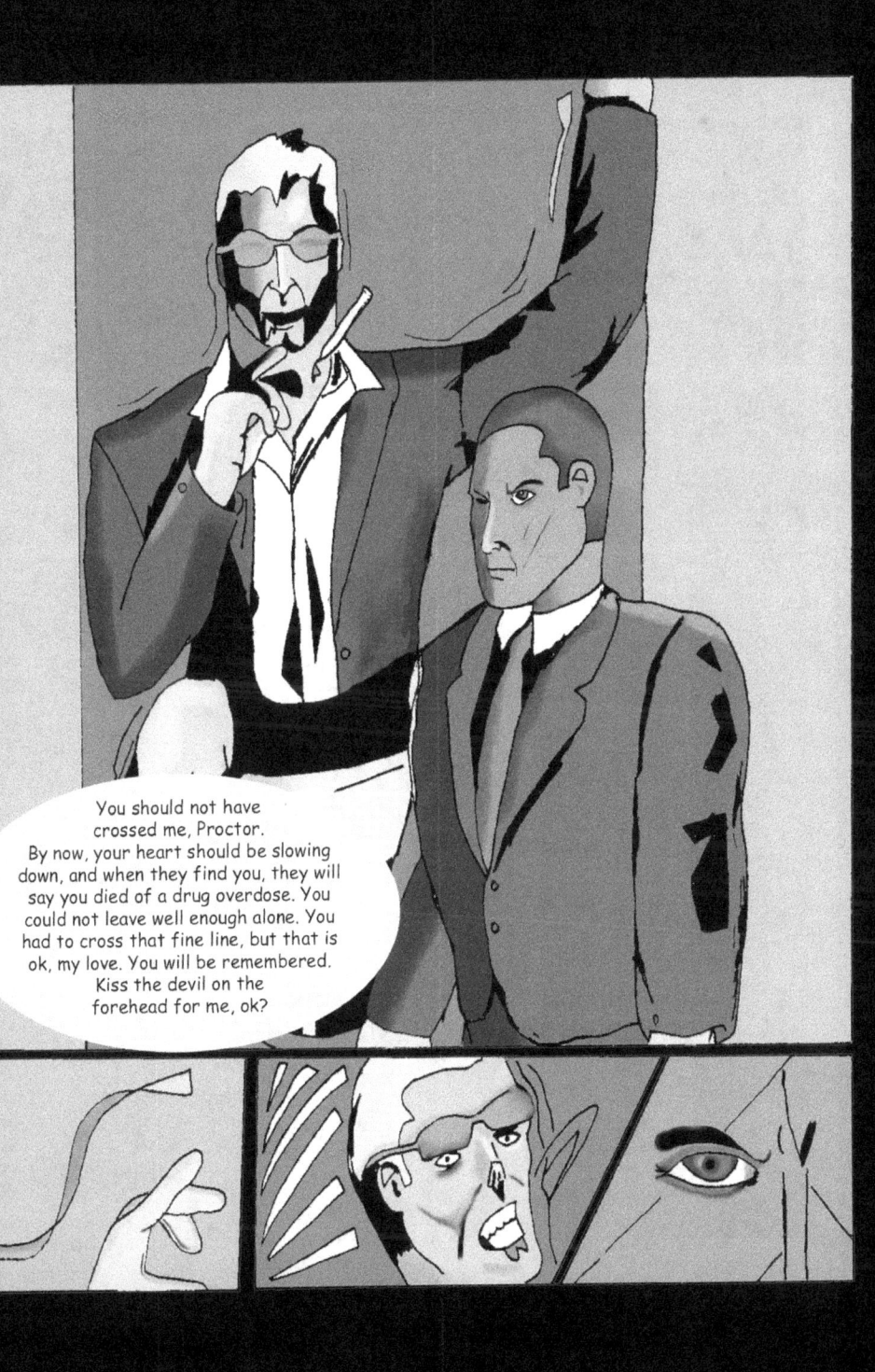

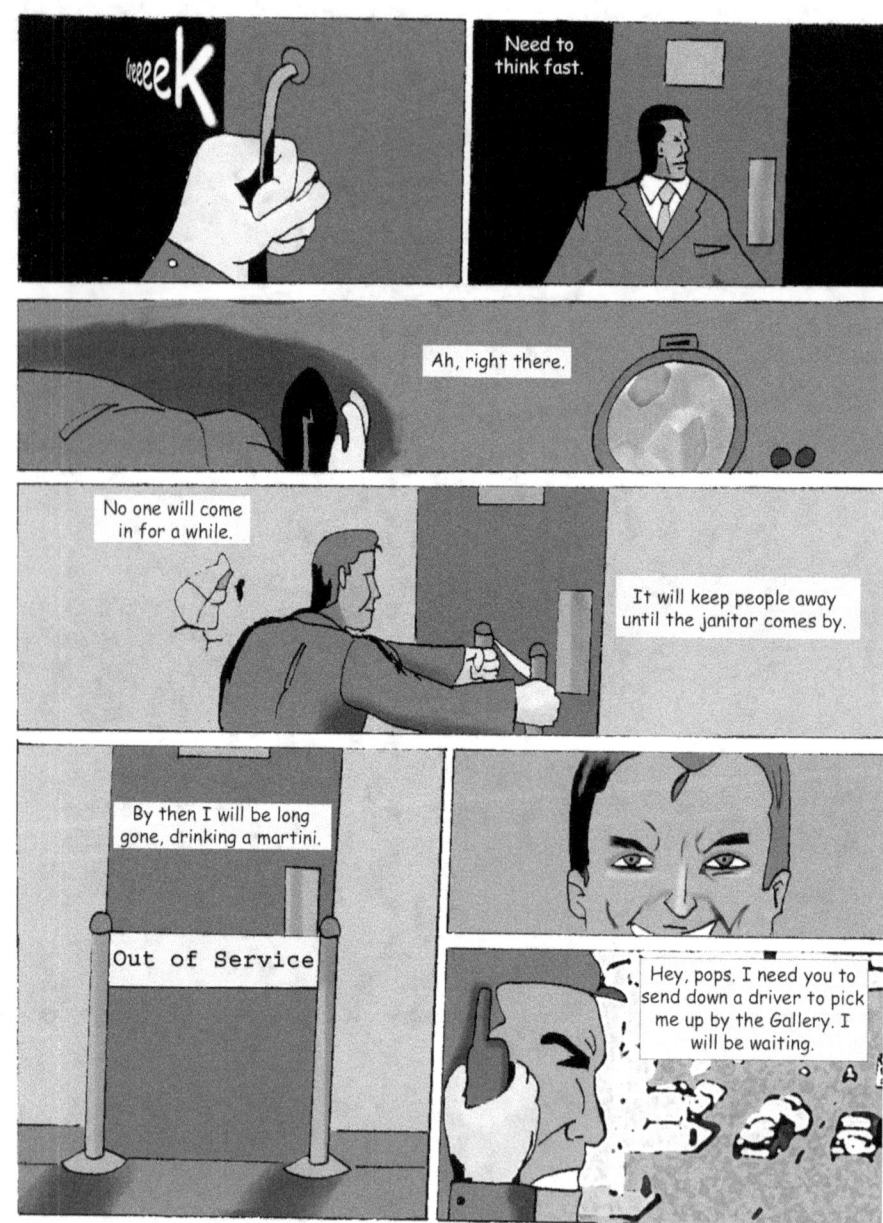

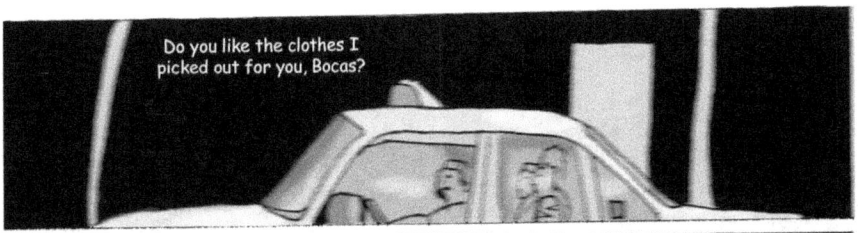

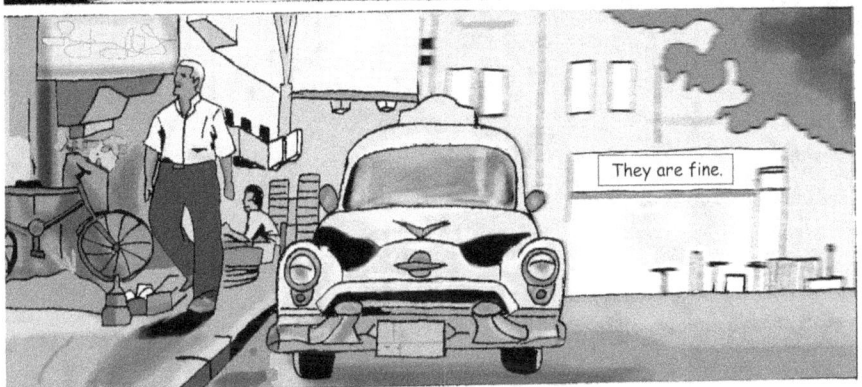

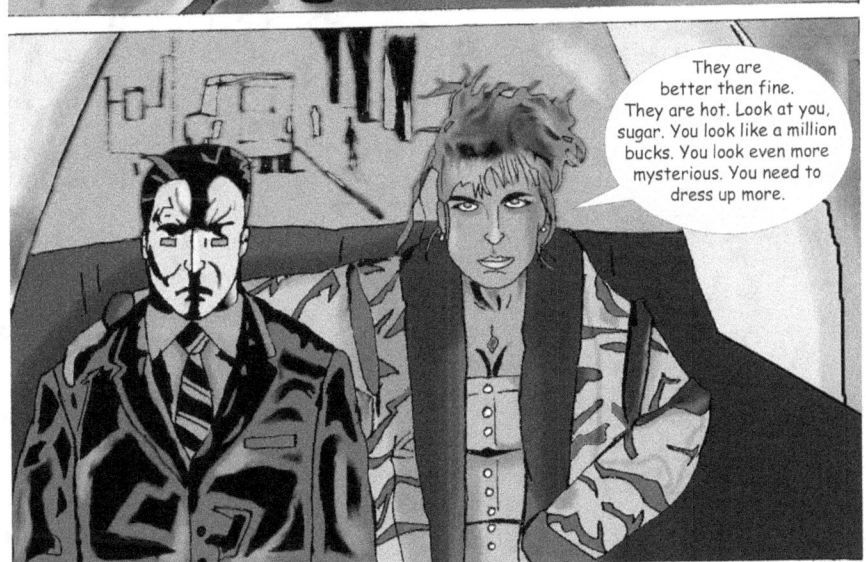

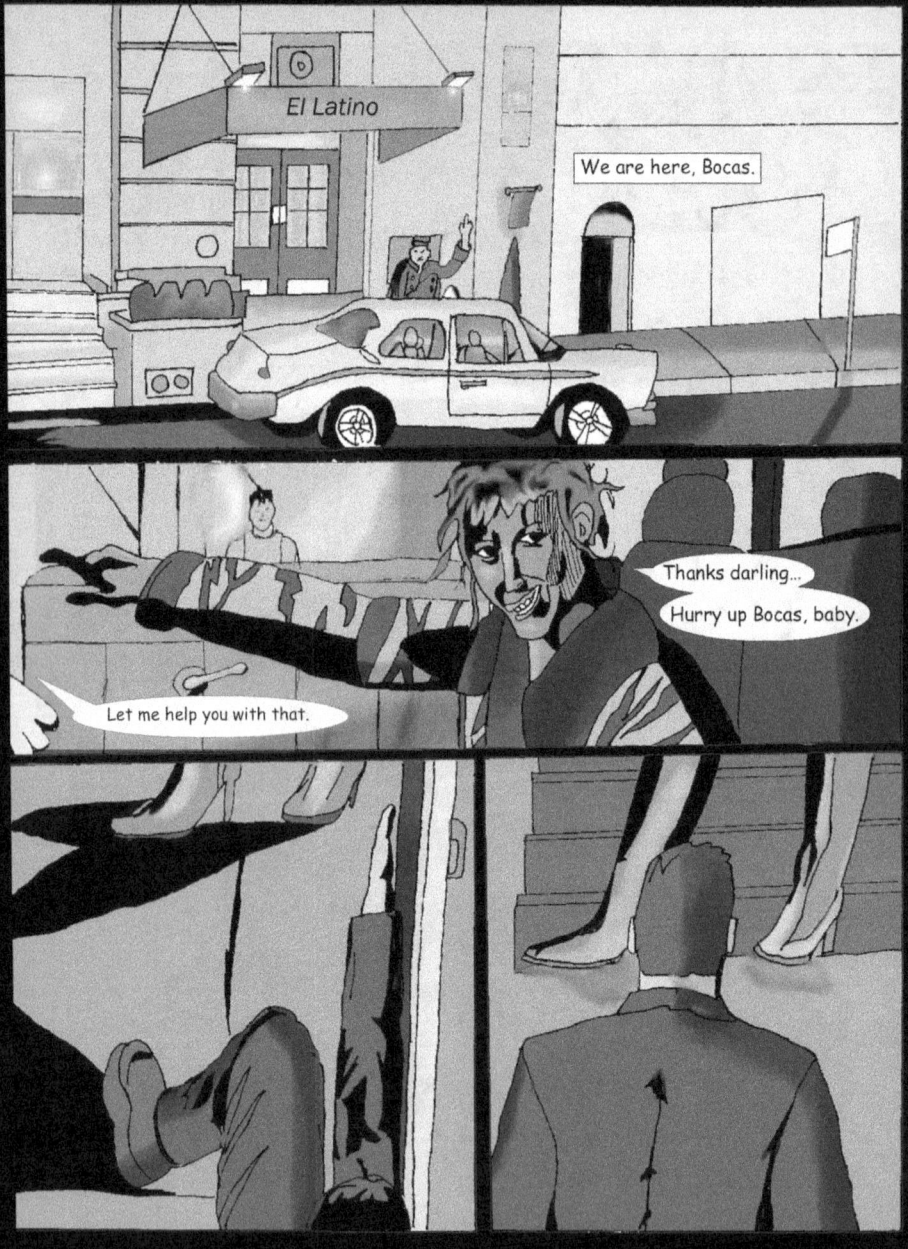

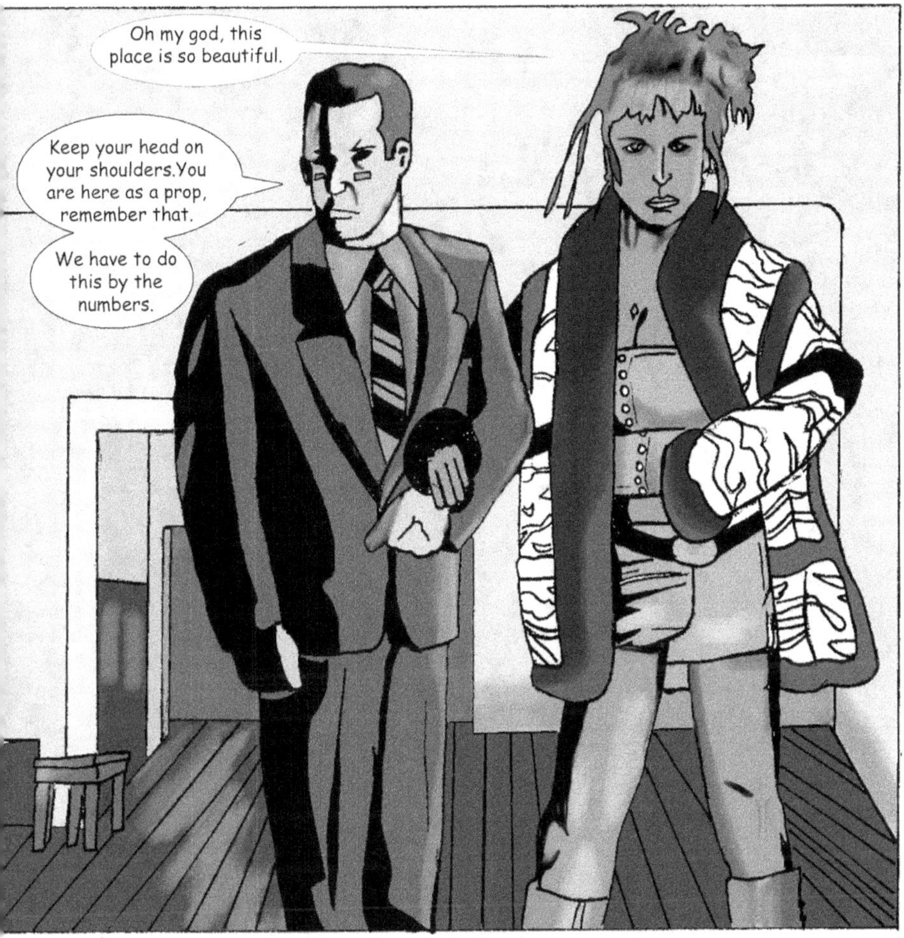

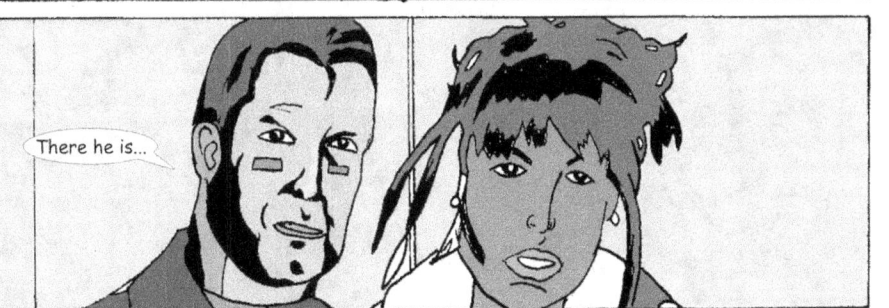

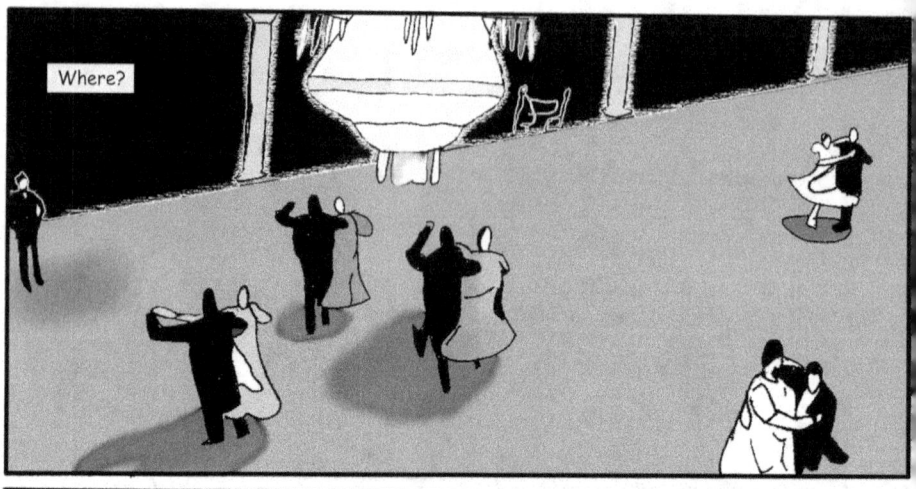

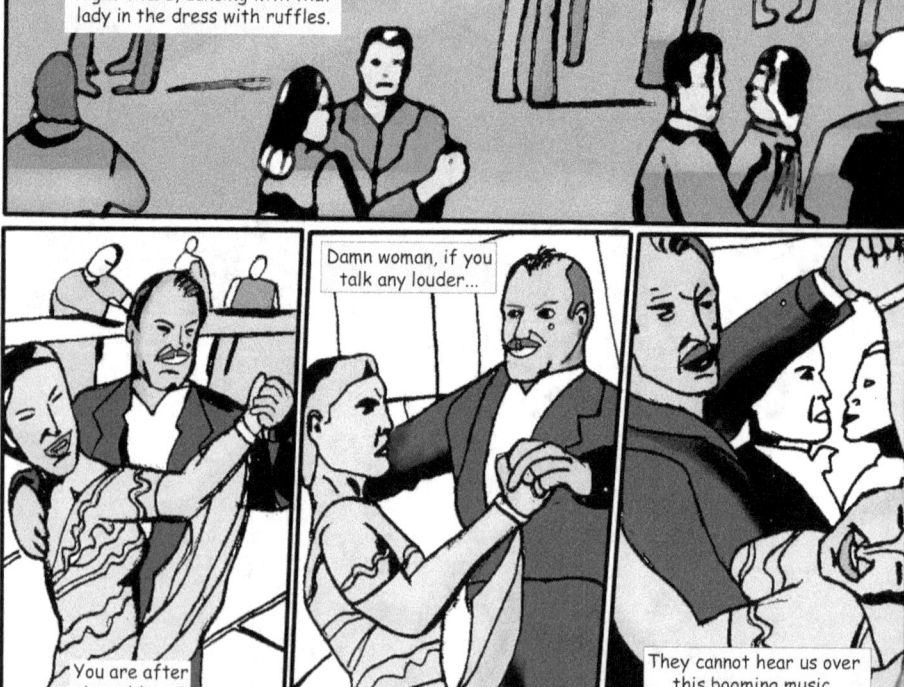

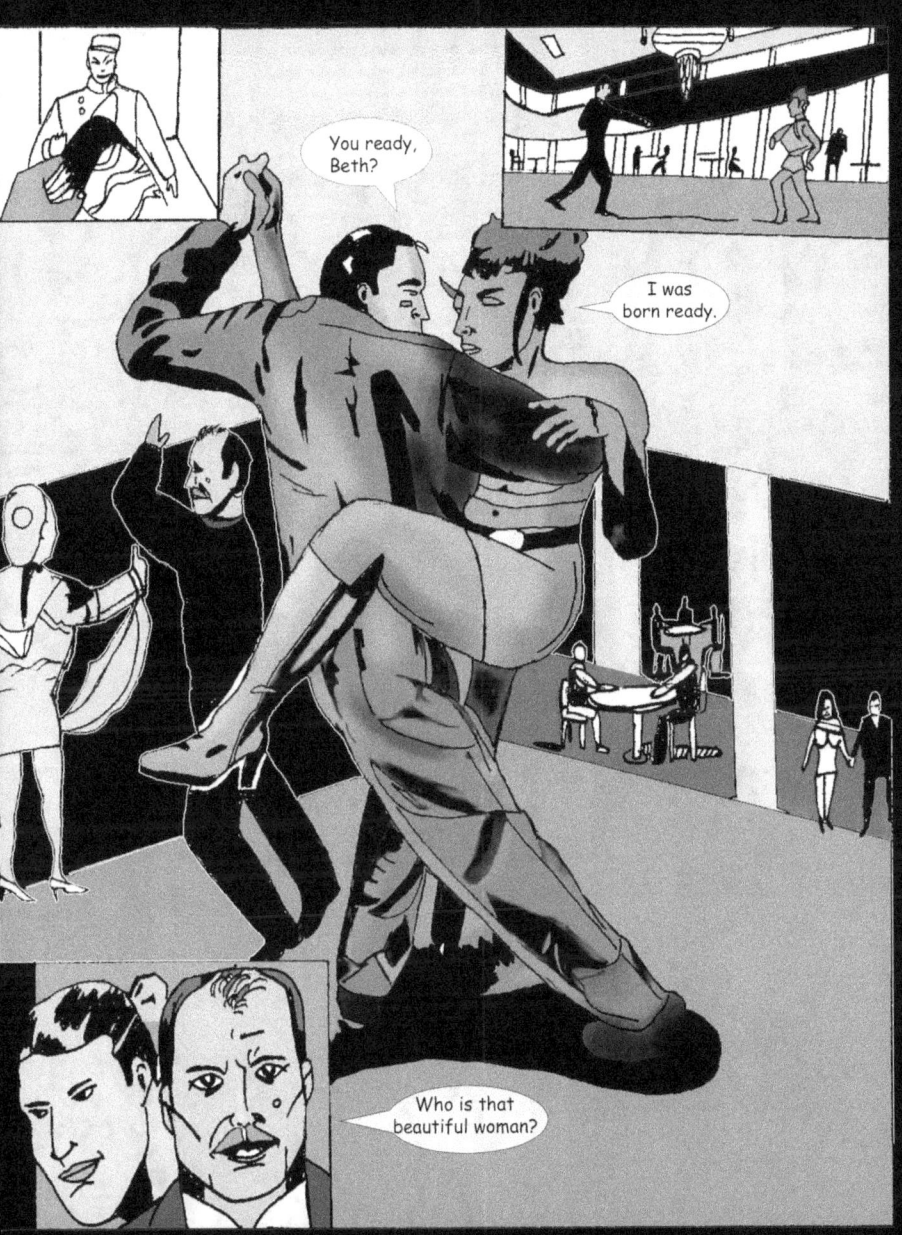

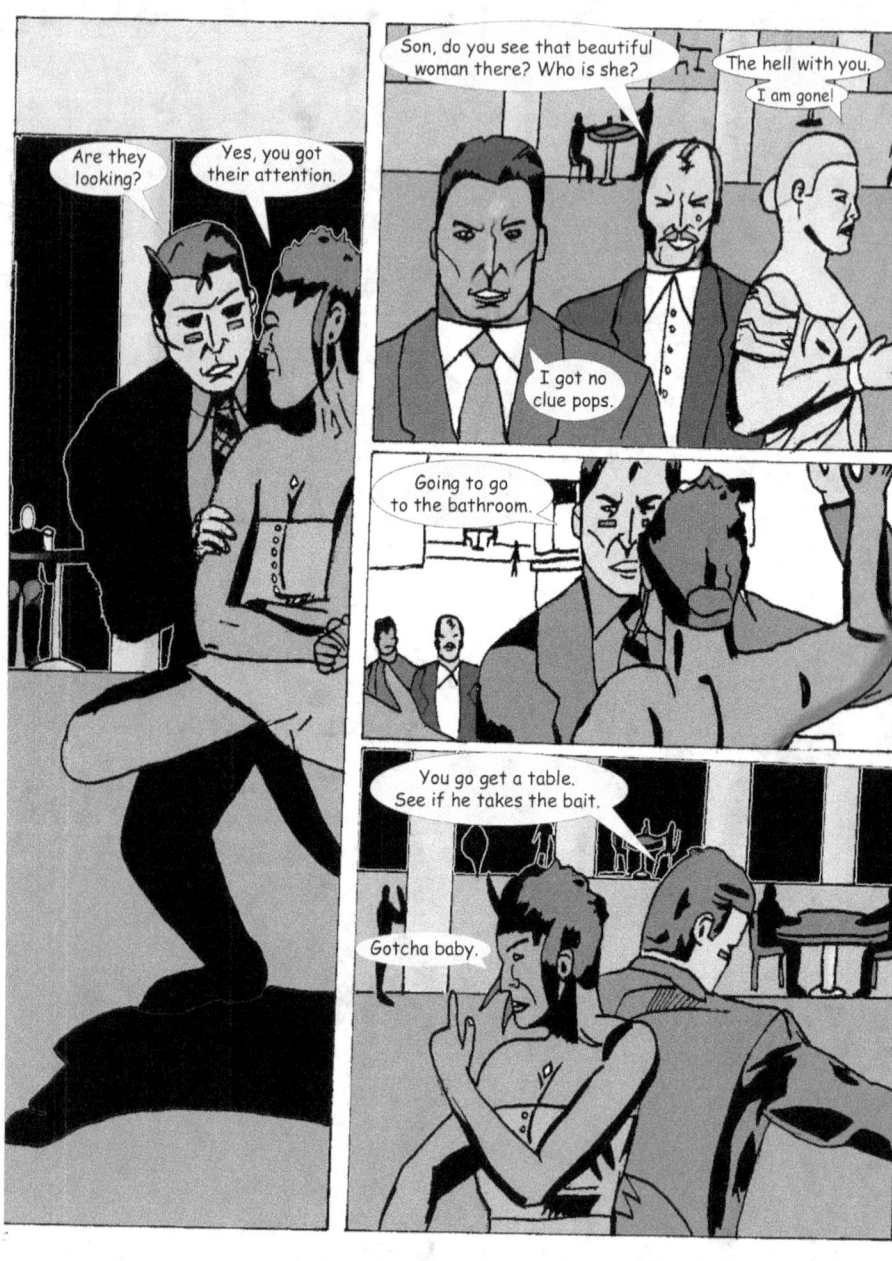

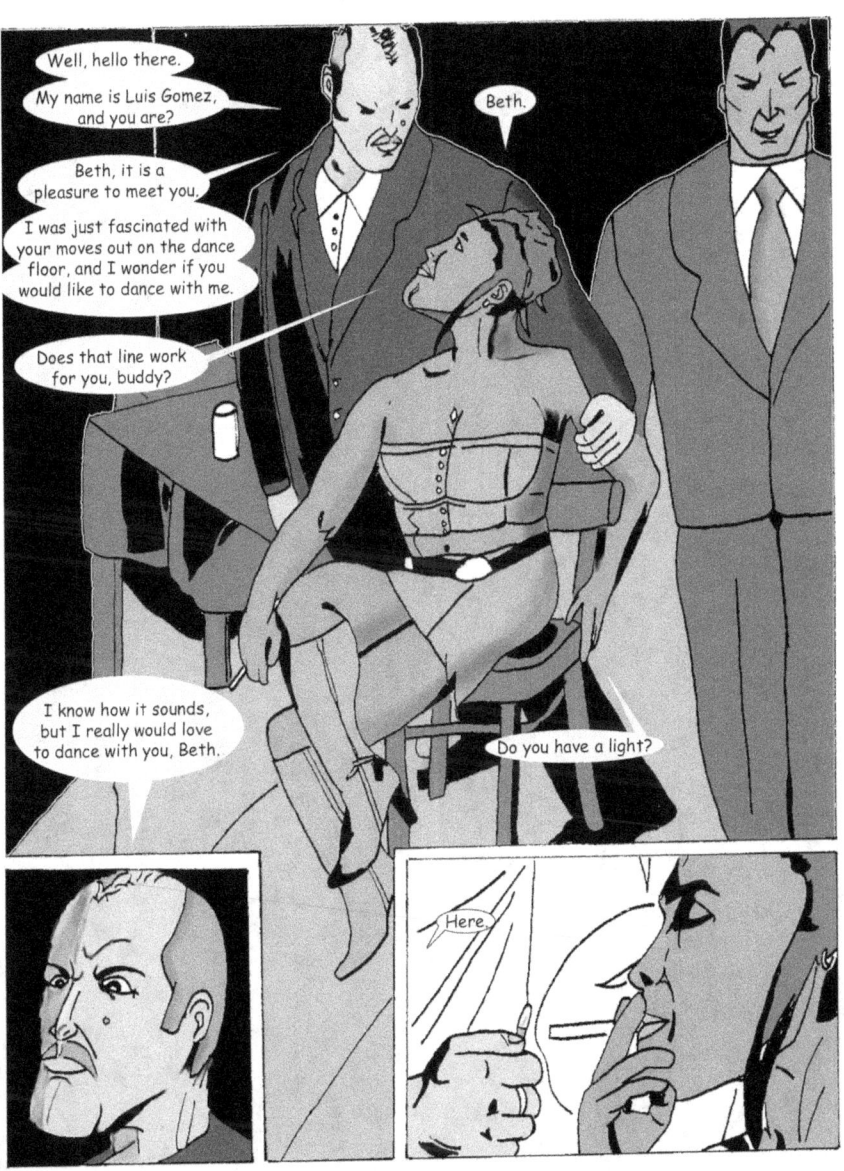

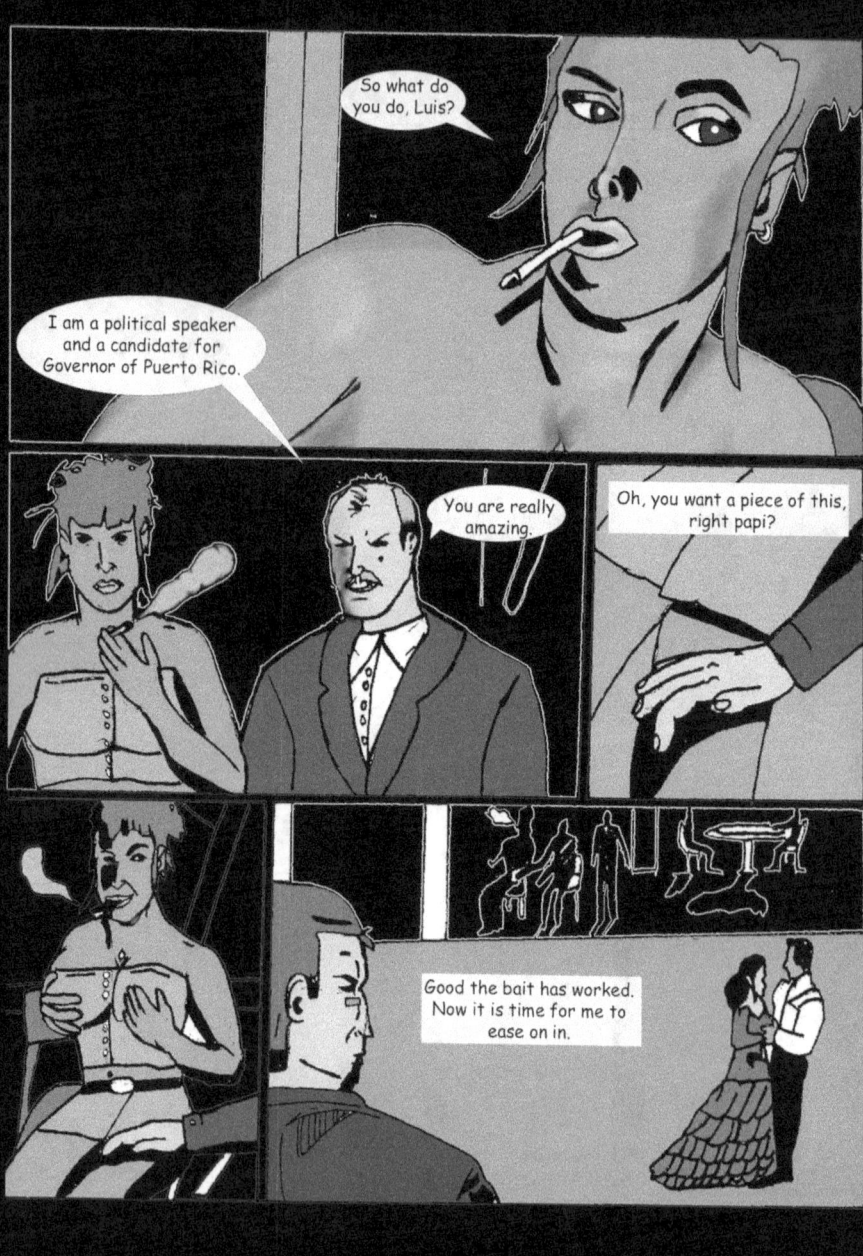

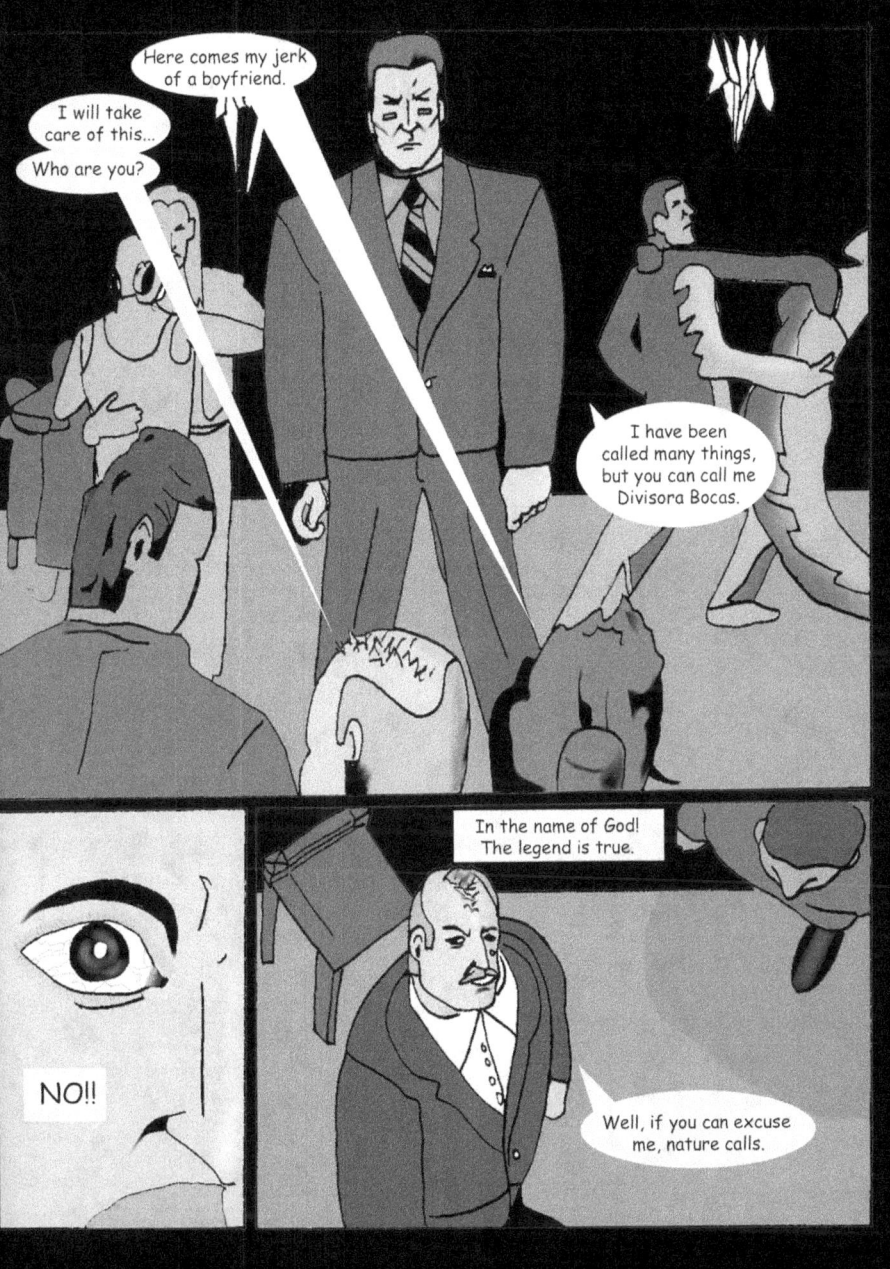

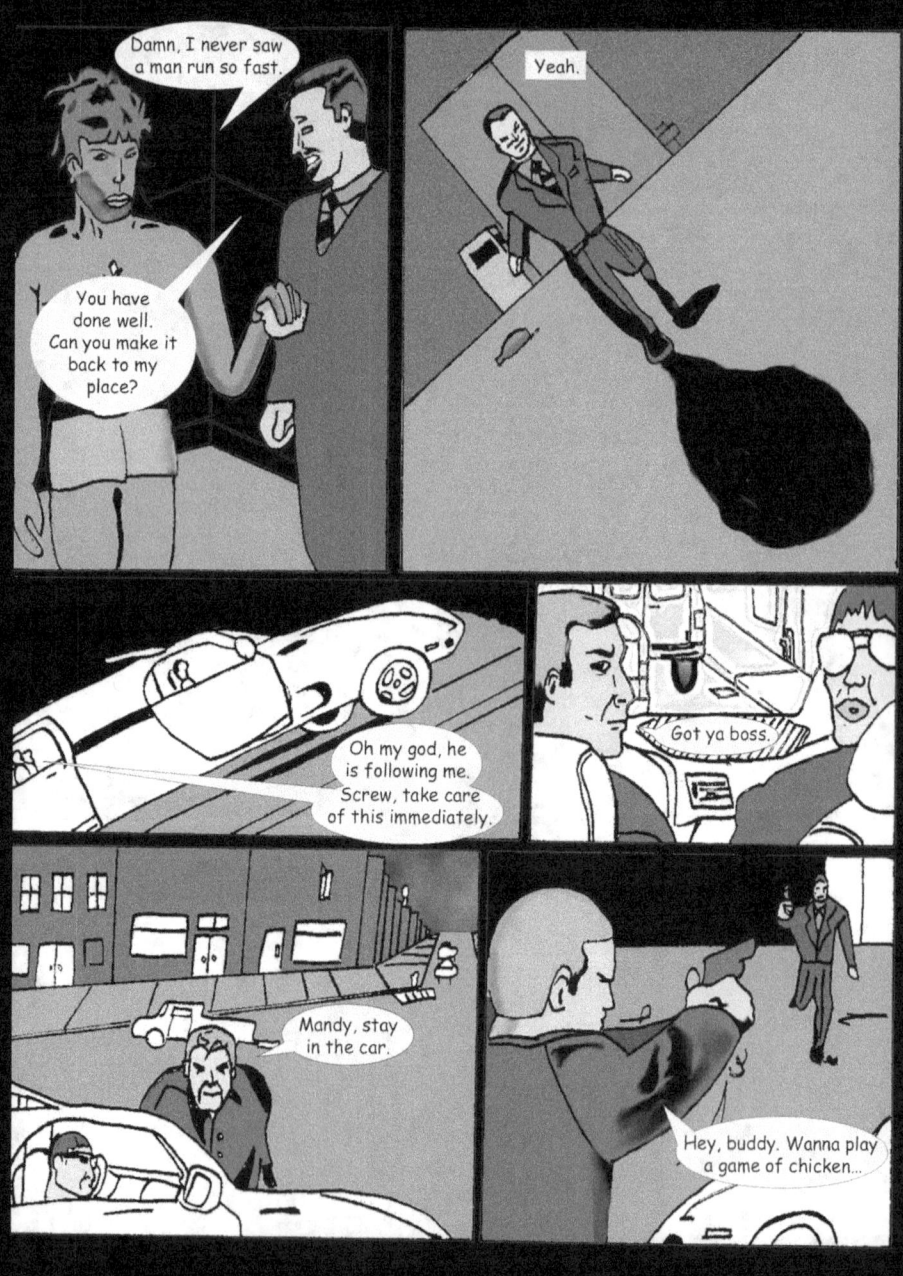

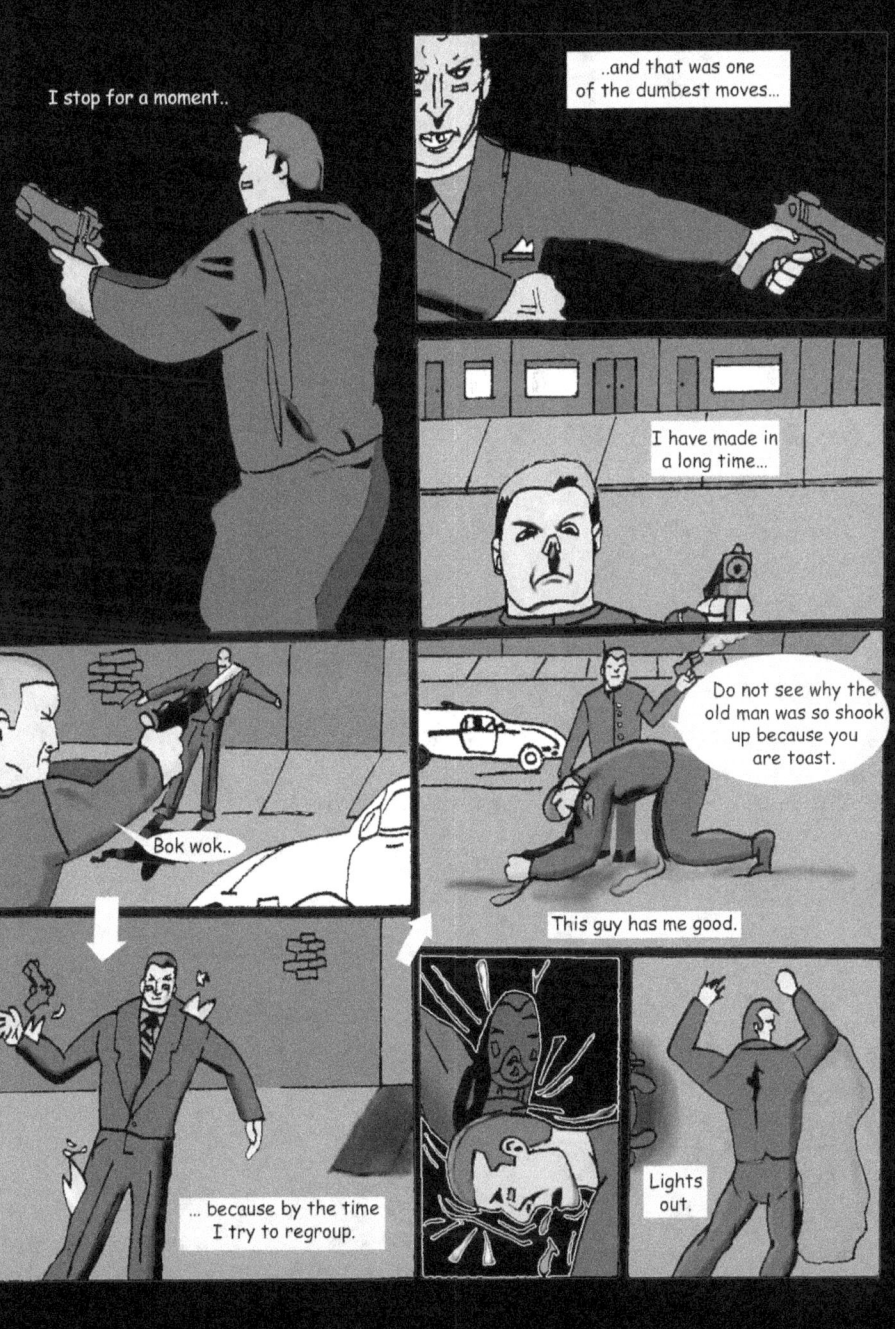

6:30 am.

So, you are trying to tell me that this guy is a myth?

No, not a myth. He's a legend, and legend goes that he hunts down those that have committed a great wrong. Most times, it is someone placing a curse on you that gets Bocas to come after you.

This sounds like a corny horror movie.

Seriously, my father used to tell me the story of the unstoppable Bocas. How he fought the Rough Riders that stormed into Puerto Rico during the late 19th century. He was compromised during the end by too many soldiers. Our father even went as far as stating that this unmarked tombstone was the final resting place of the legendary Bocas, and all you had to do was call his name, and he would be resurrected. Of course, I didn't believe it, but my brother Alberto ate it up.

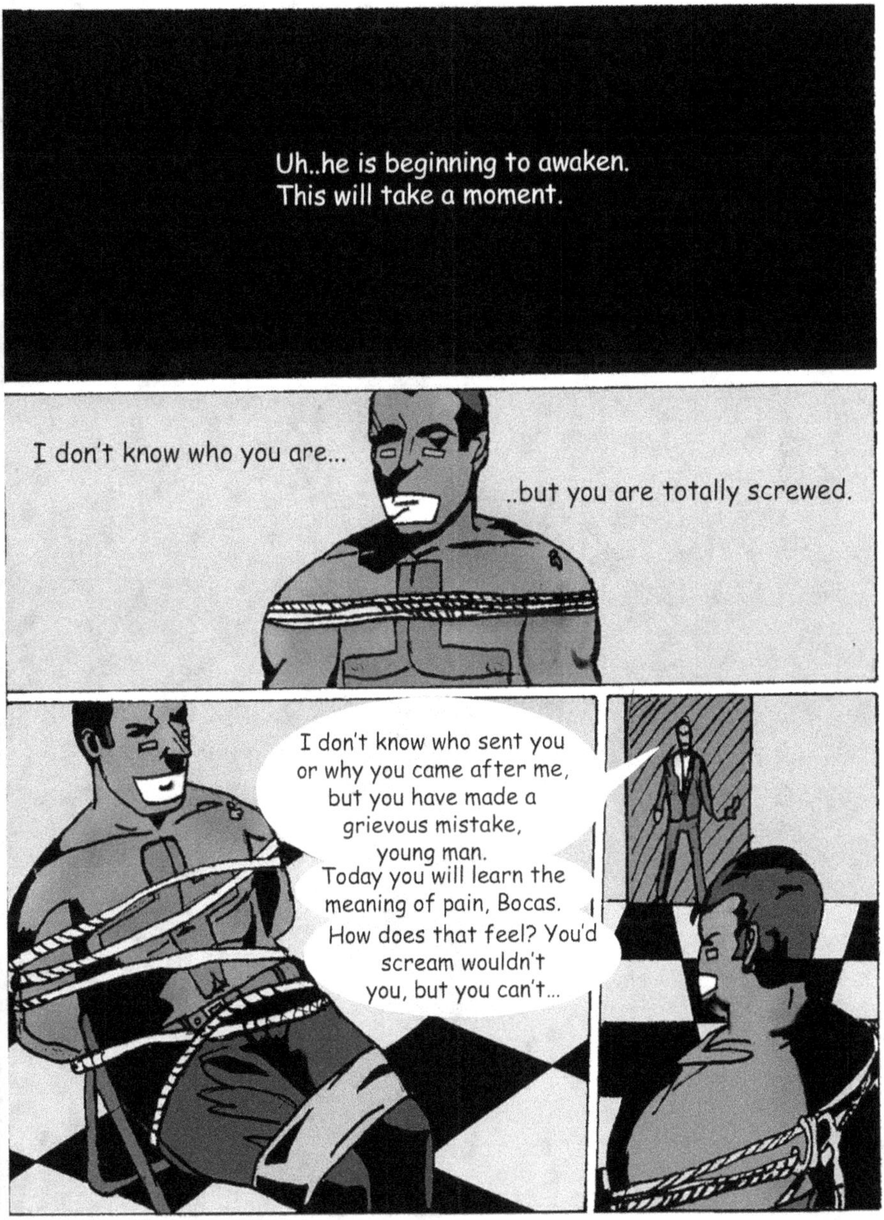

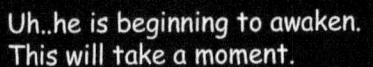

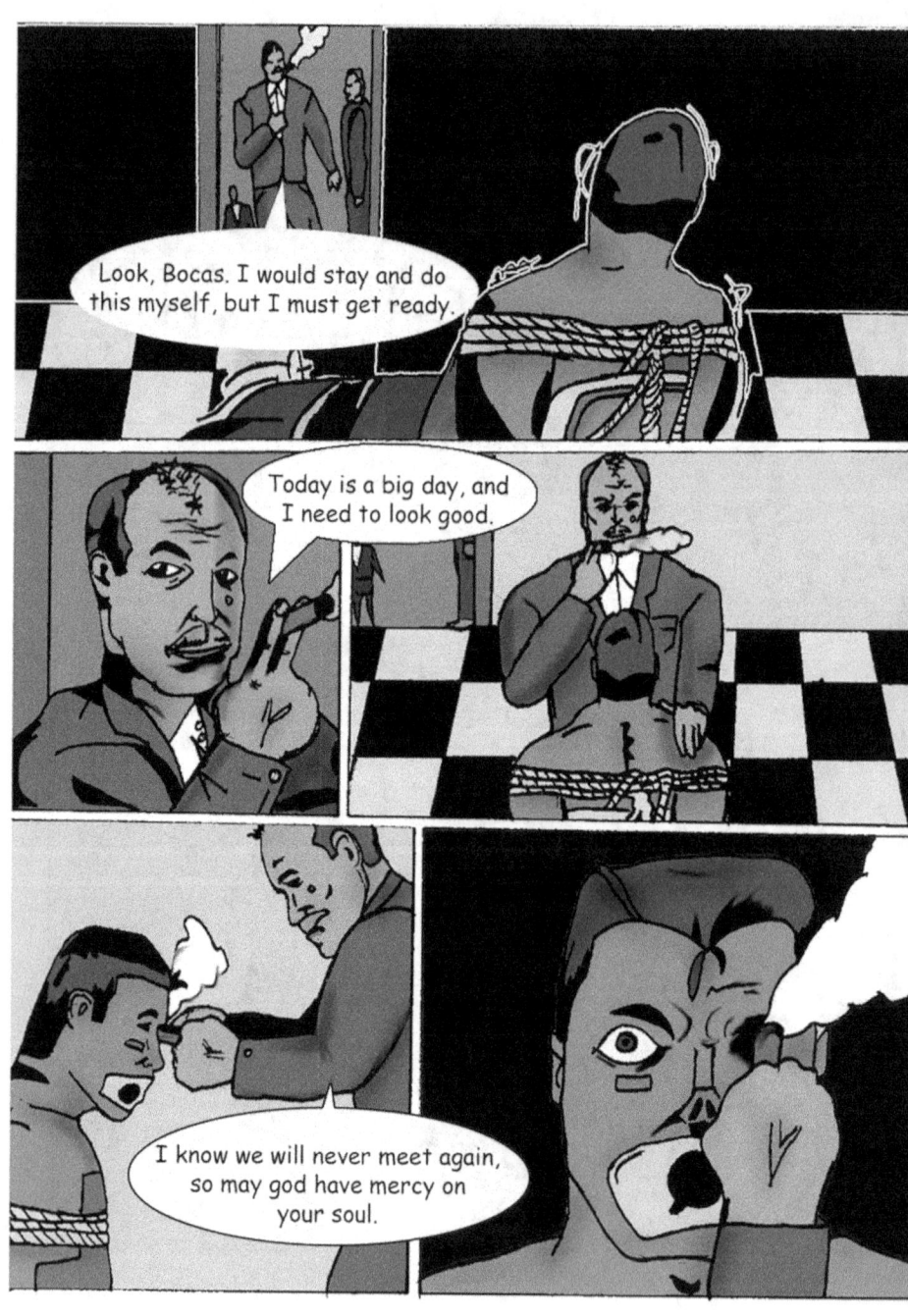

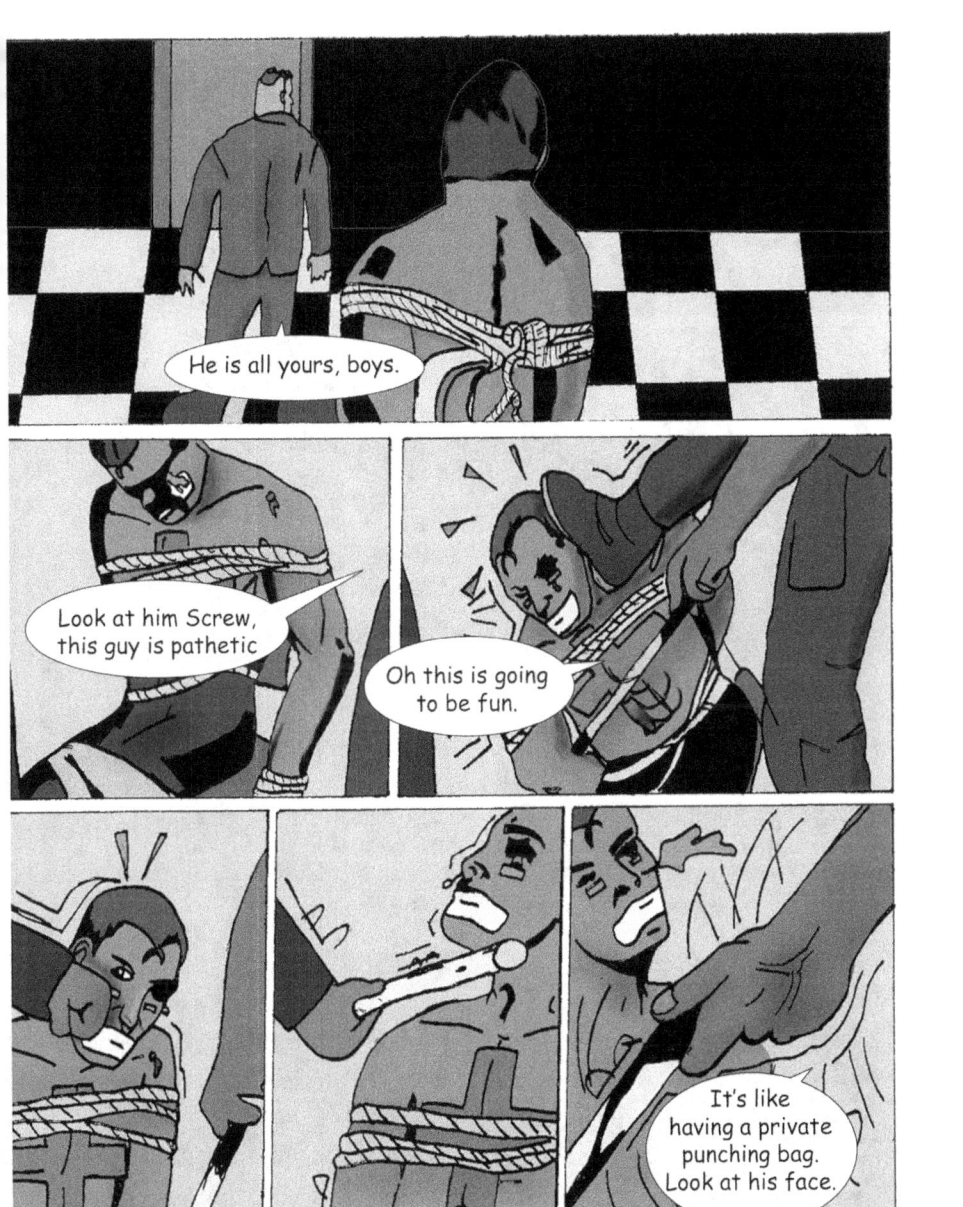

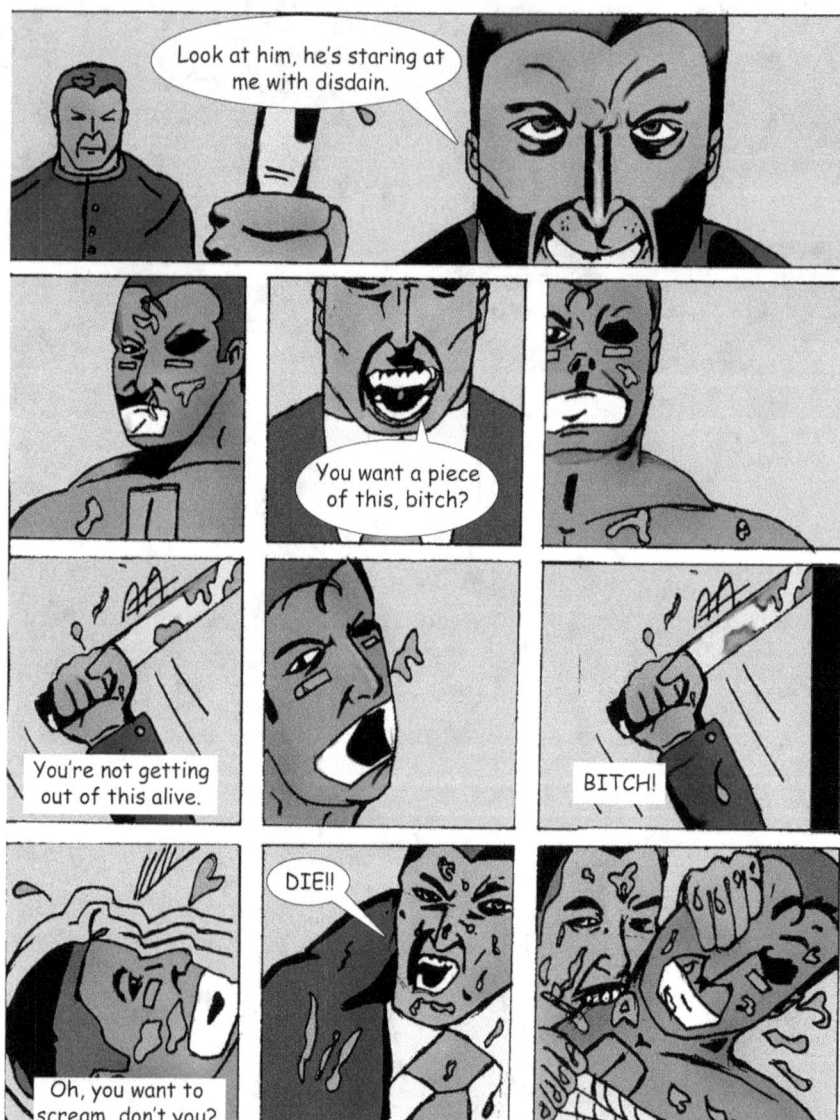

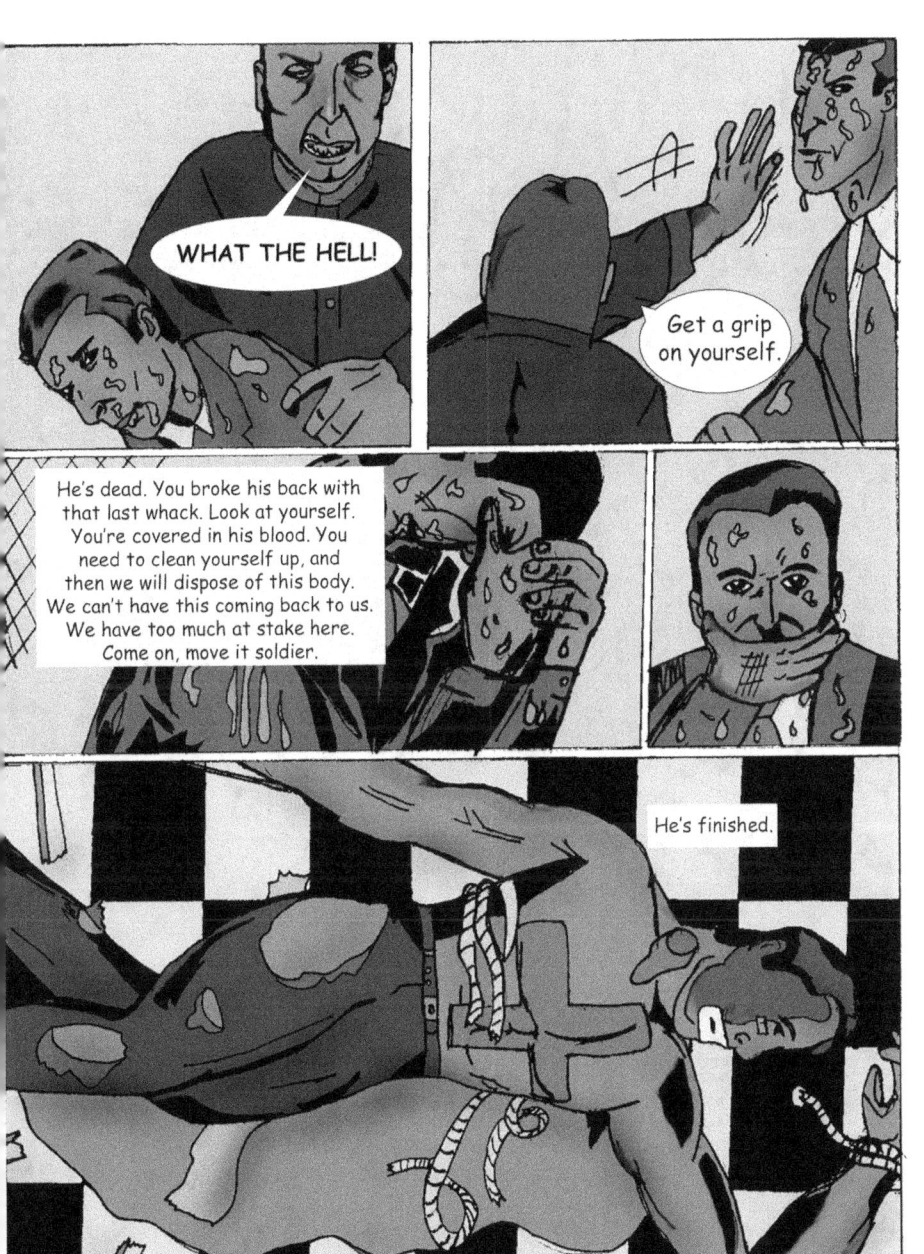

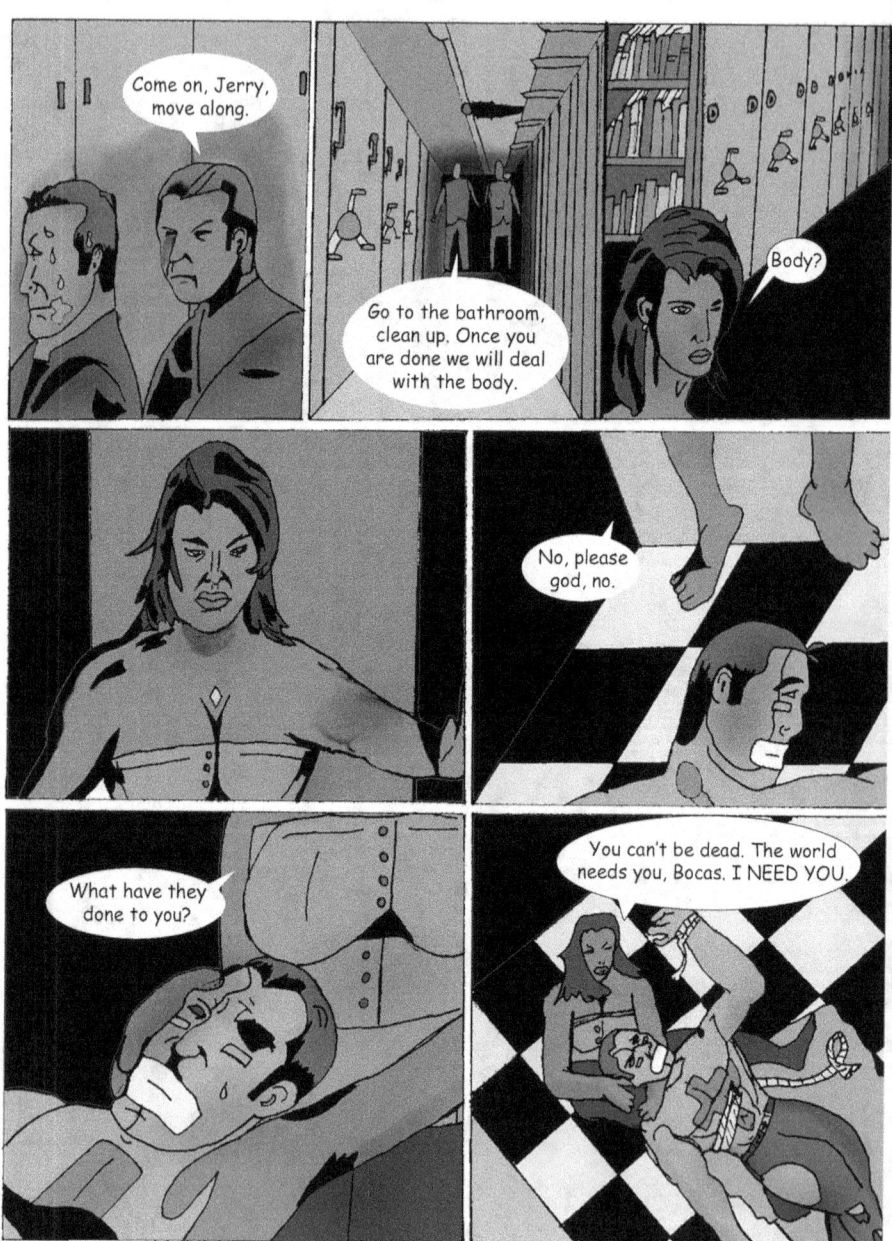

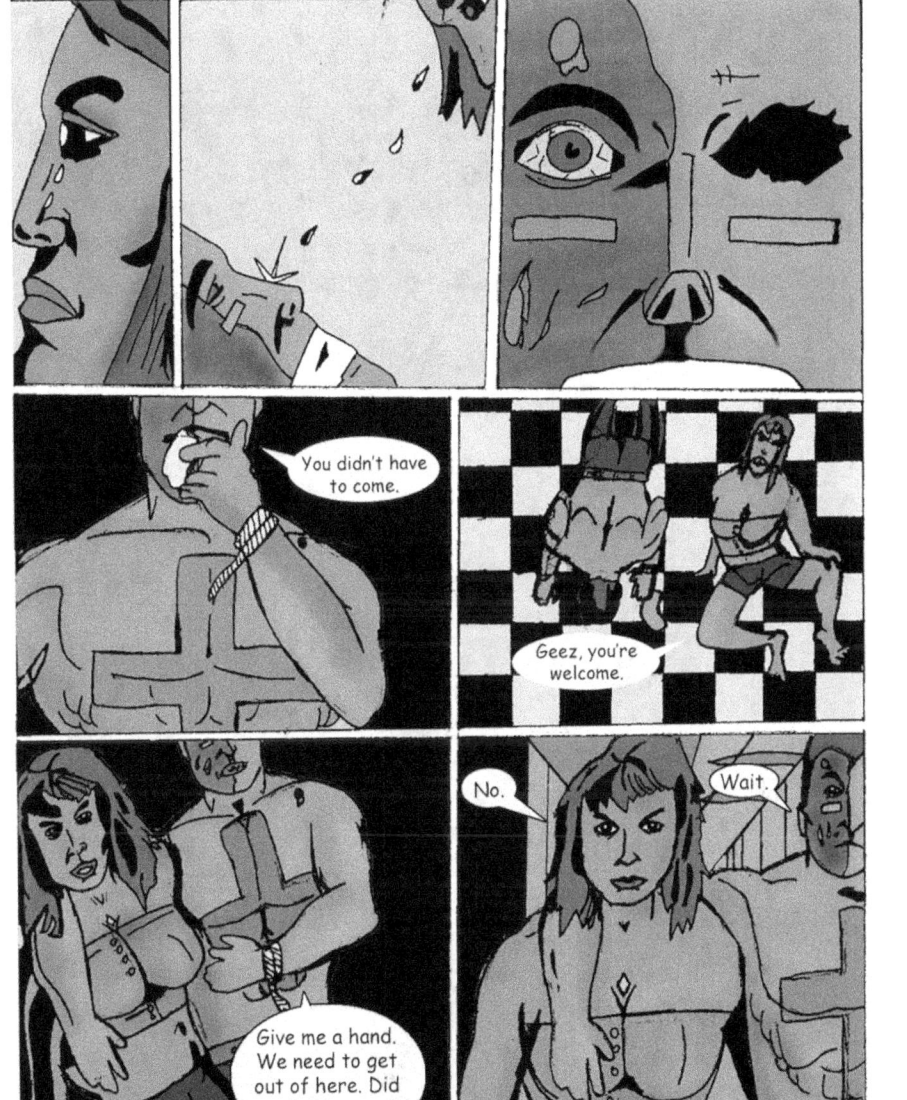

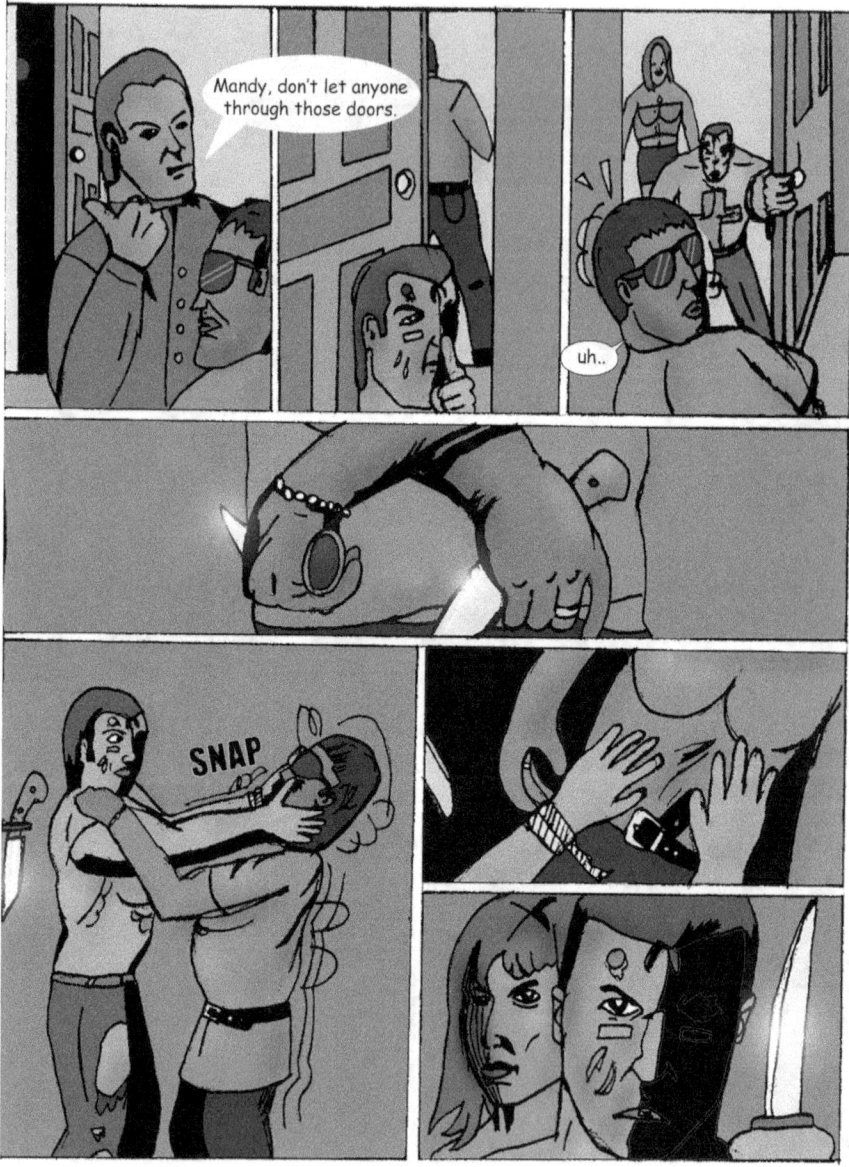

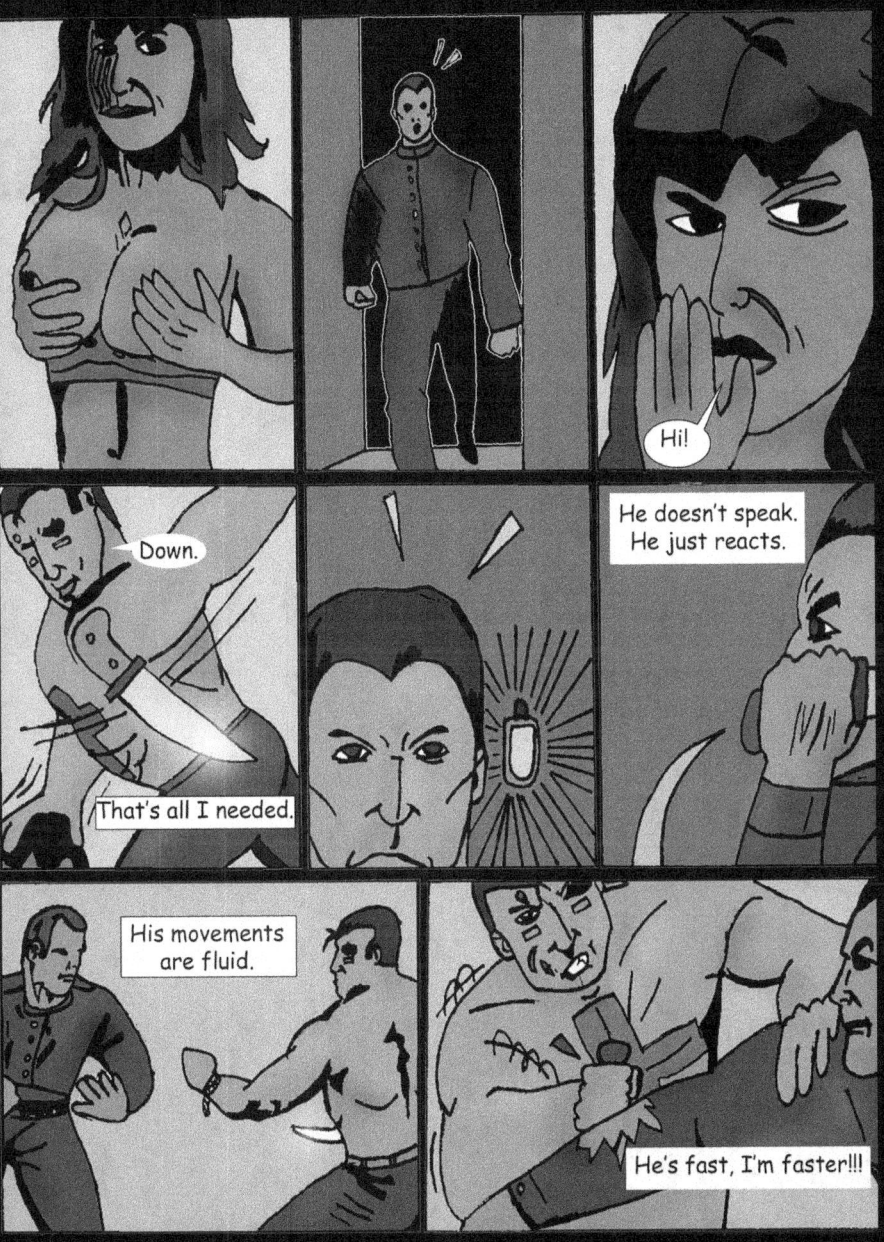

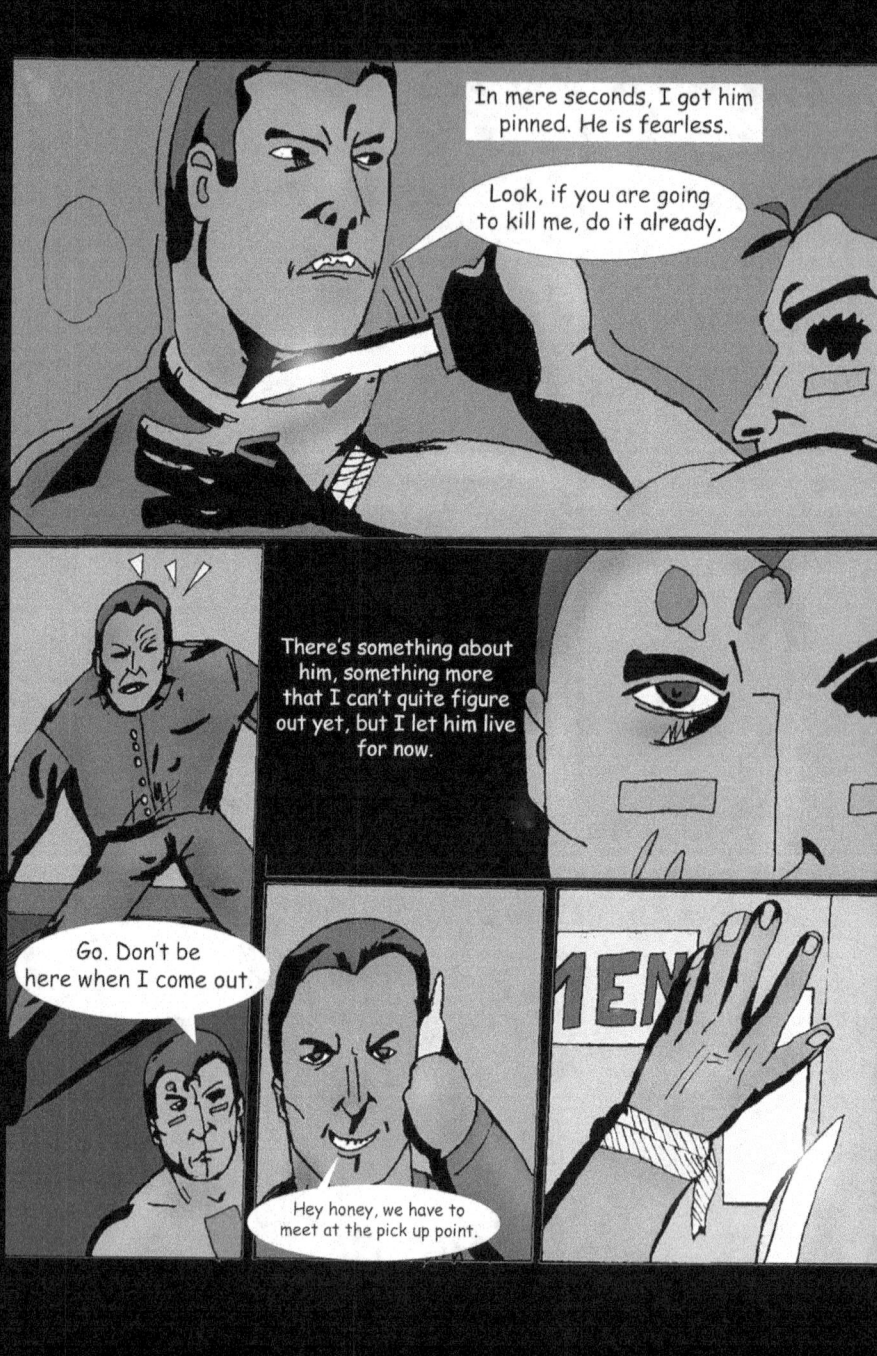

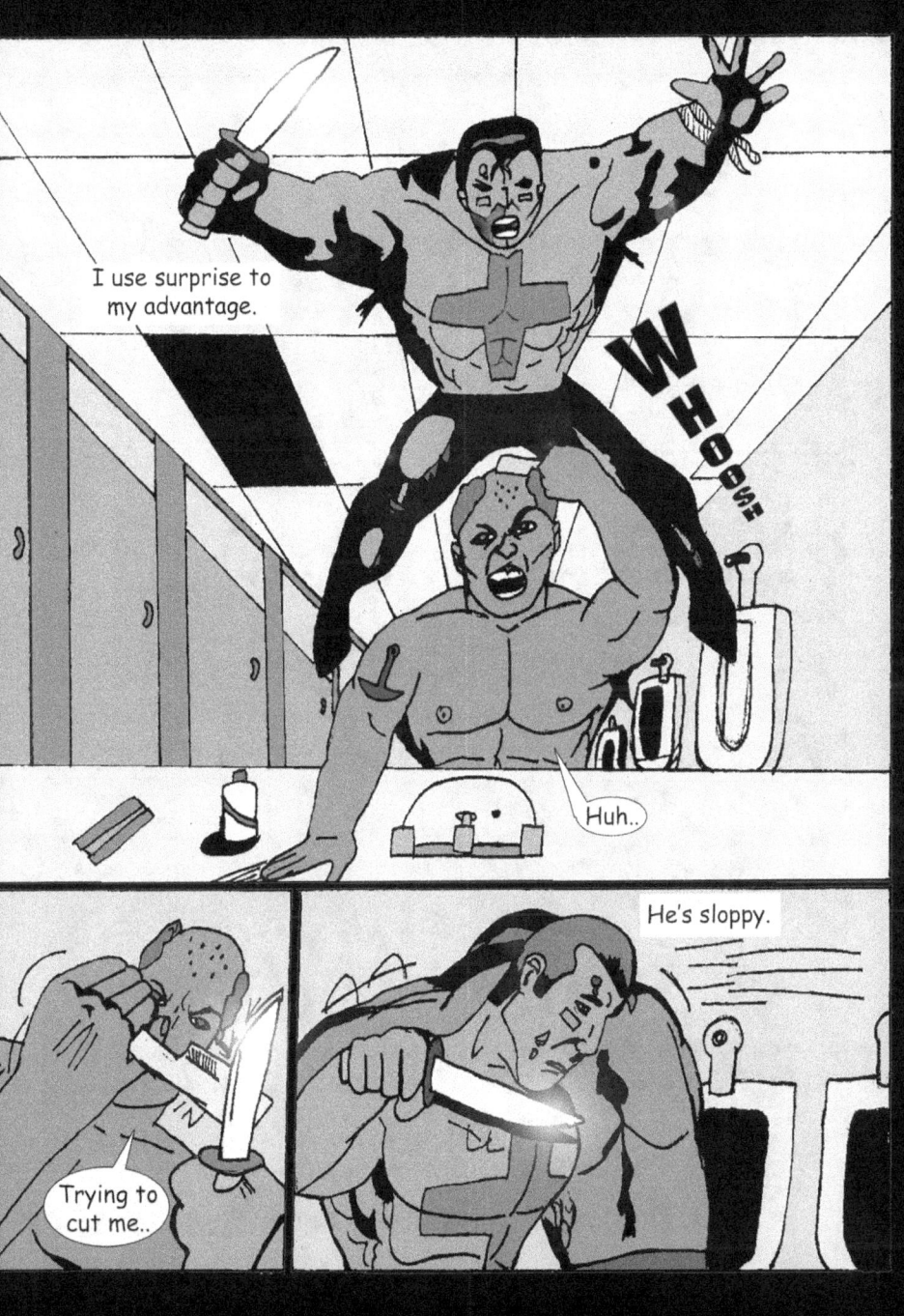

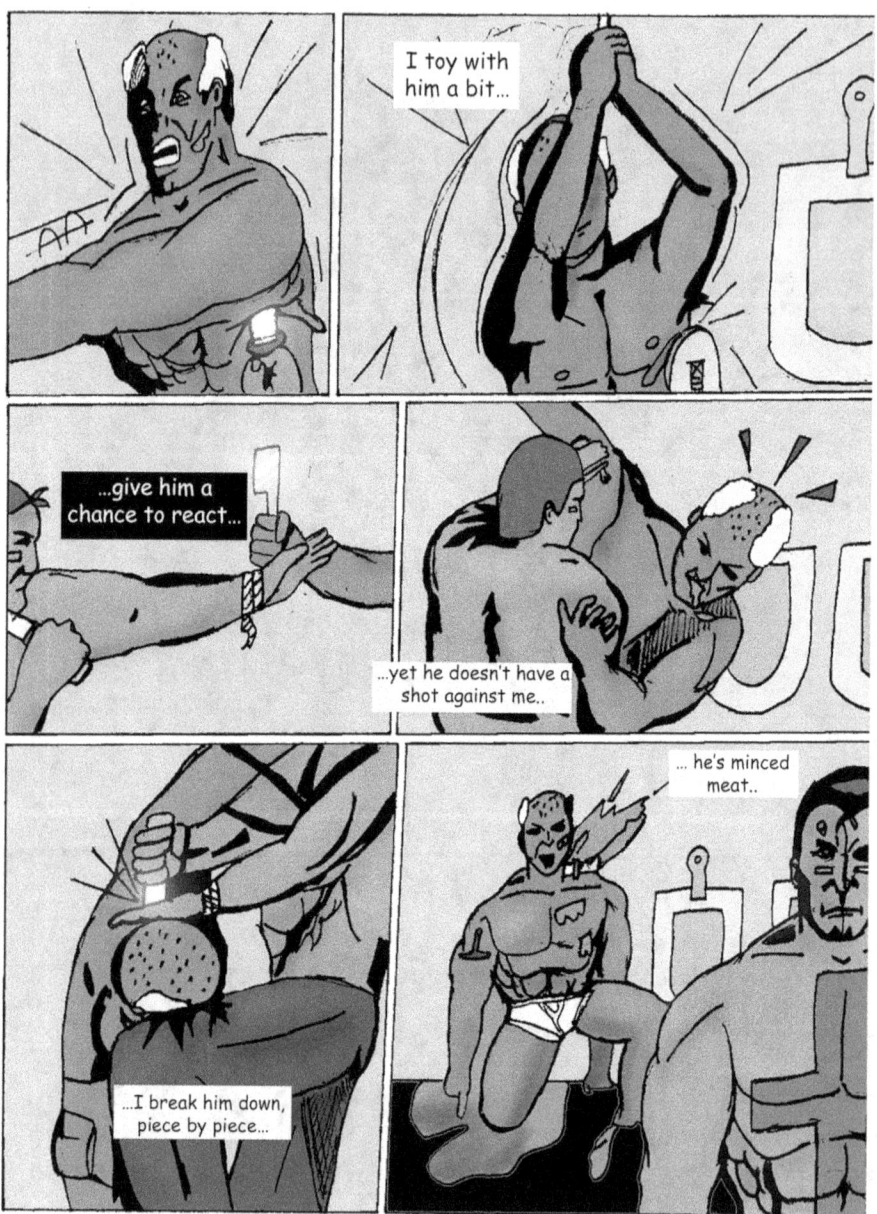

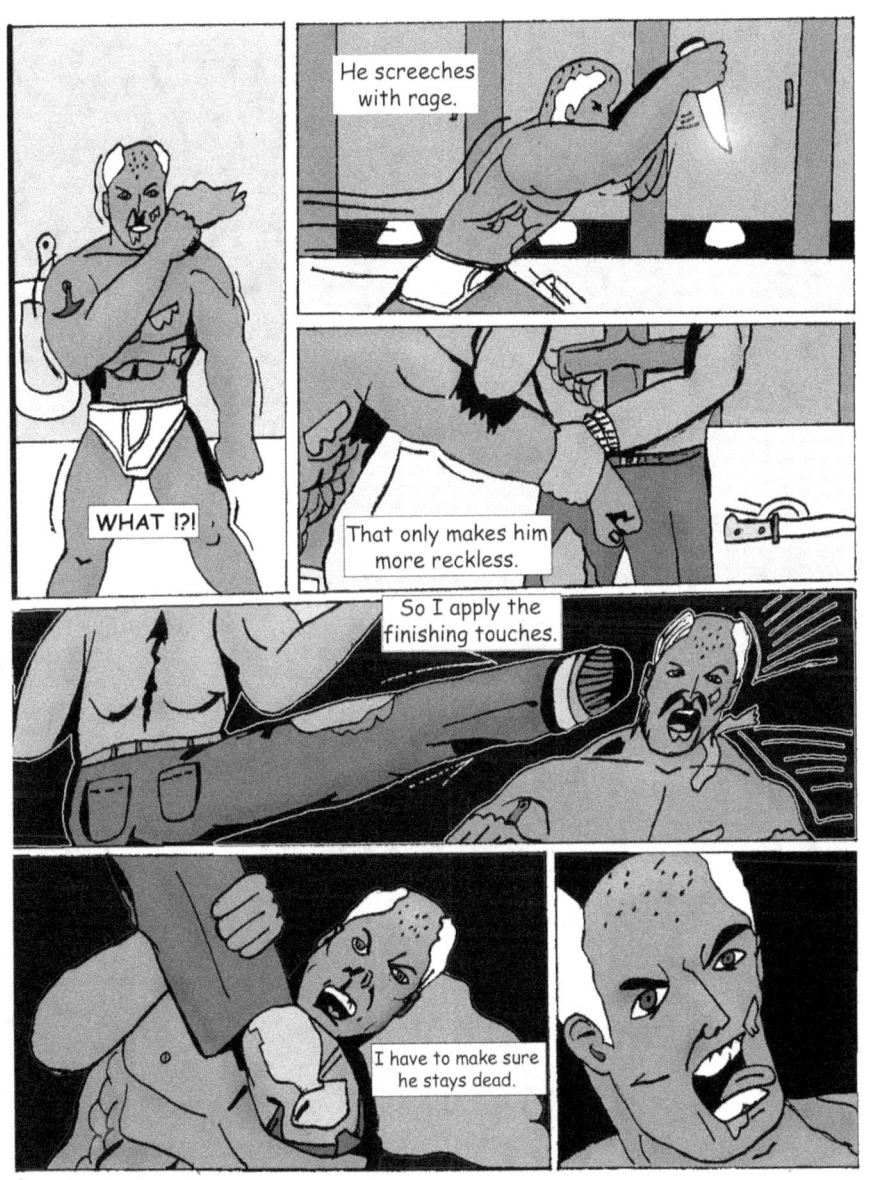

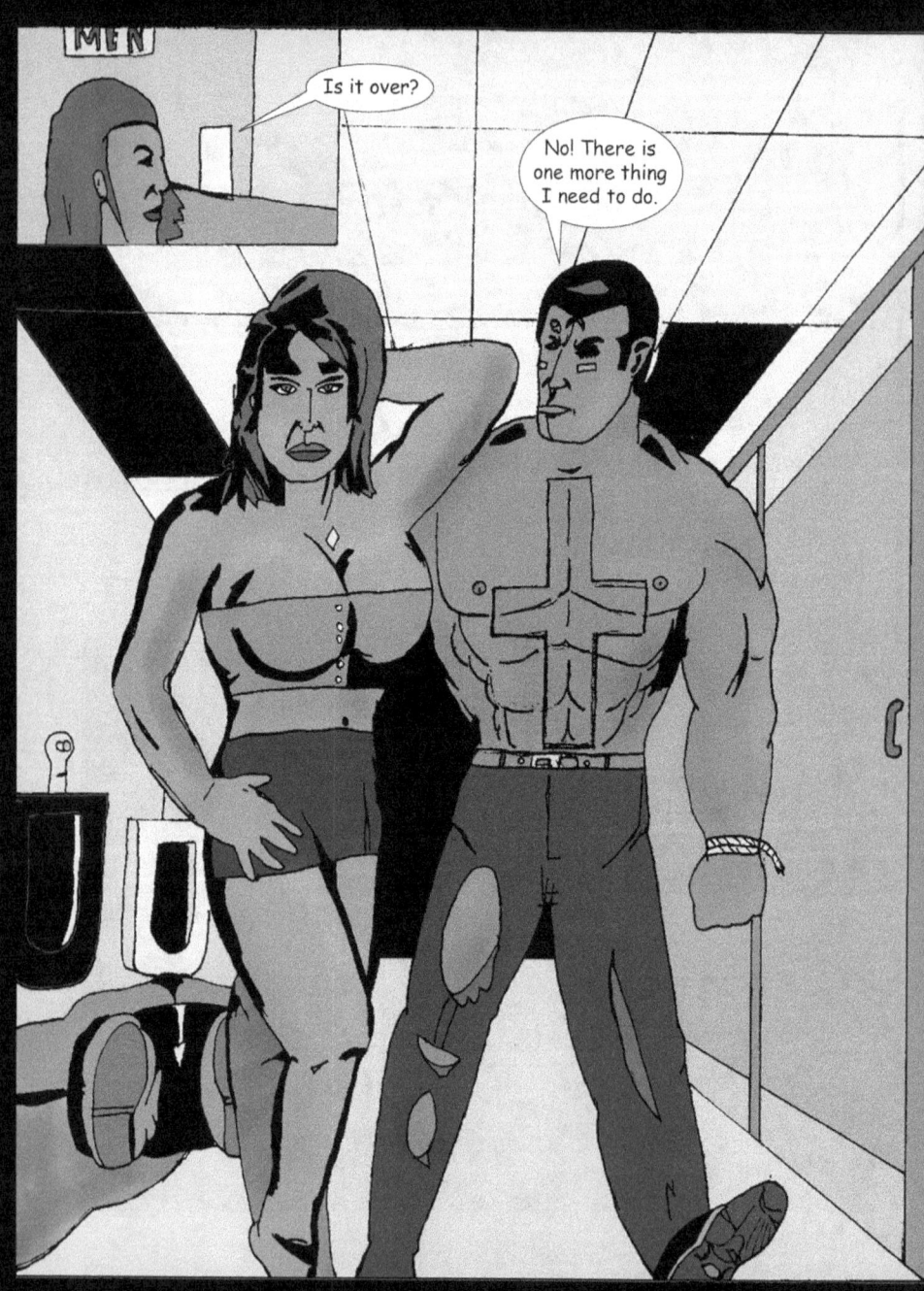

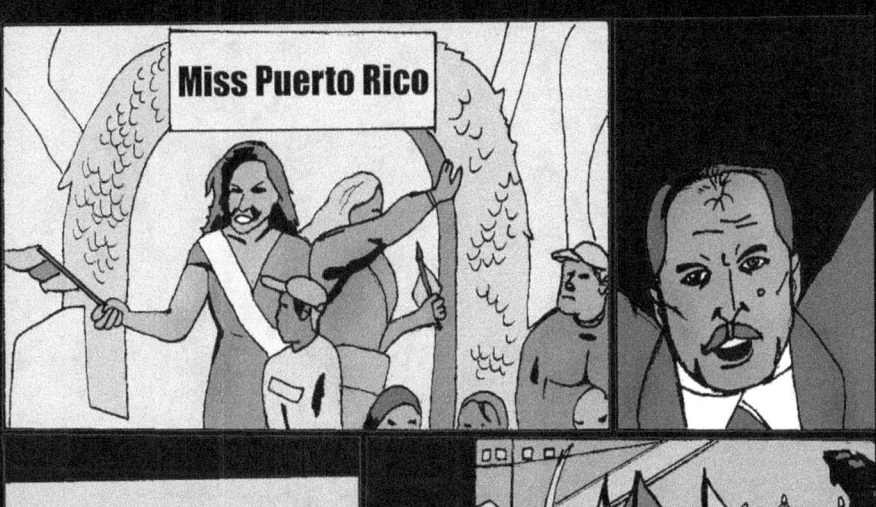

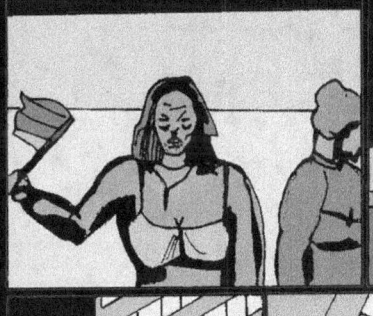

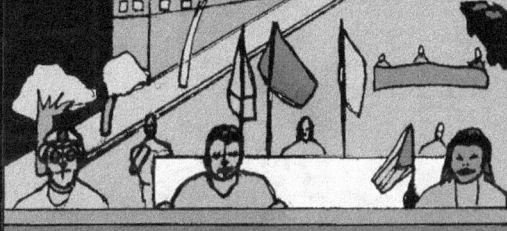

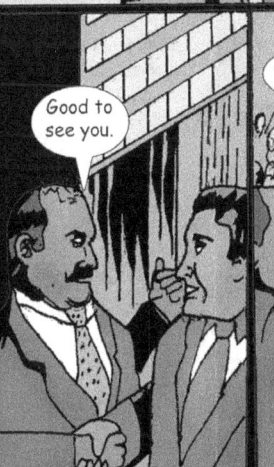

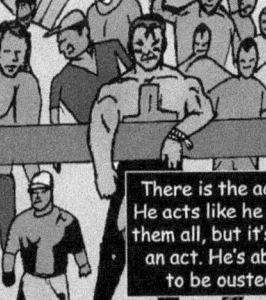

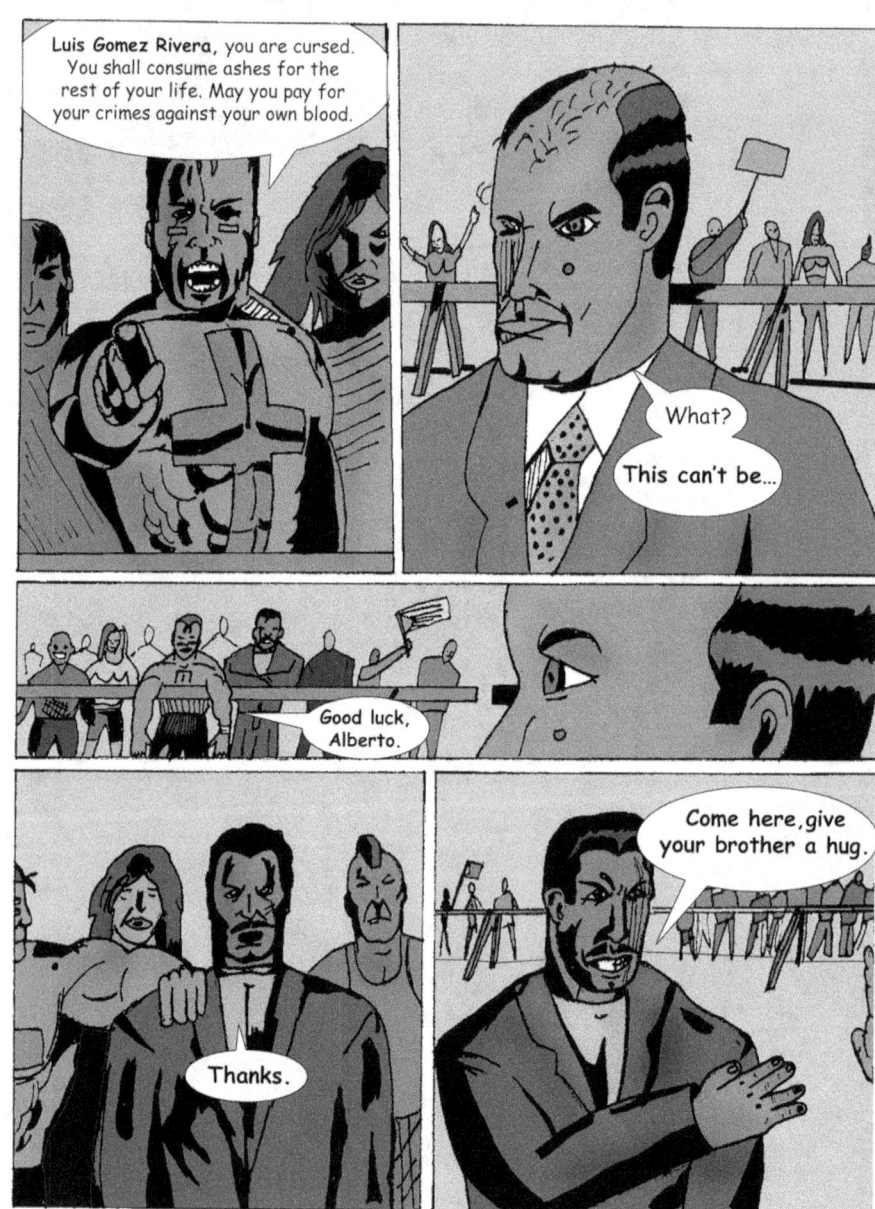

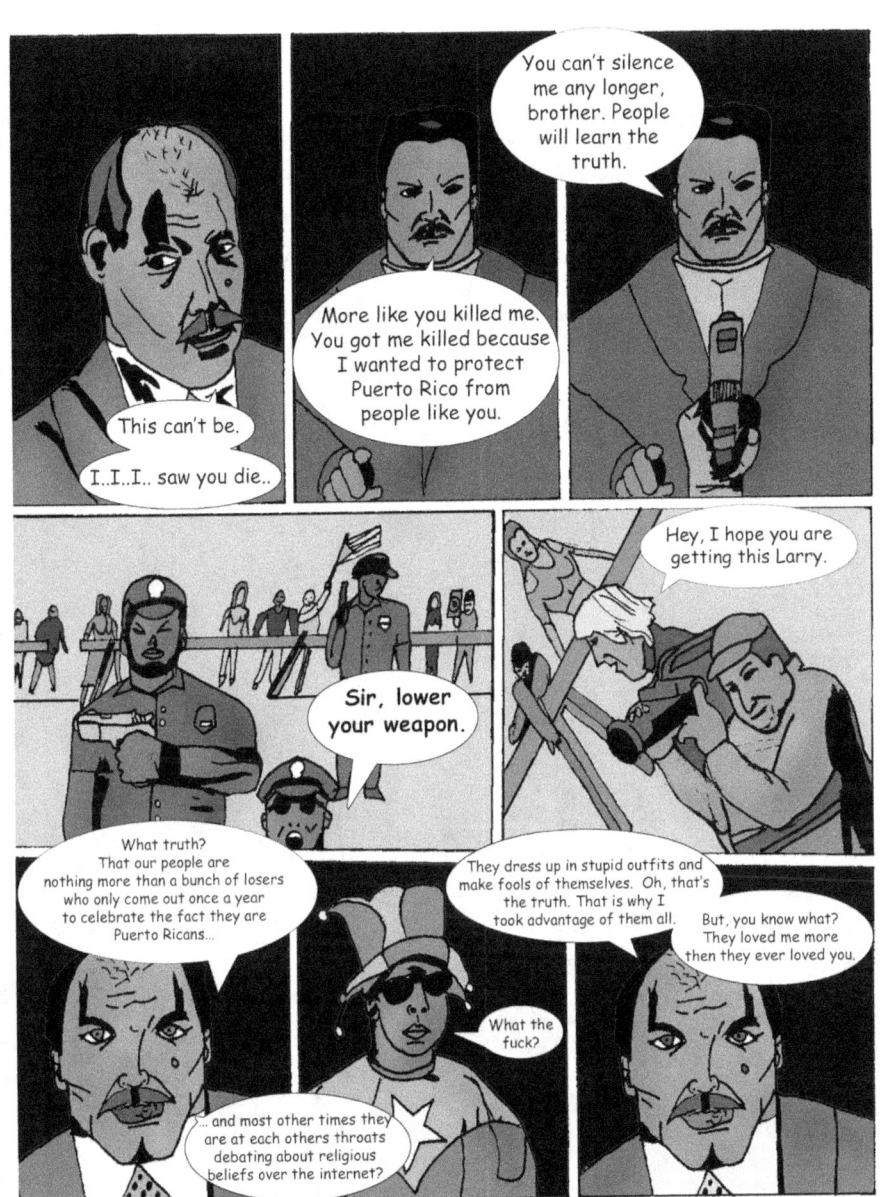

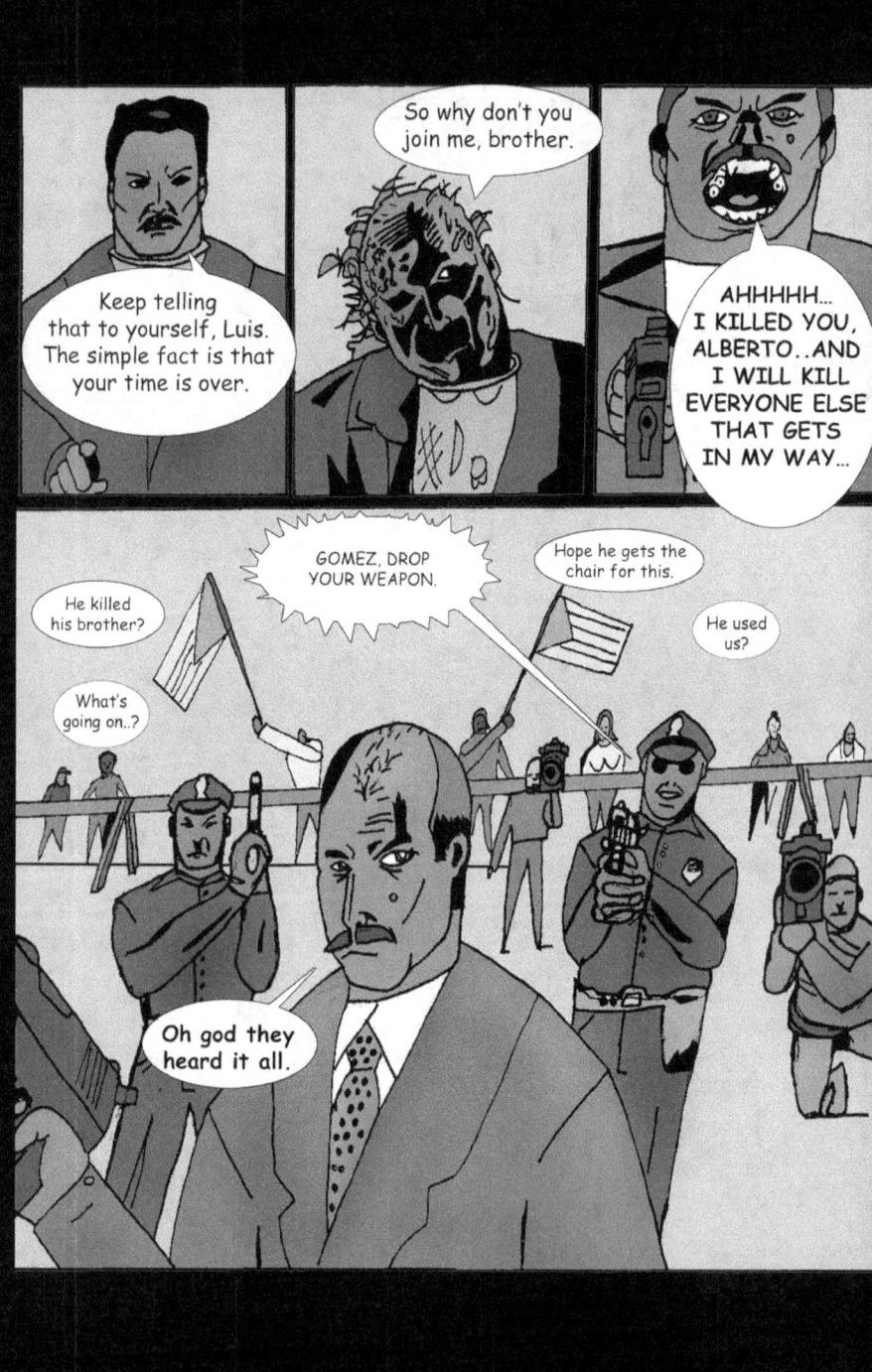

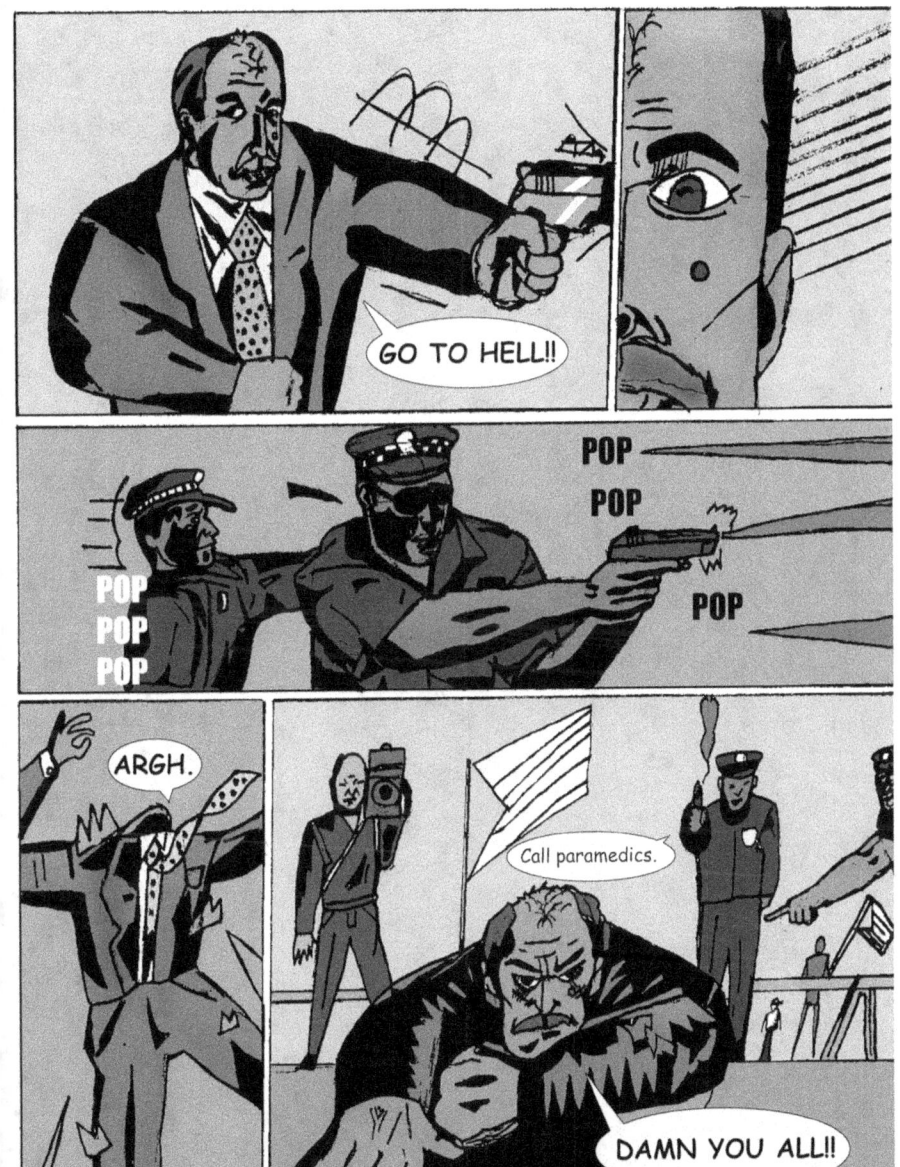

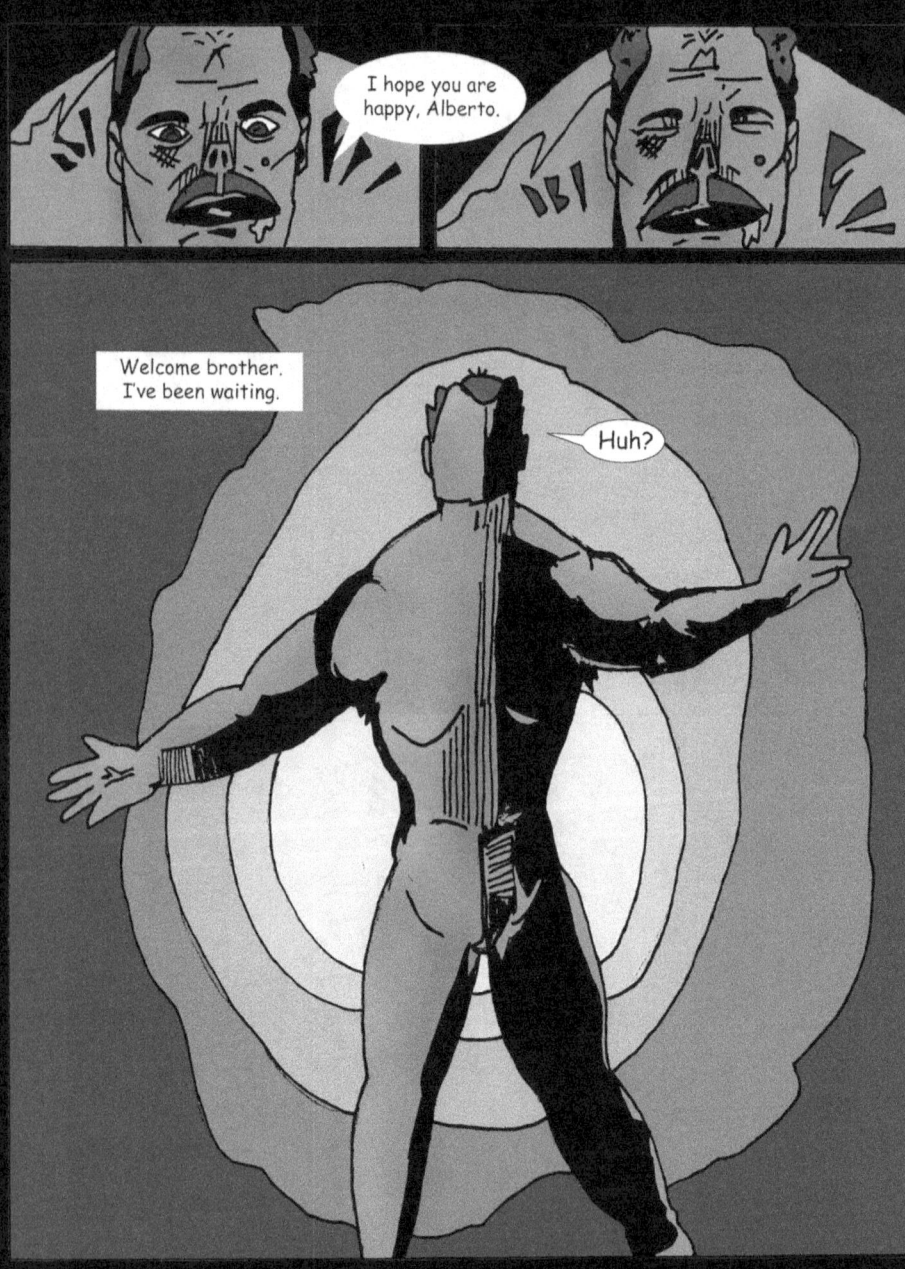

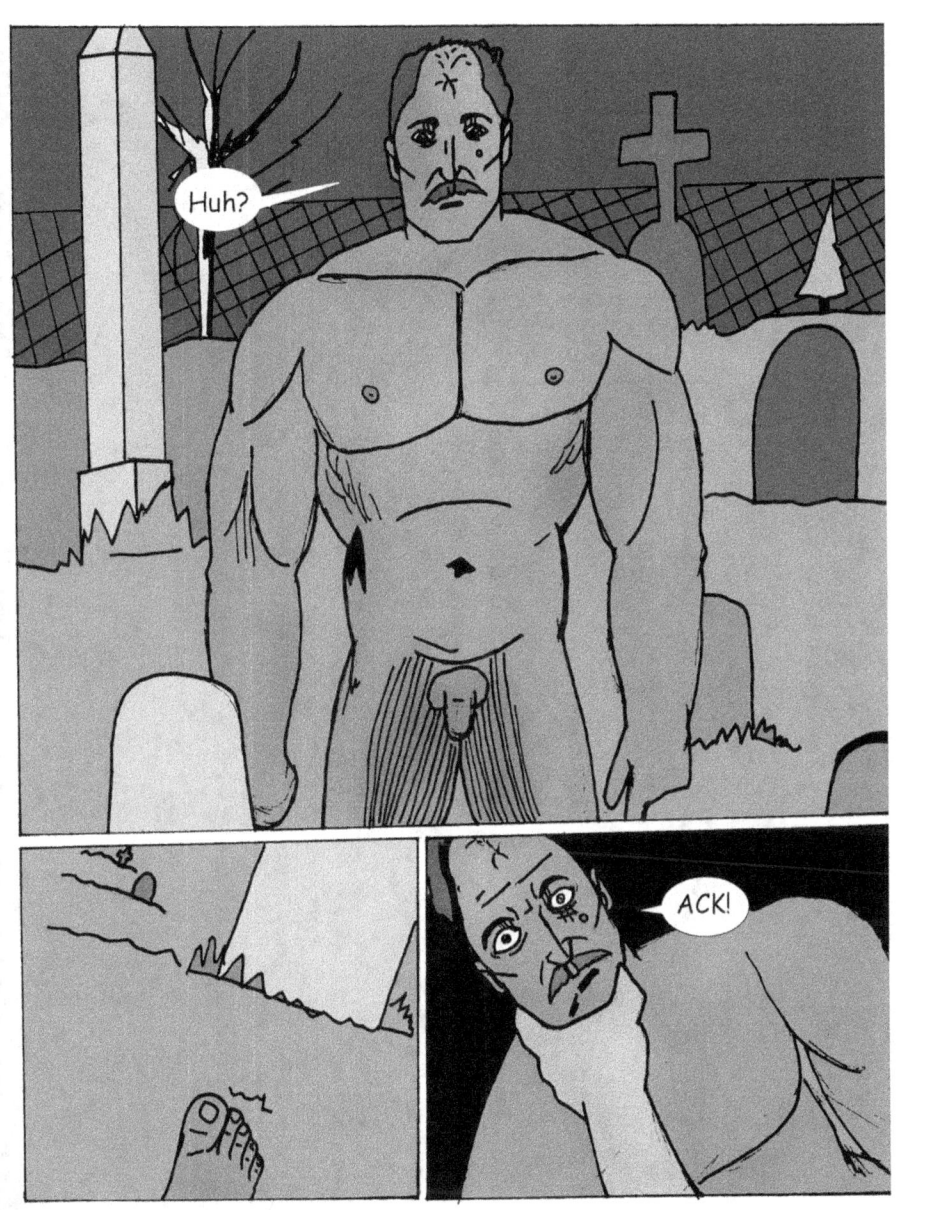

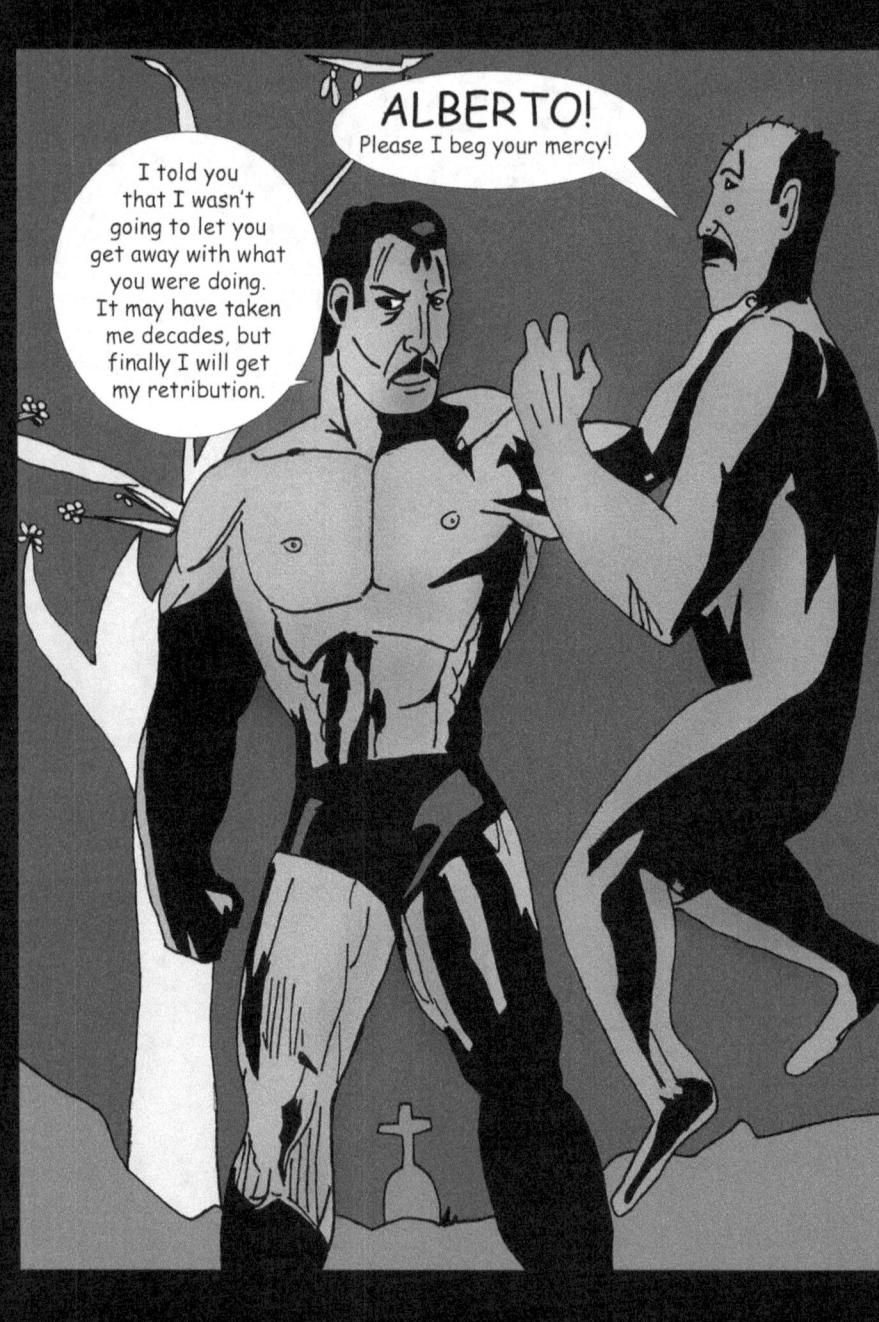

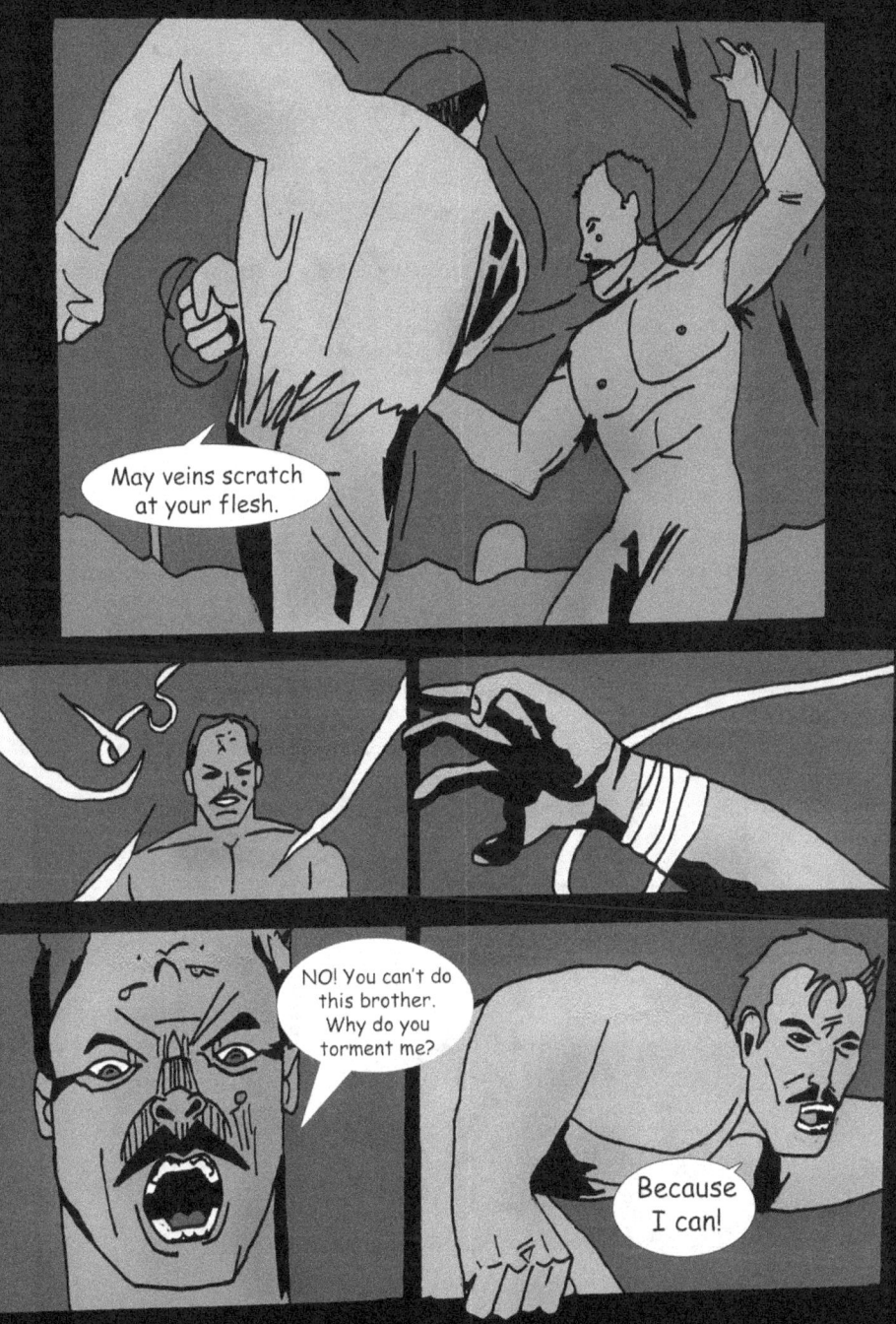

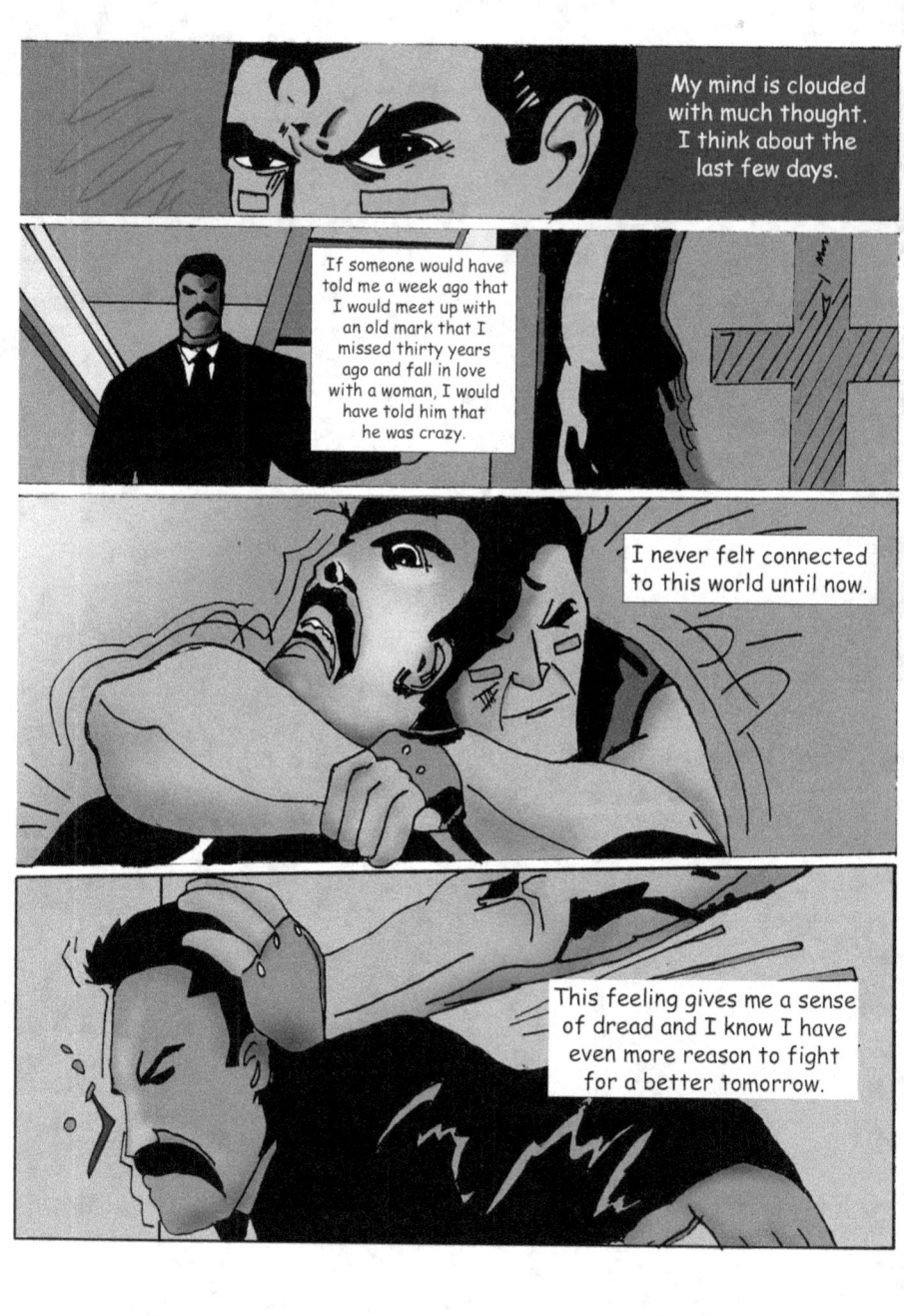

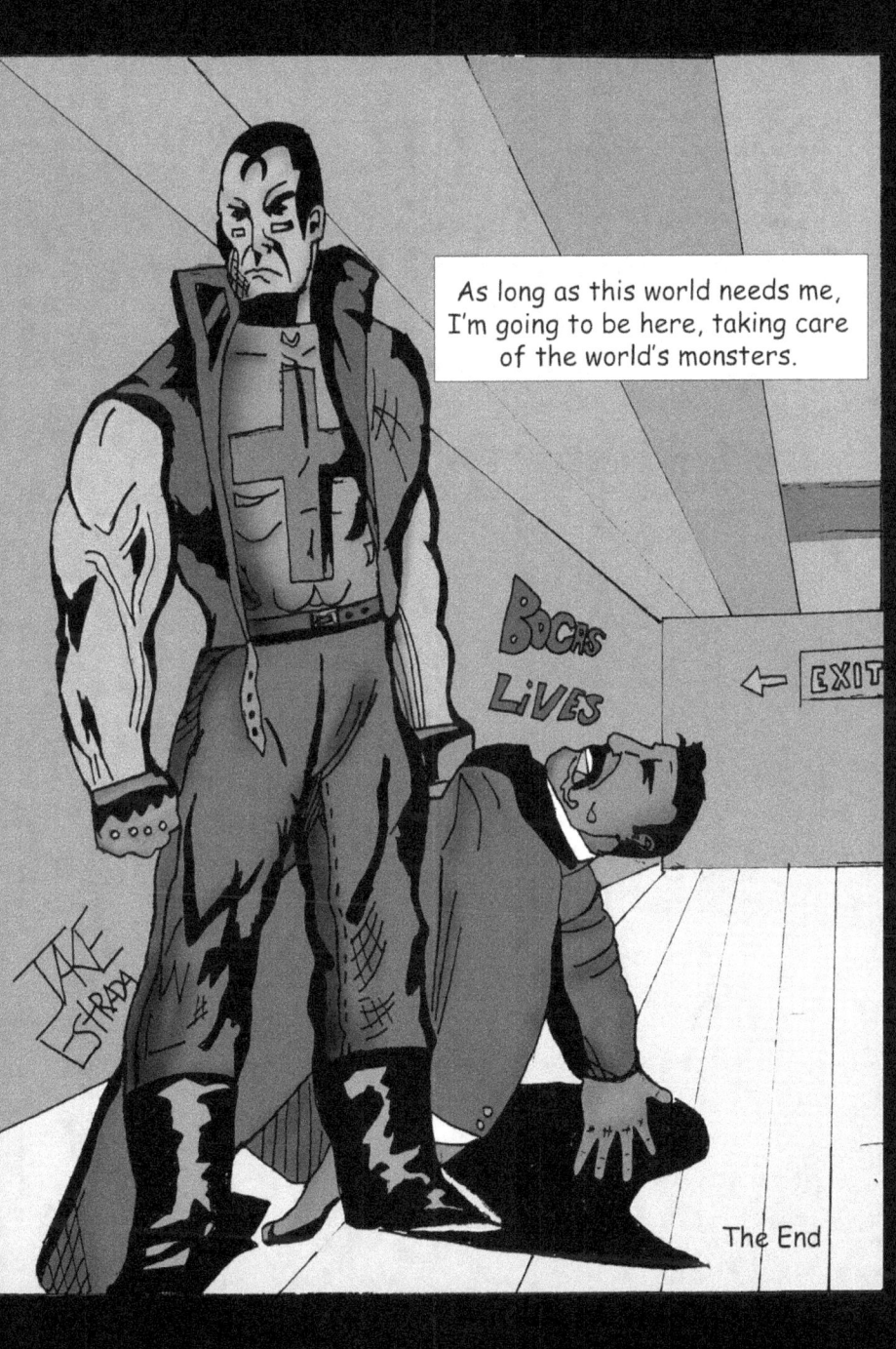

ENTER THE EVIL DOCTOR HEEL!

When innocent blood was spilled, a curse was born. This curse's name is **BOCAS.**

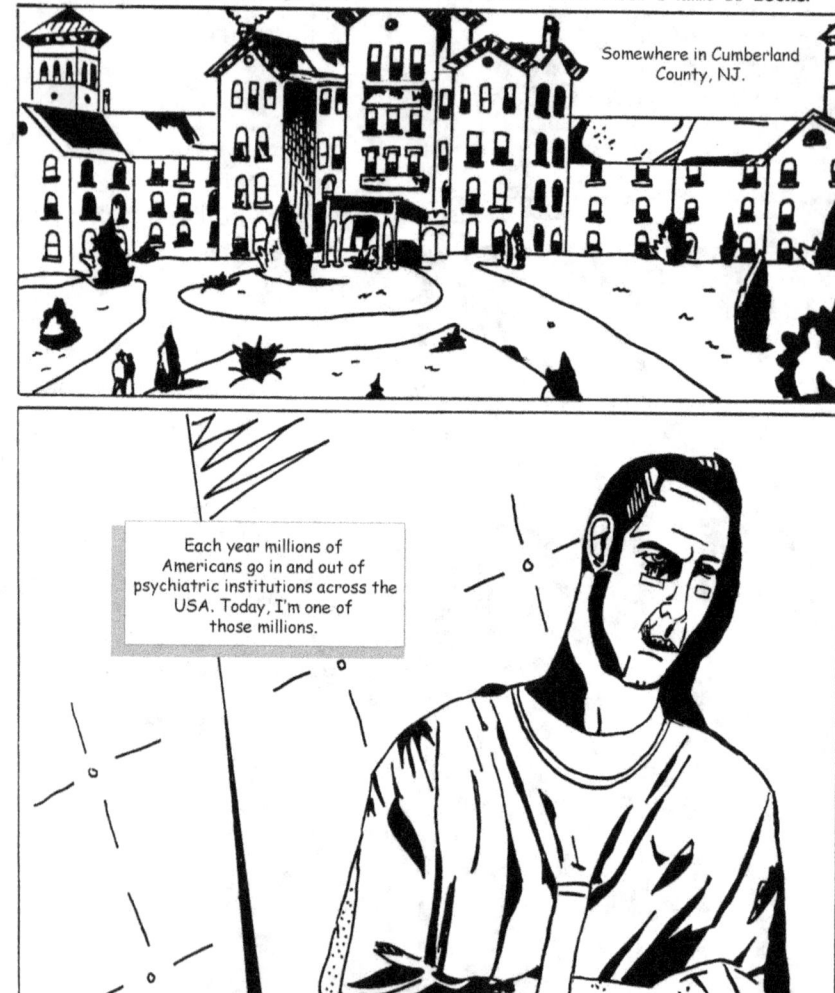

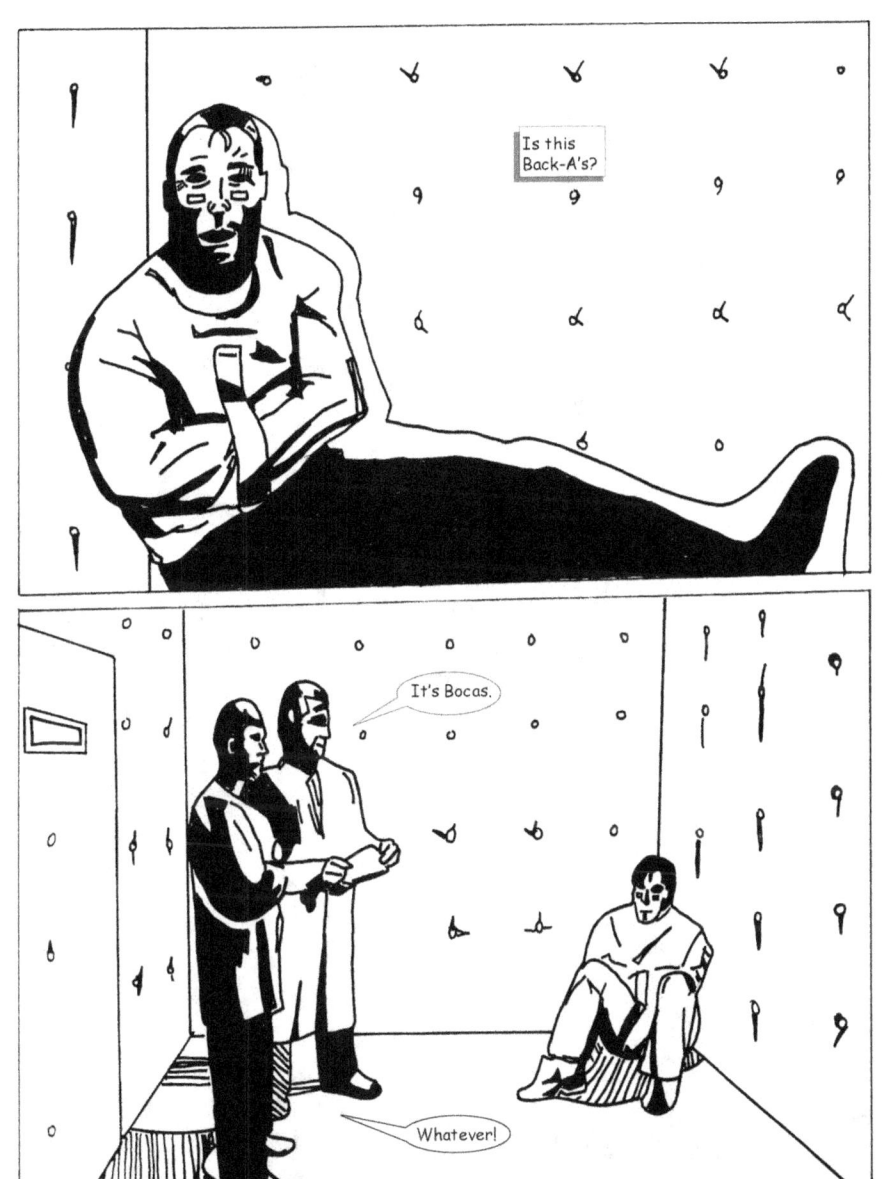

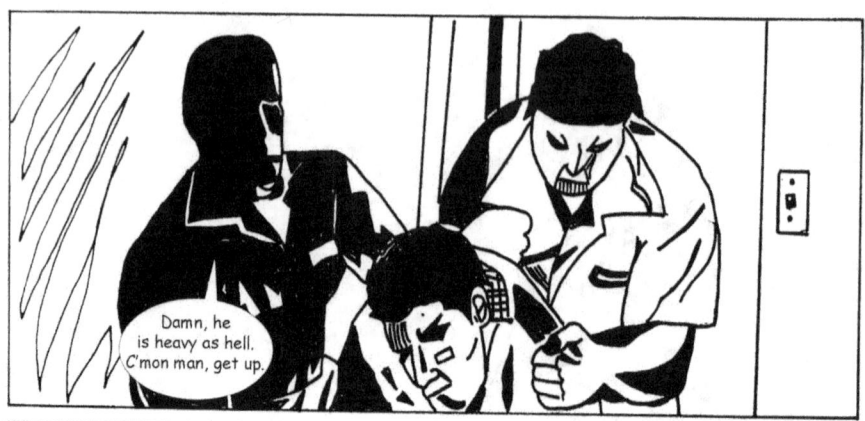

Damn, he is heavy as hell. C'mon man, get up.

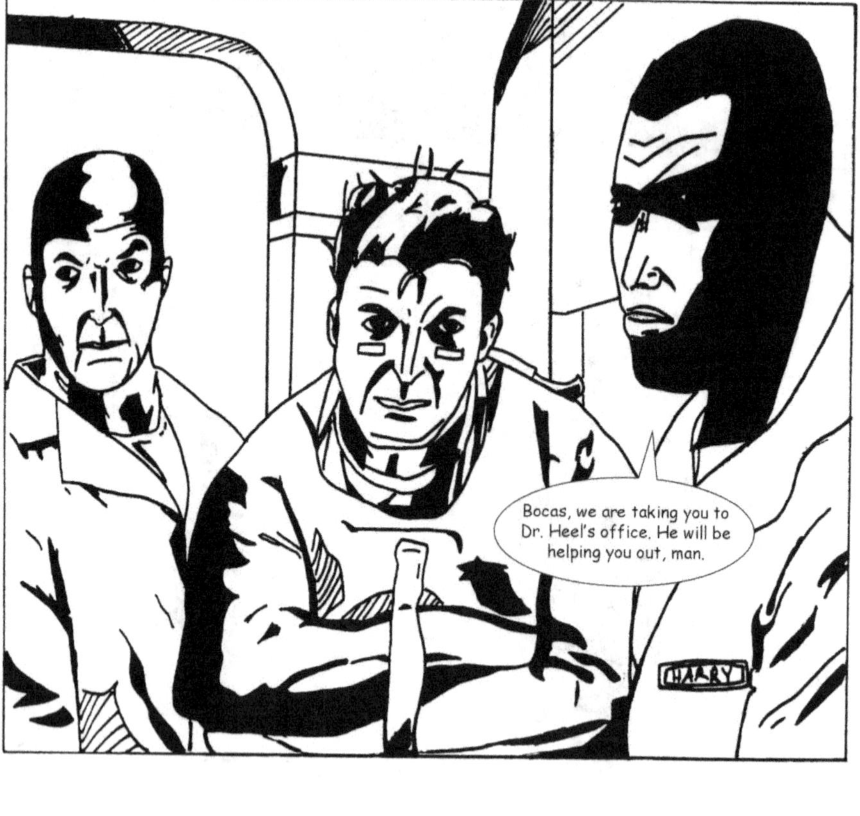

Bocas, we are taking you to Dr. Heel's office. He will be helping you out, man.

HARRY

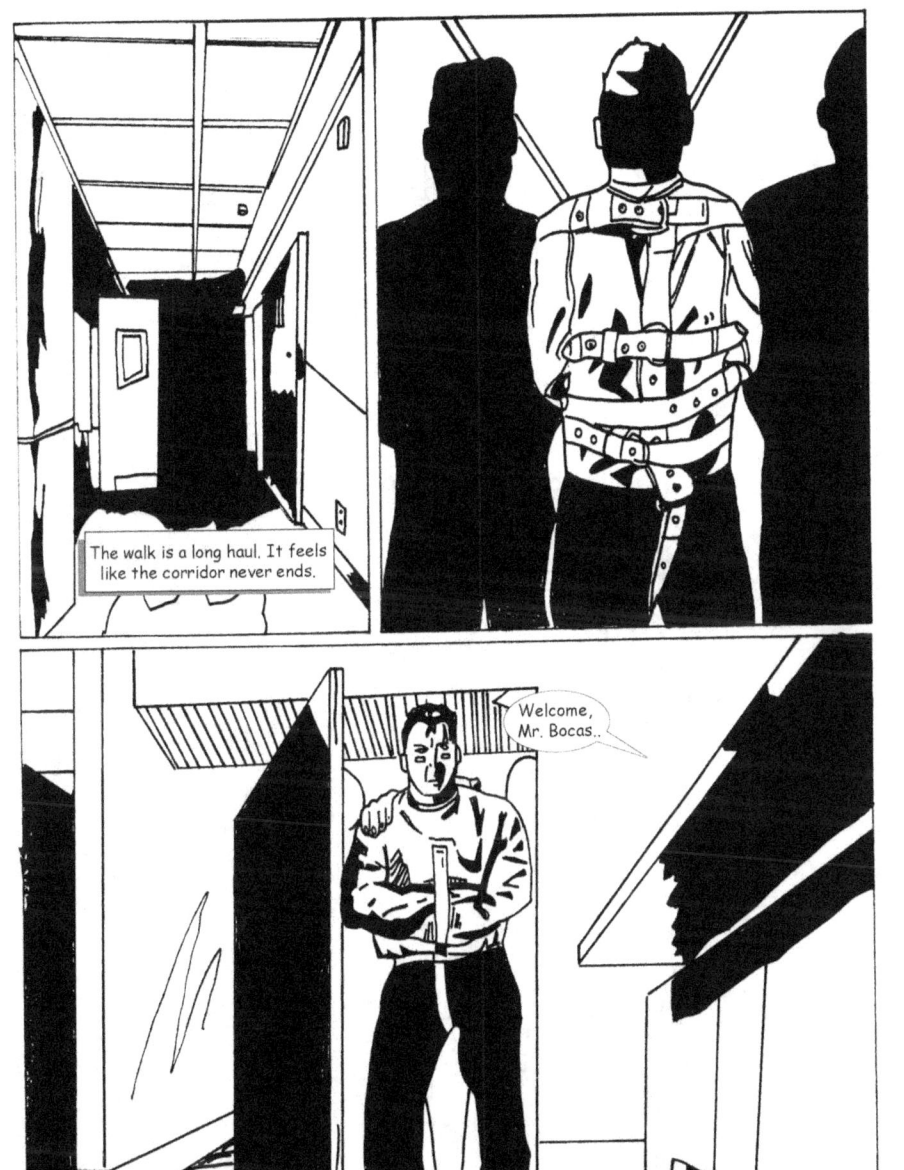

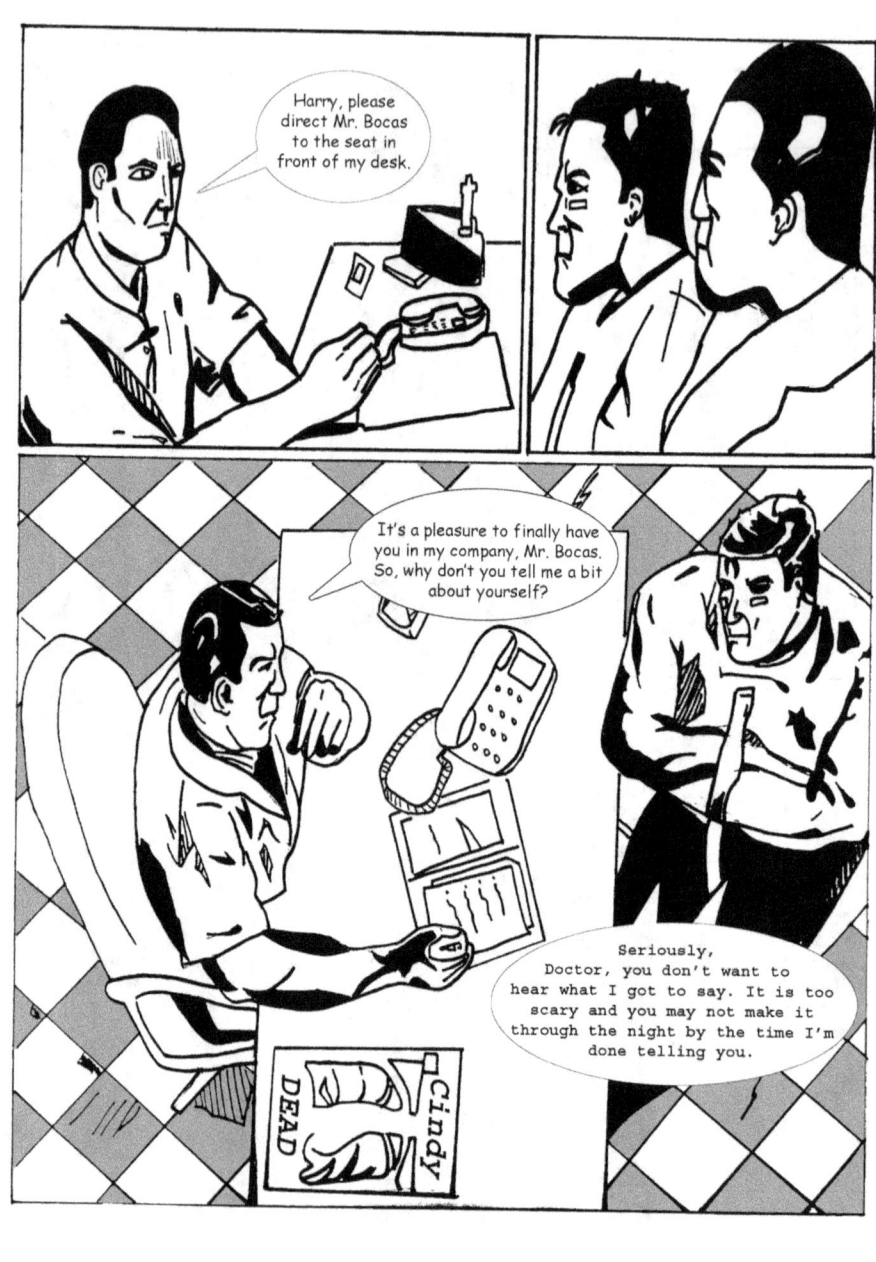

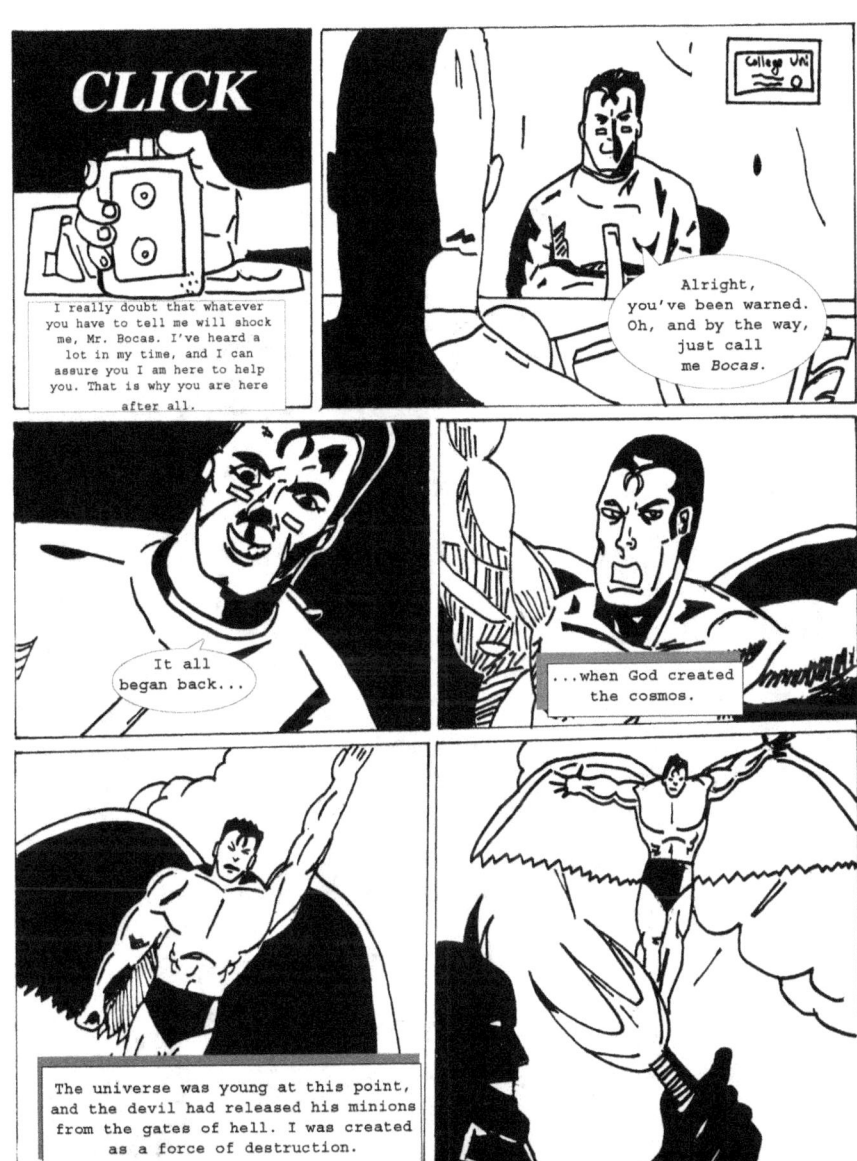

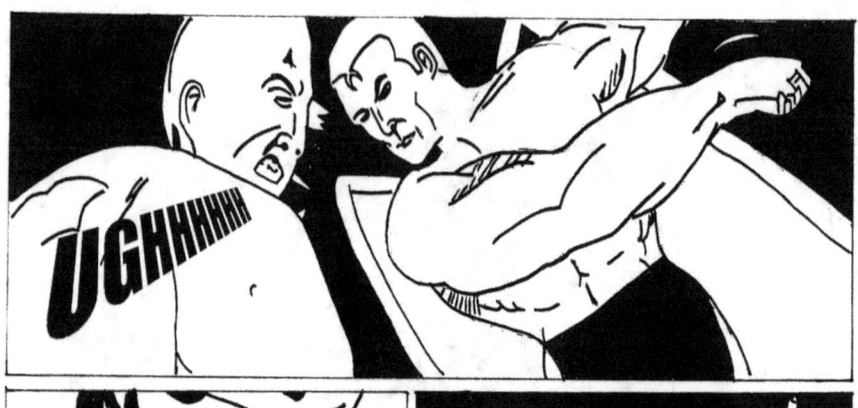

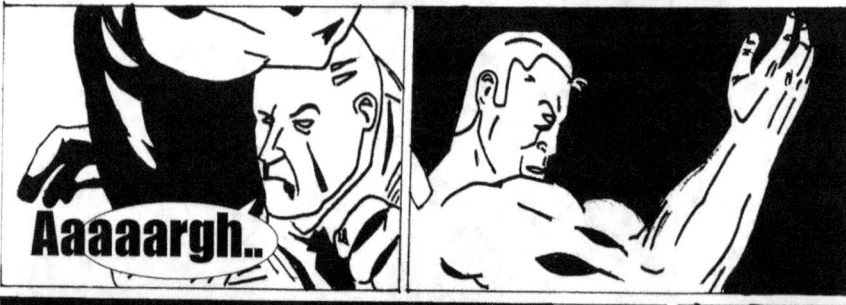

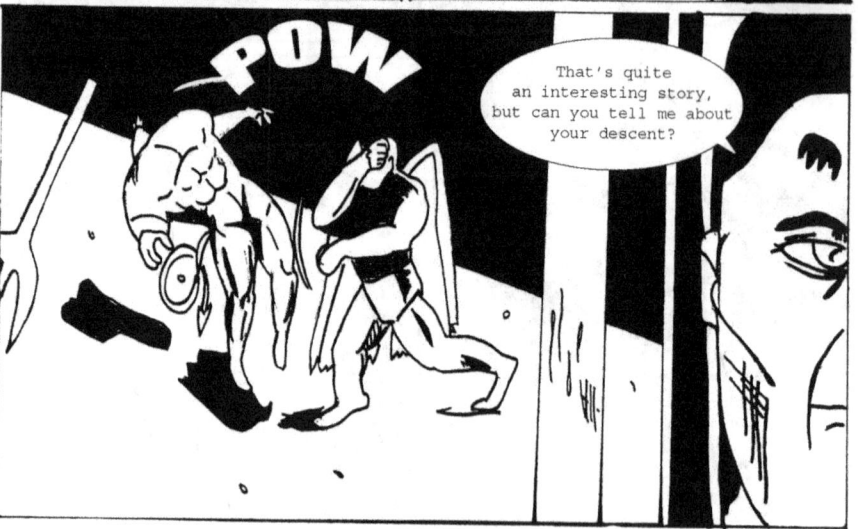

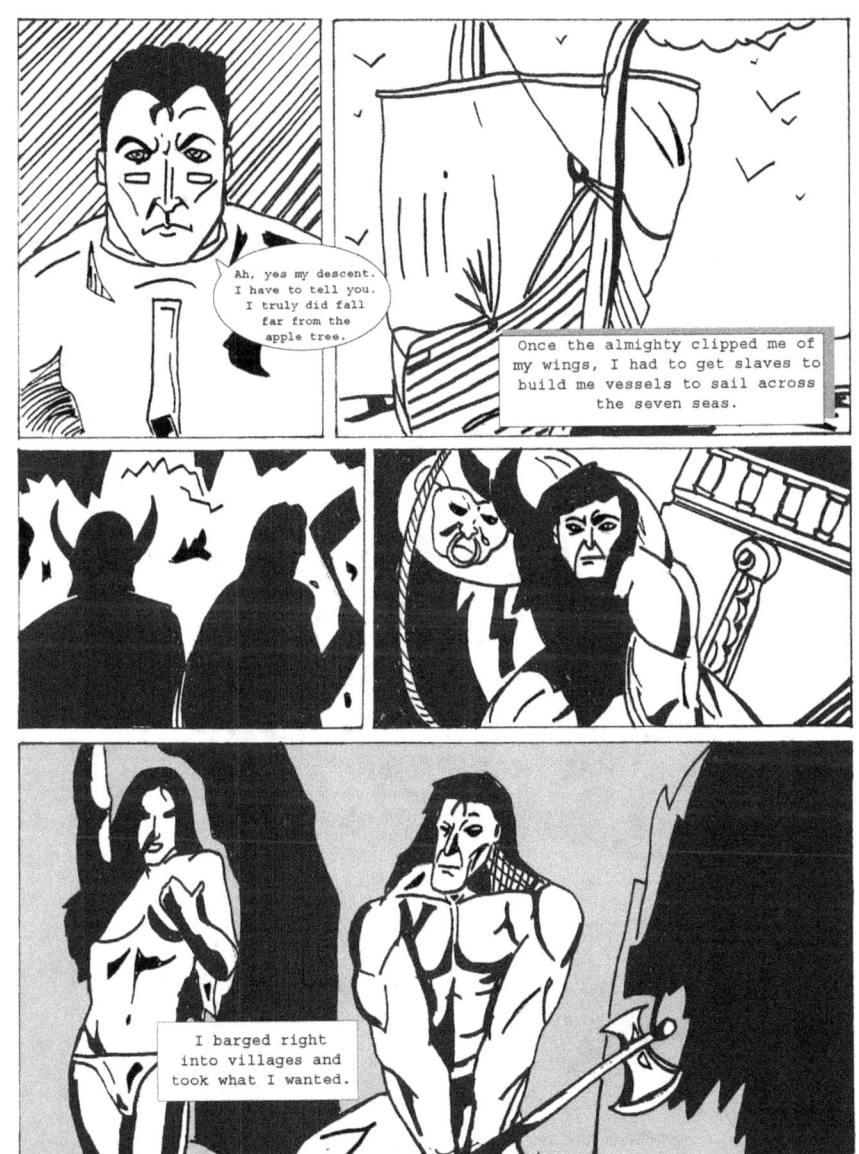

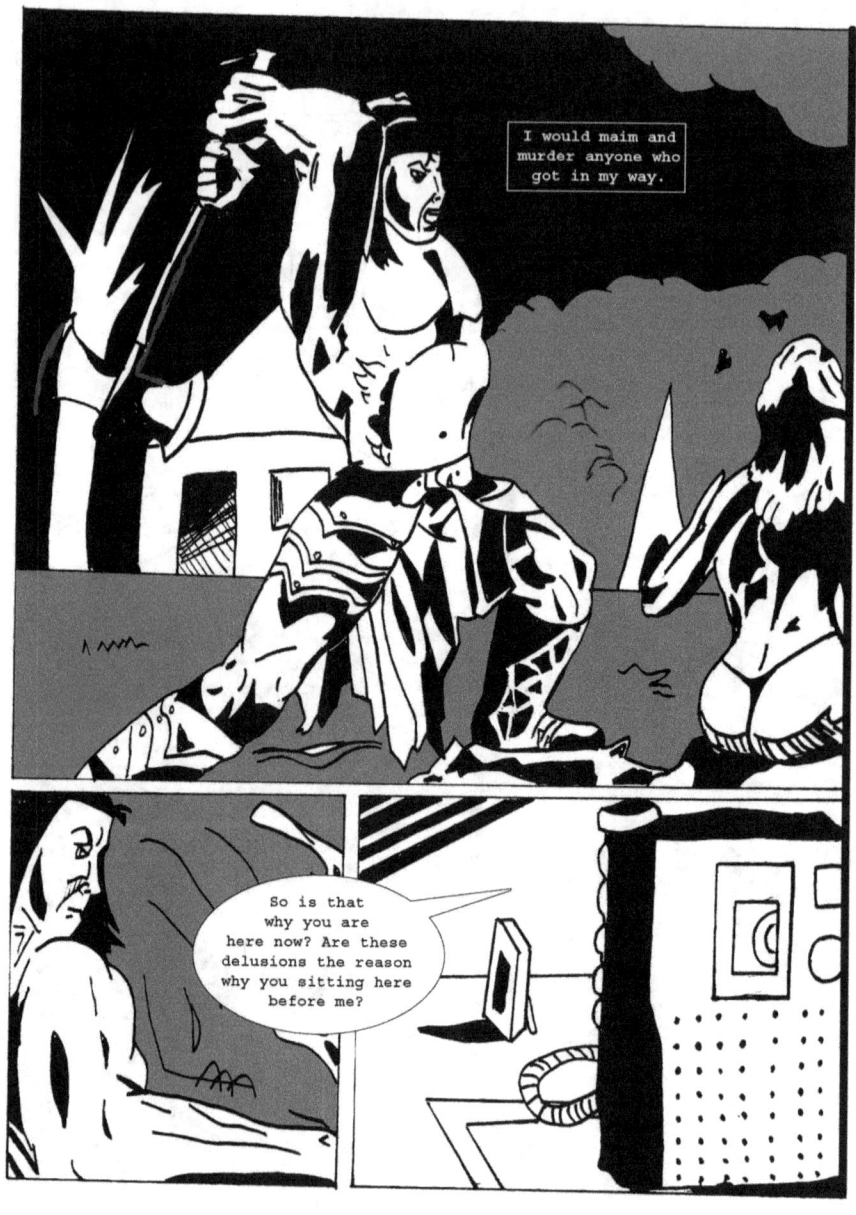

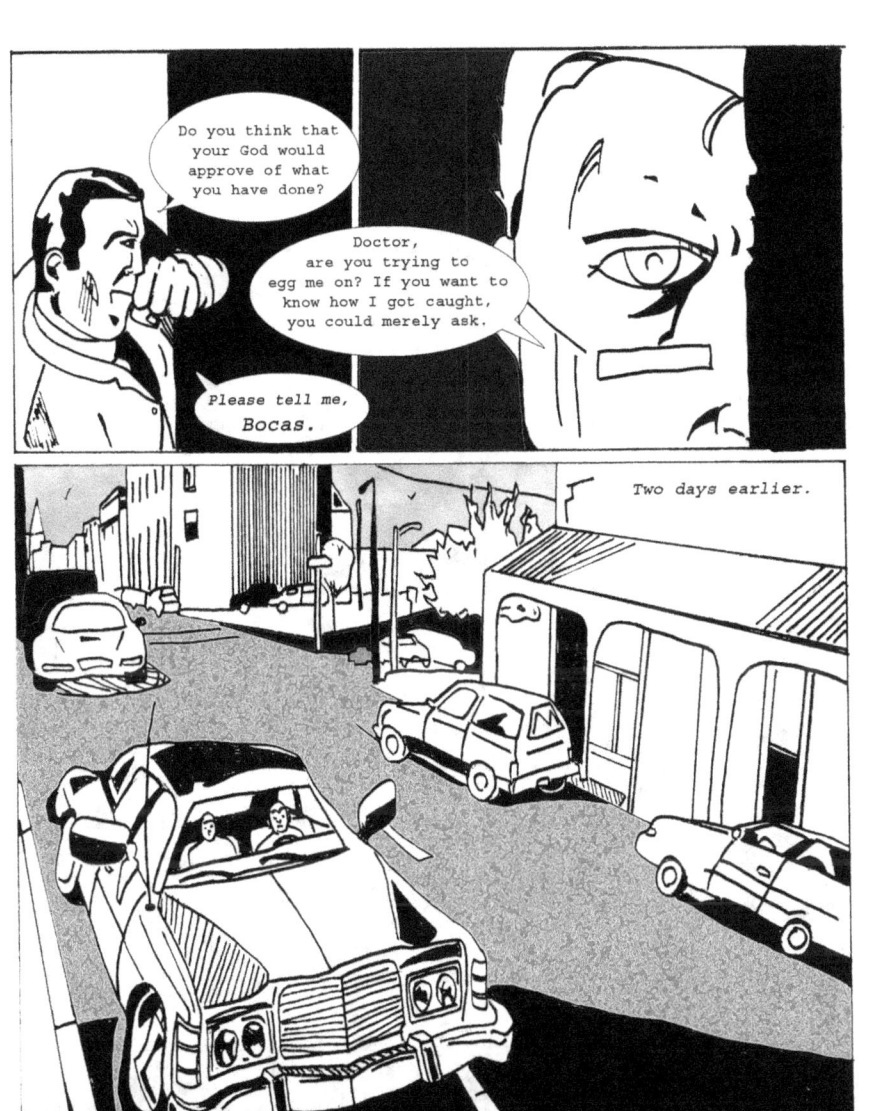

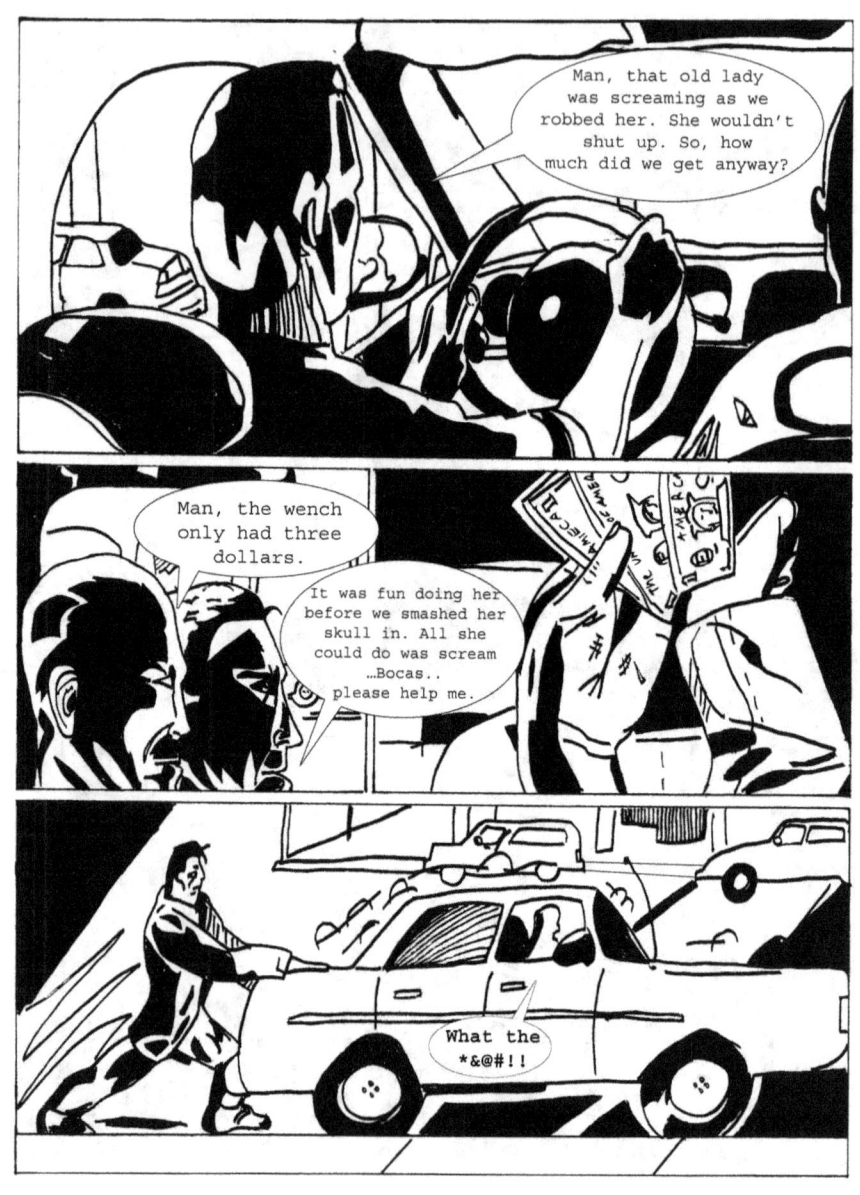

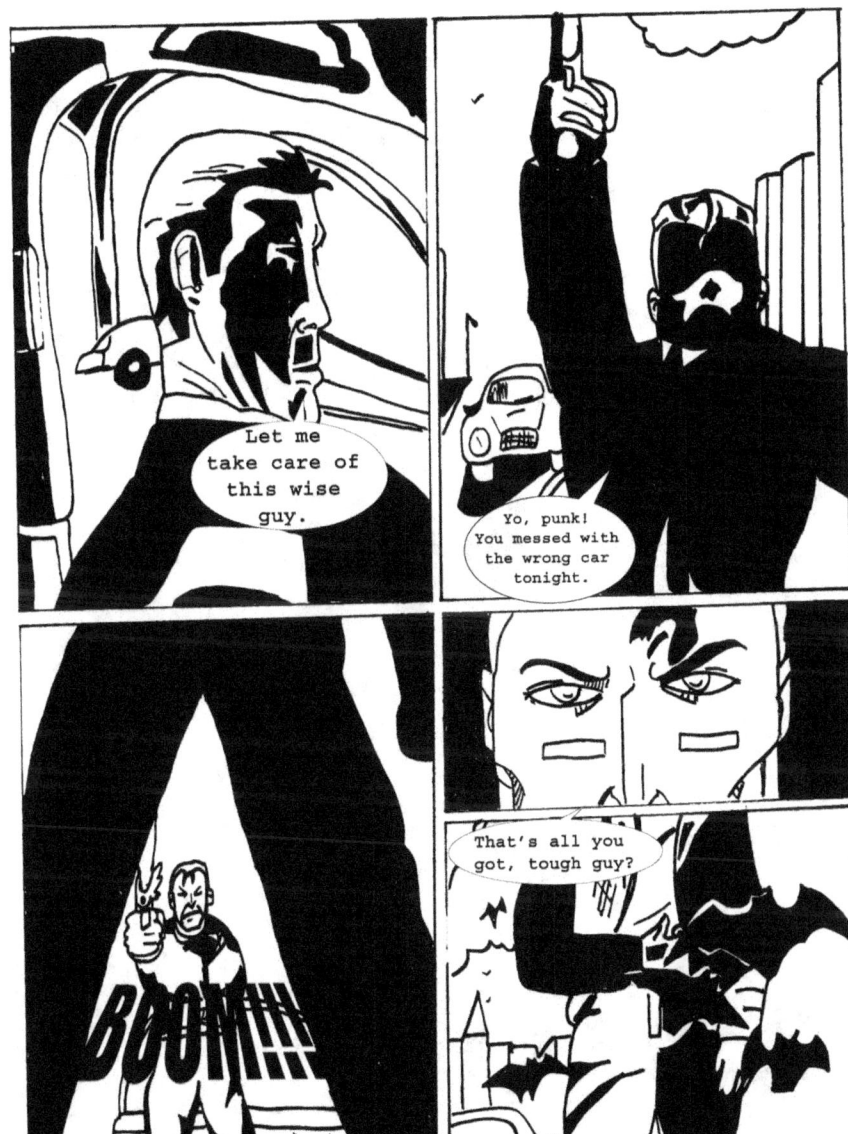

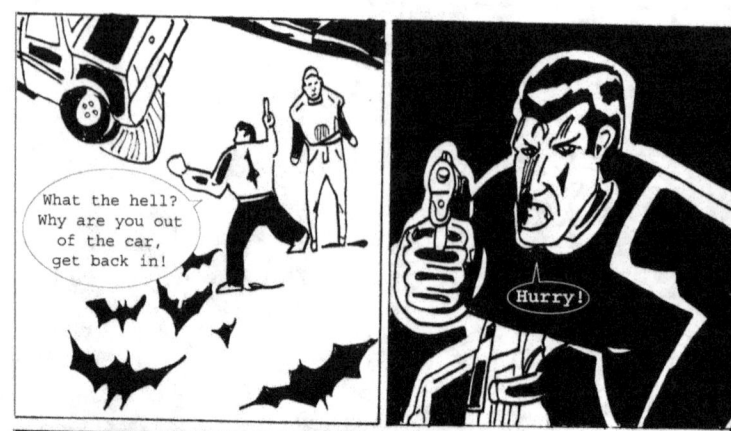

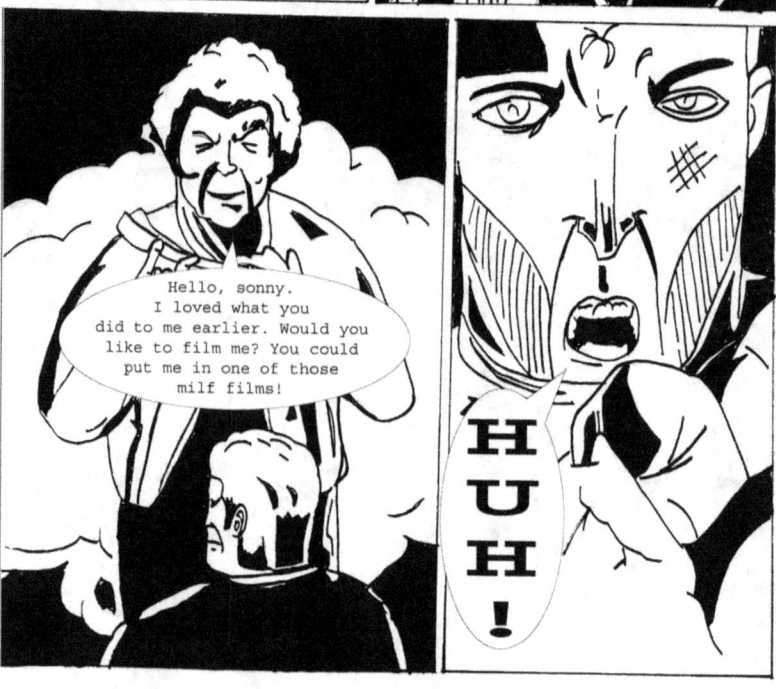

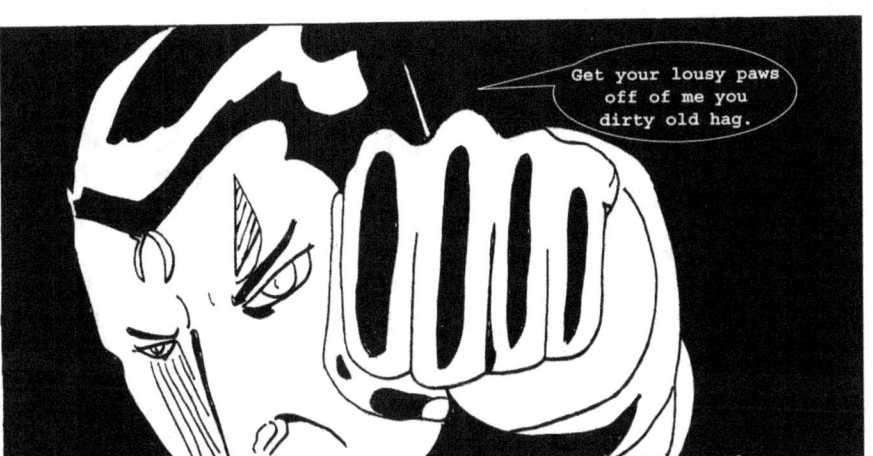

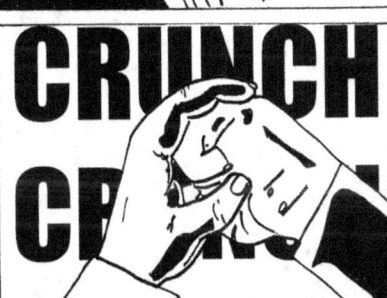

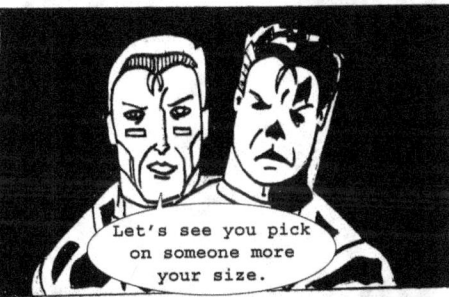

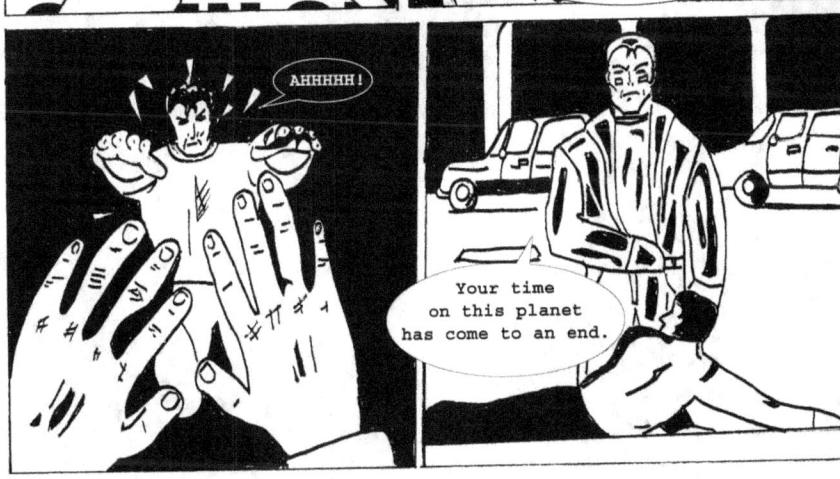

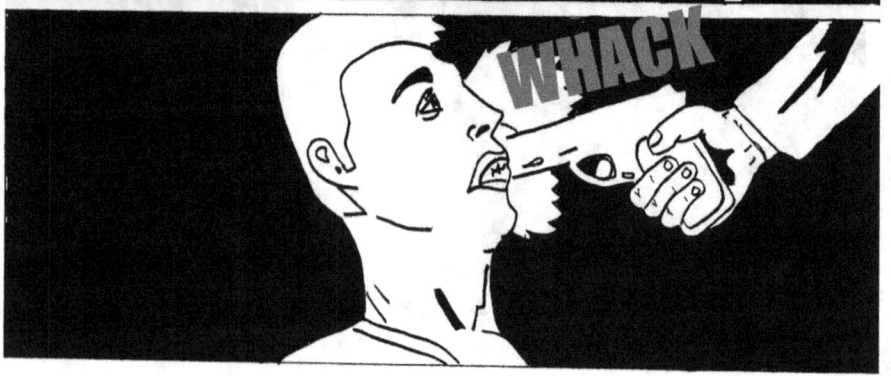

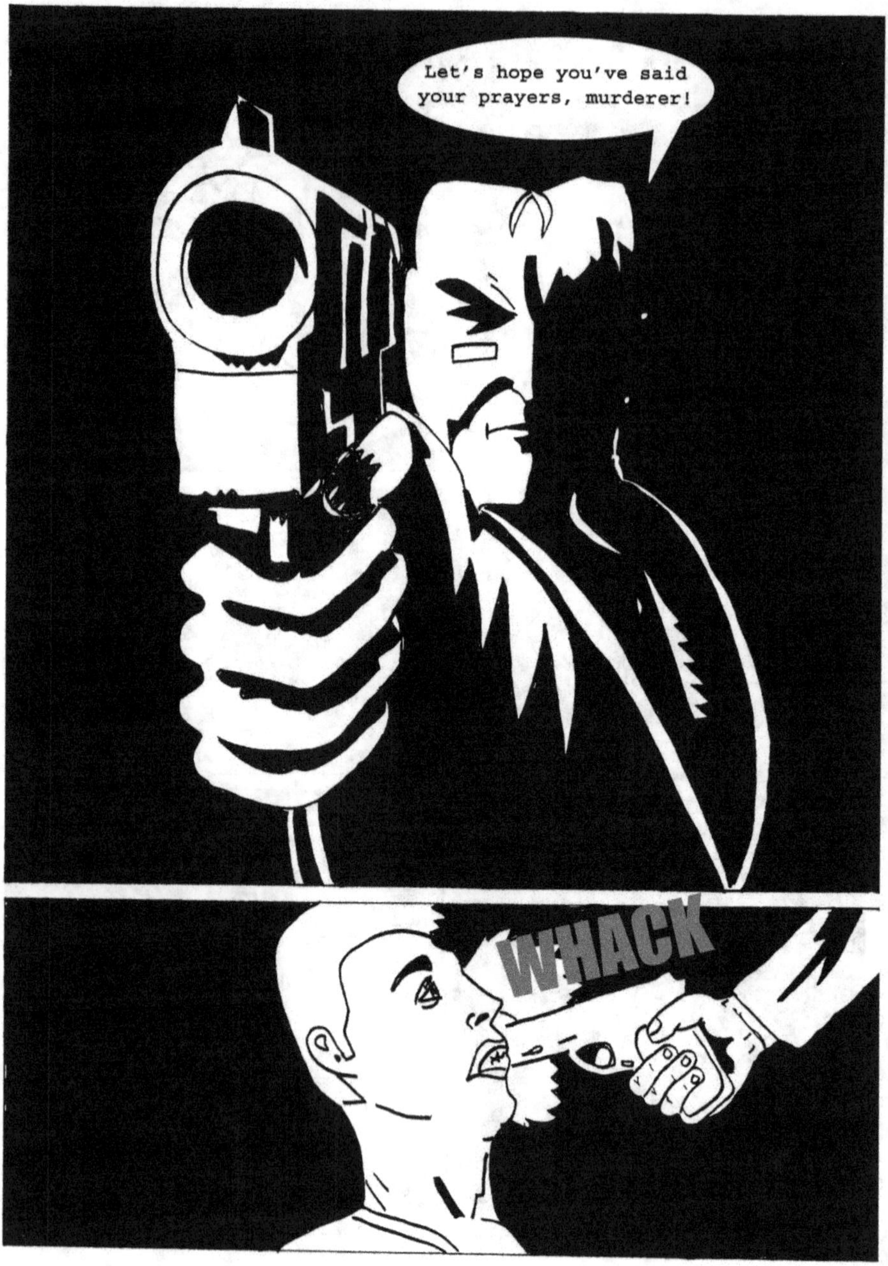

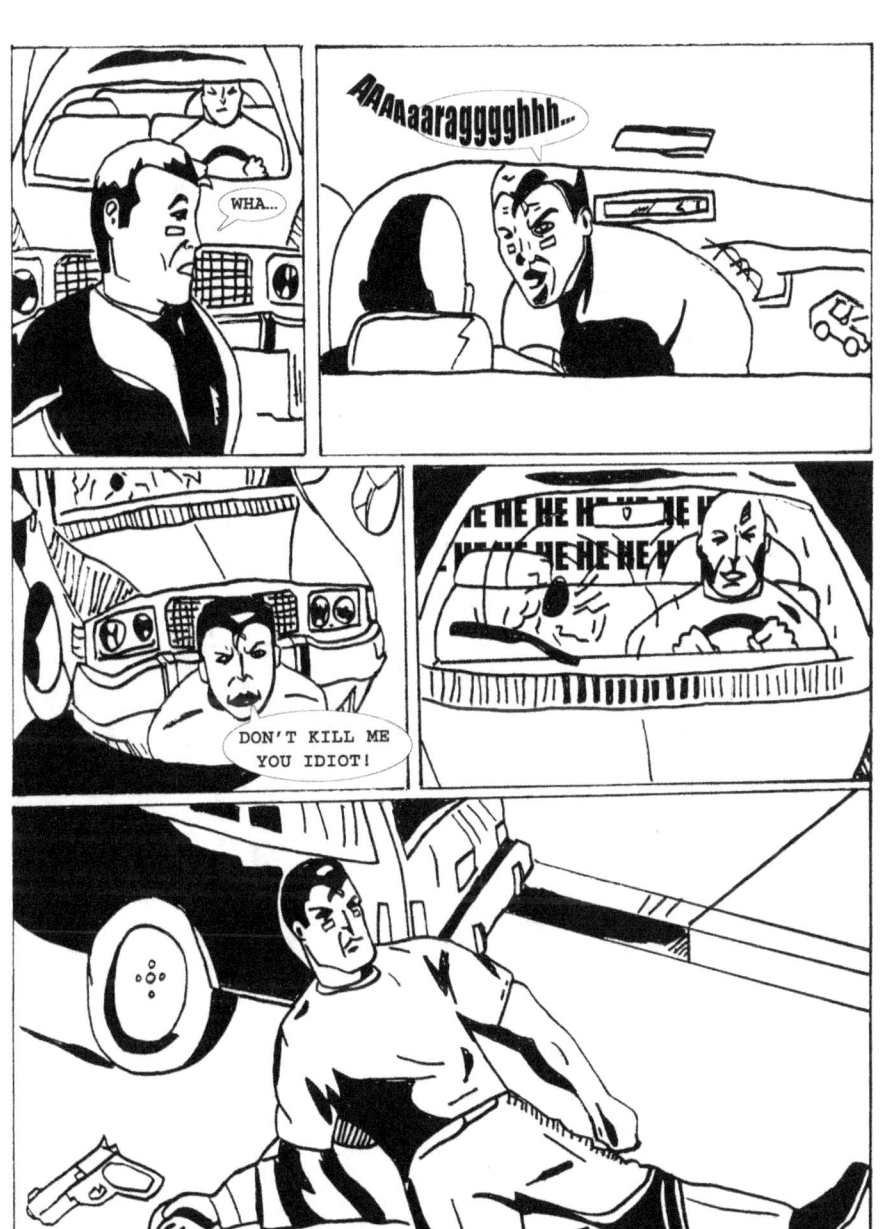

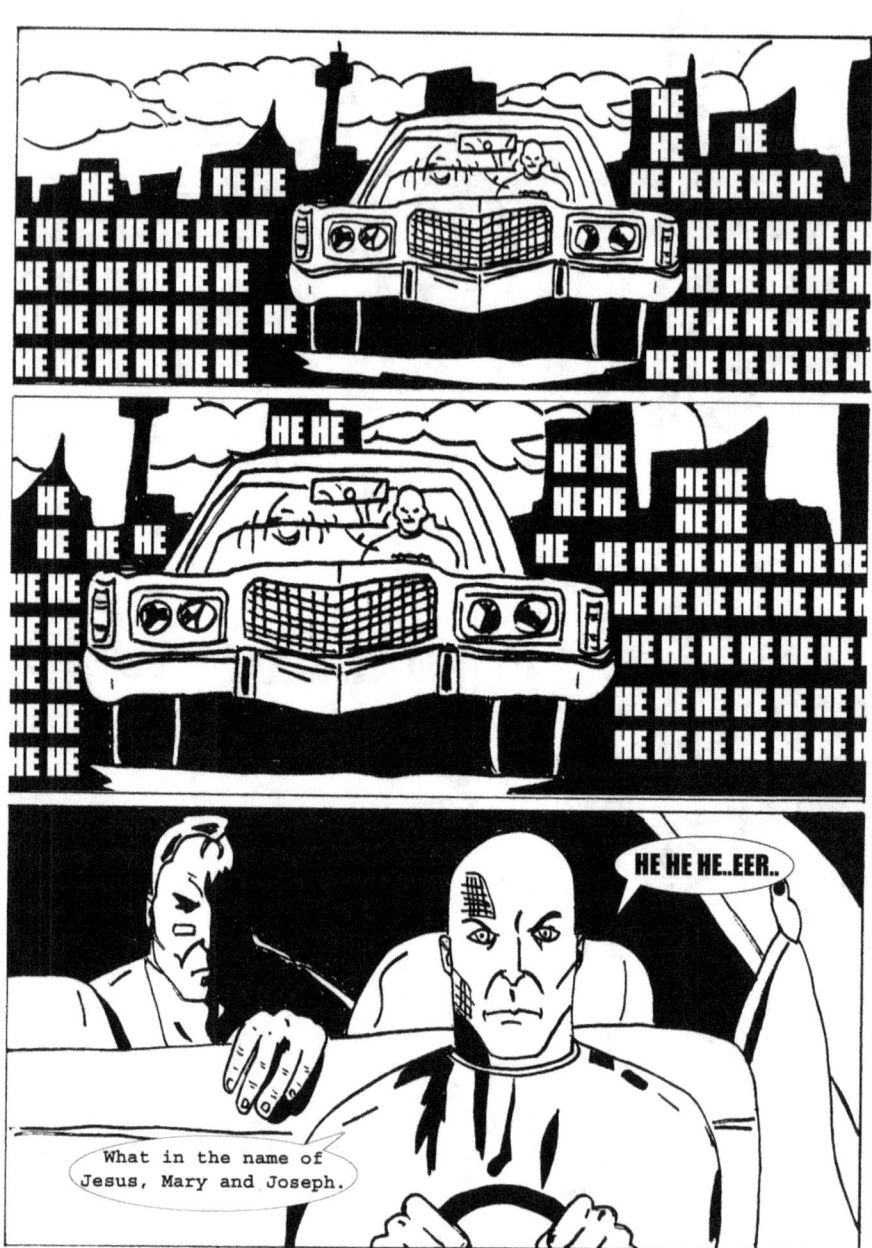

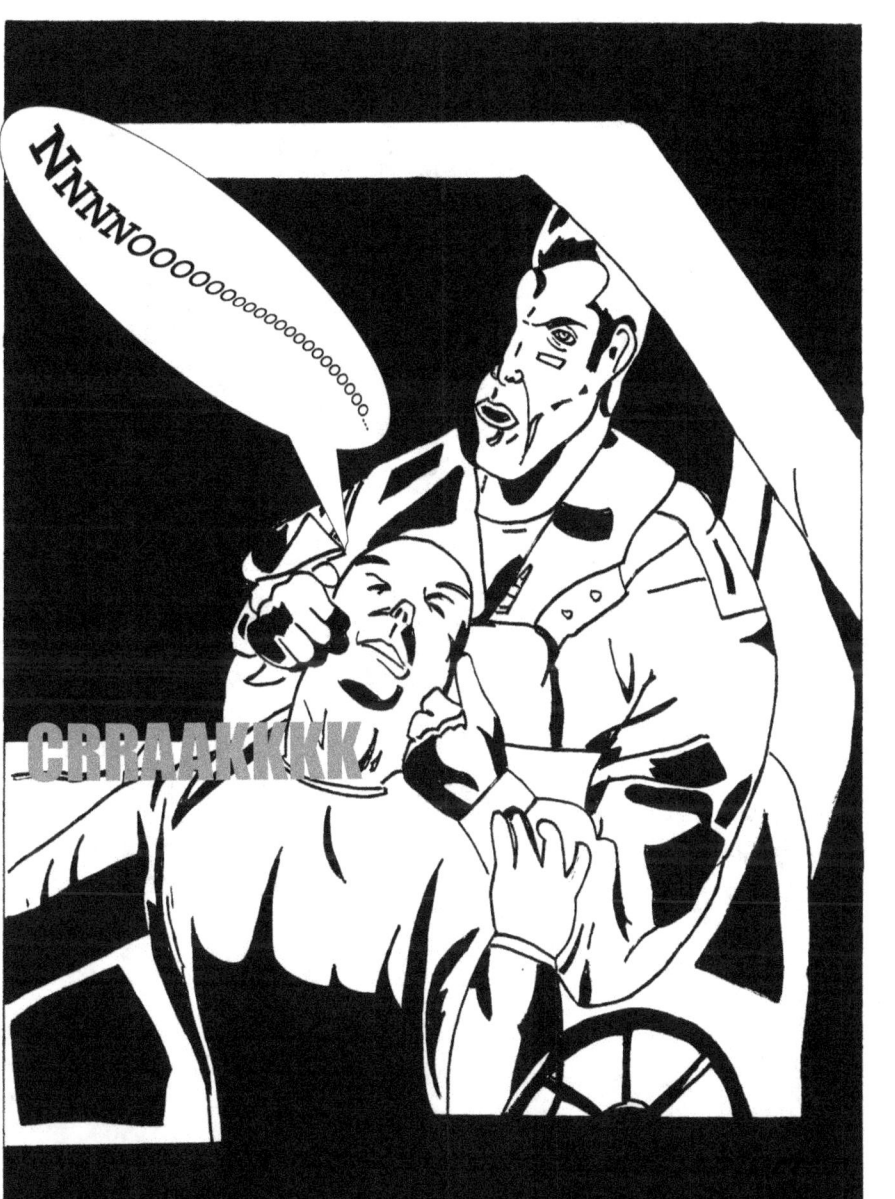

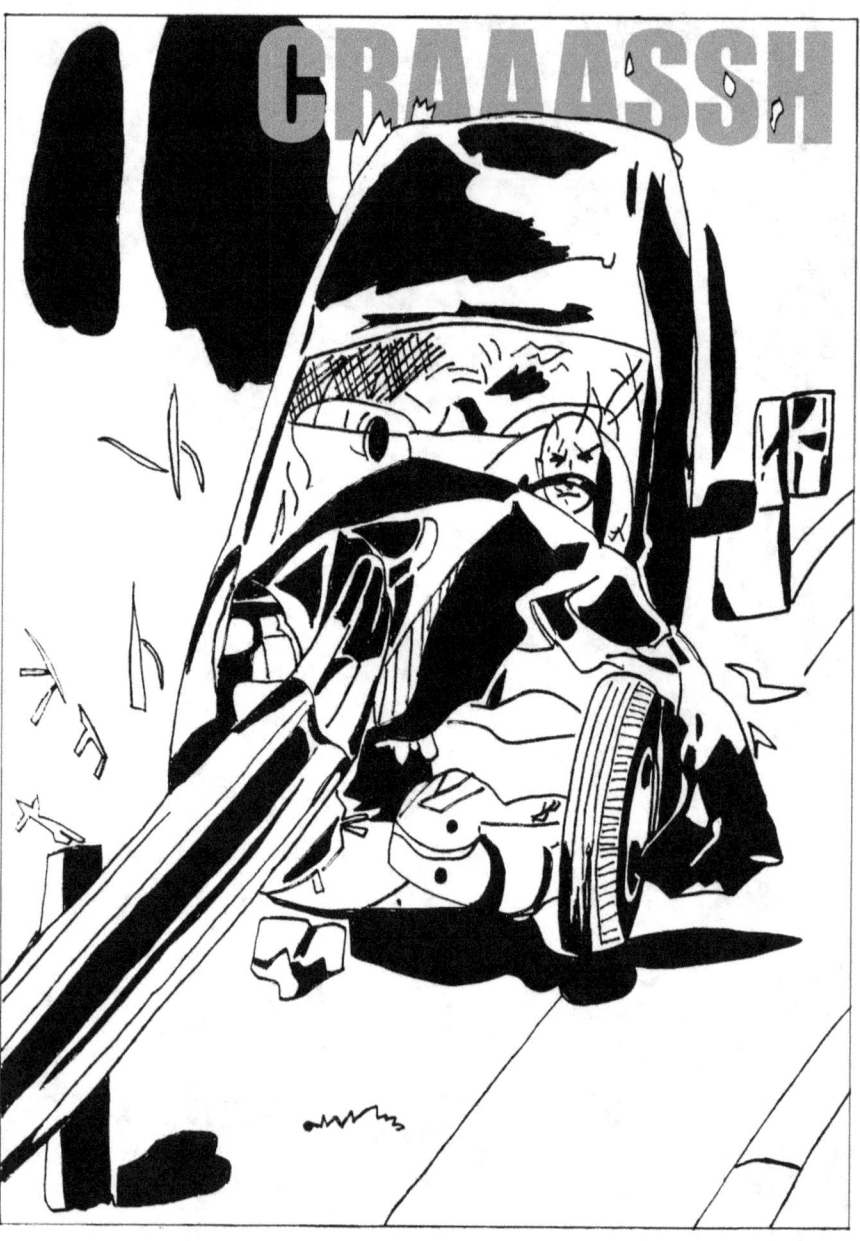

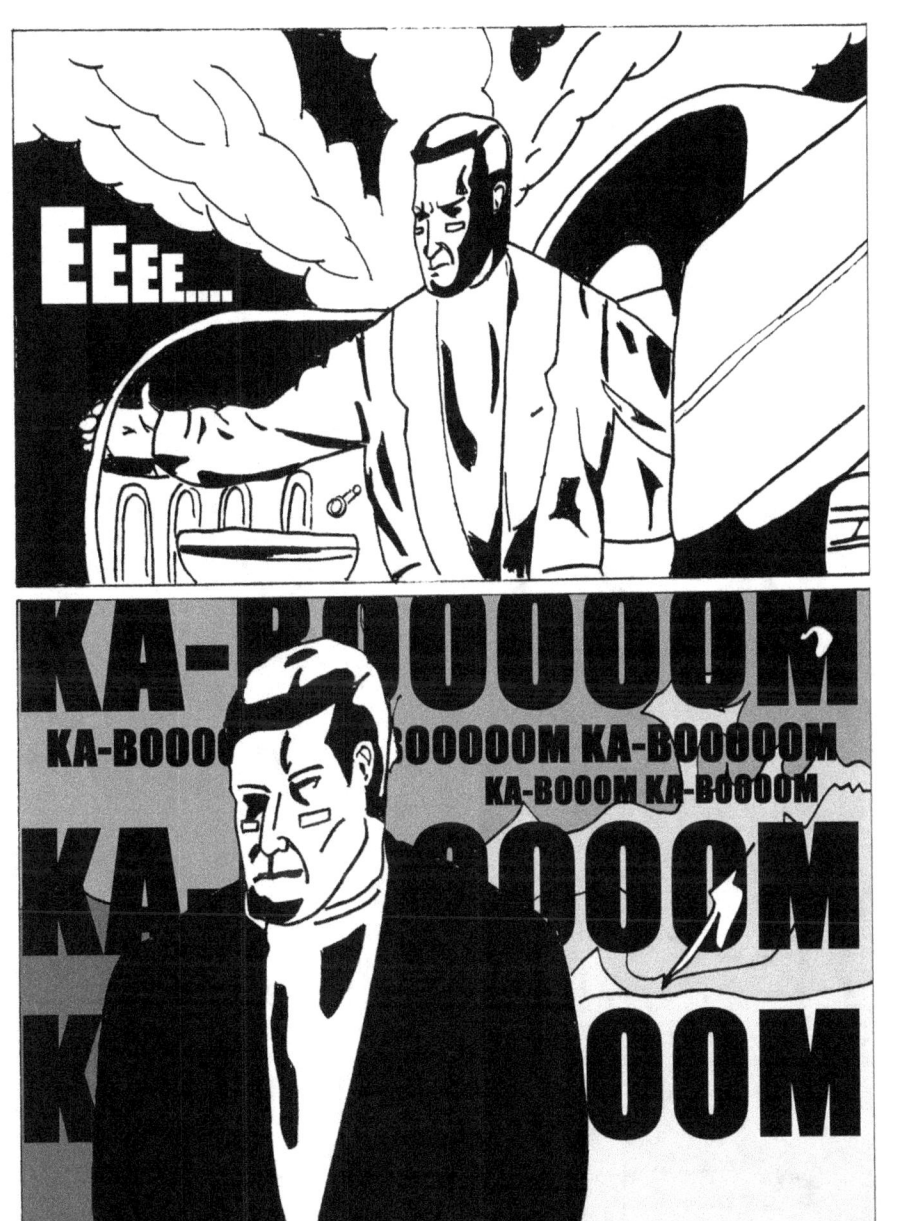

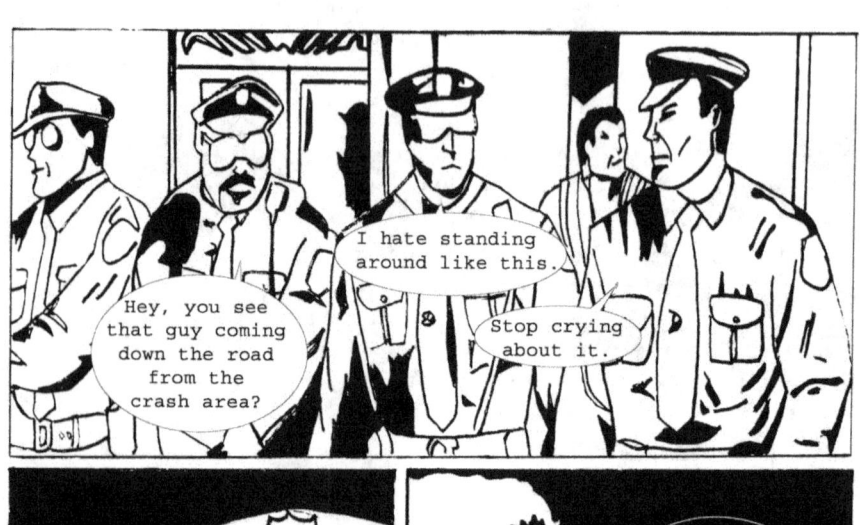

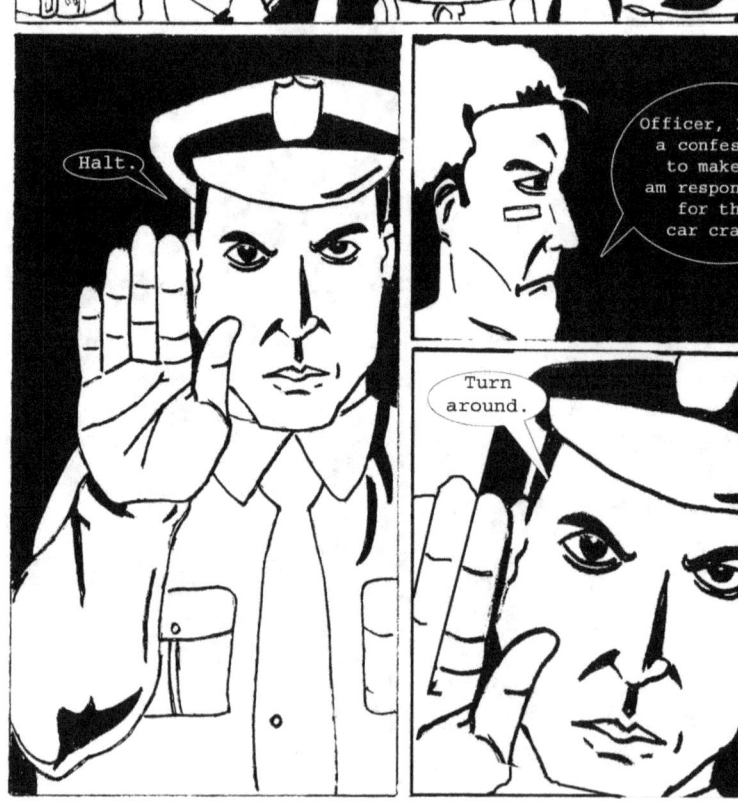

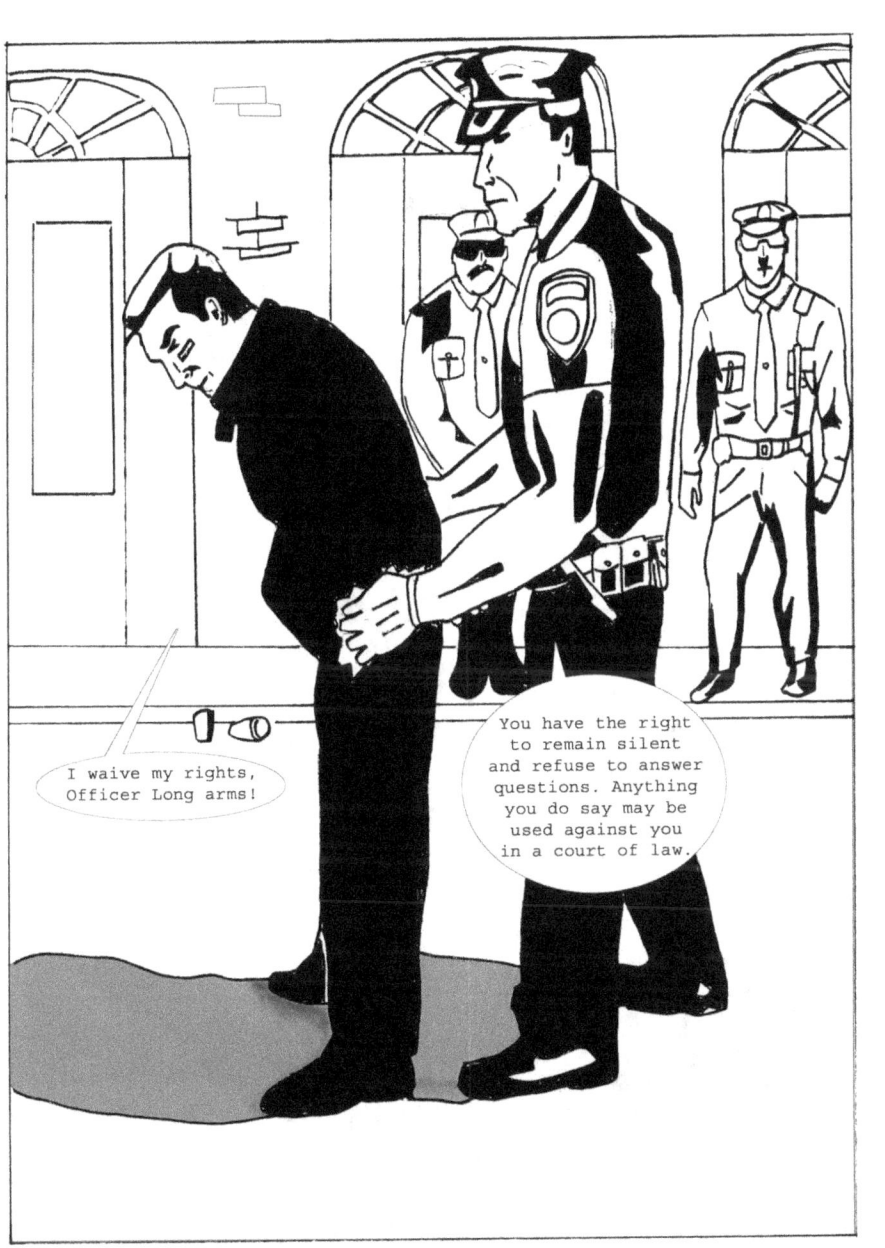

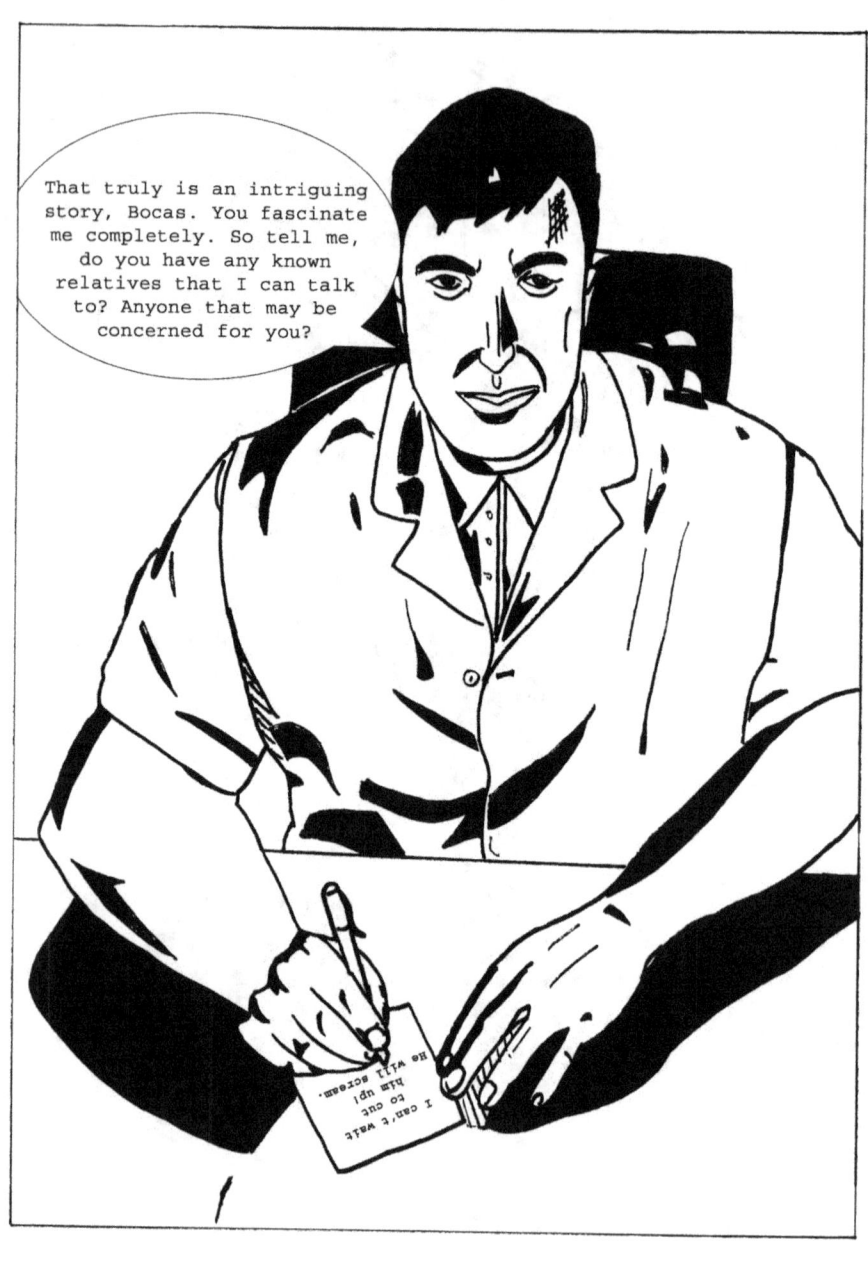

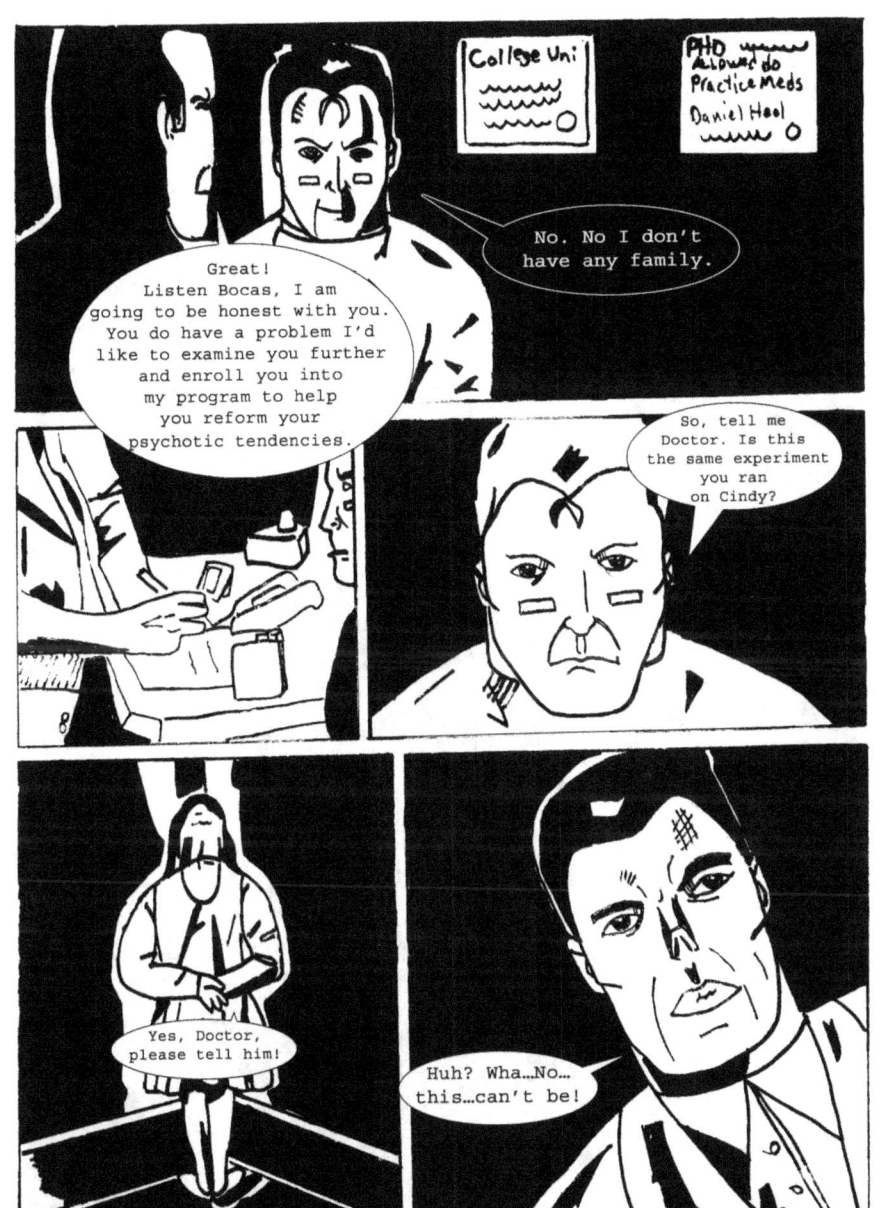

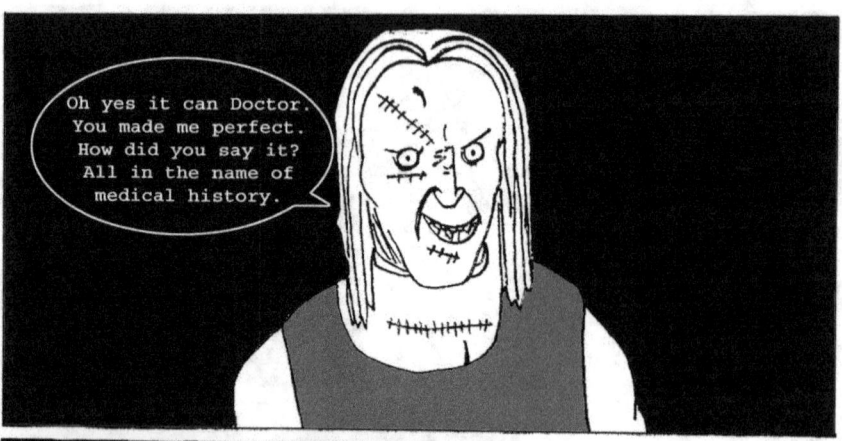

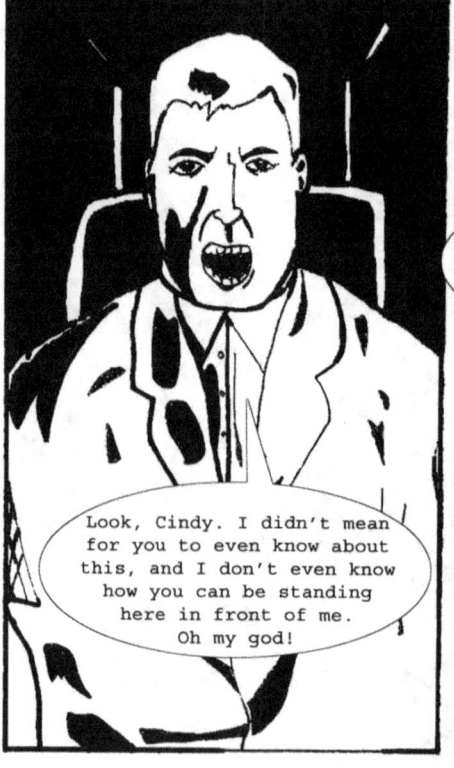

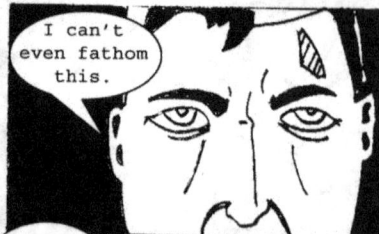

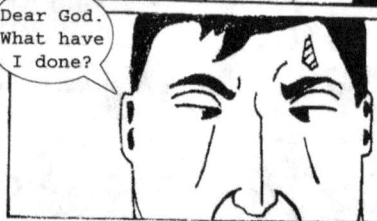

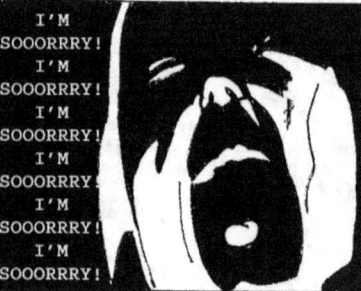

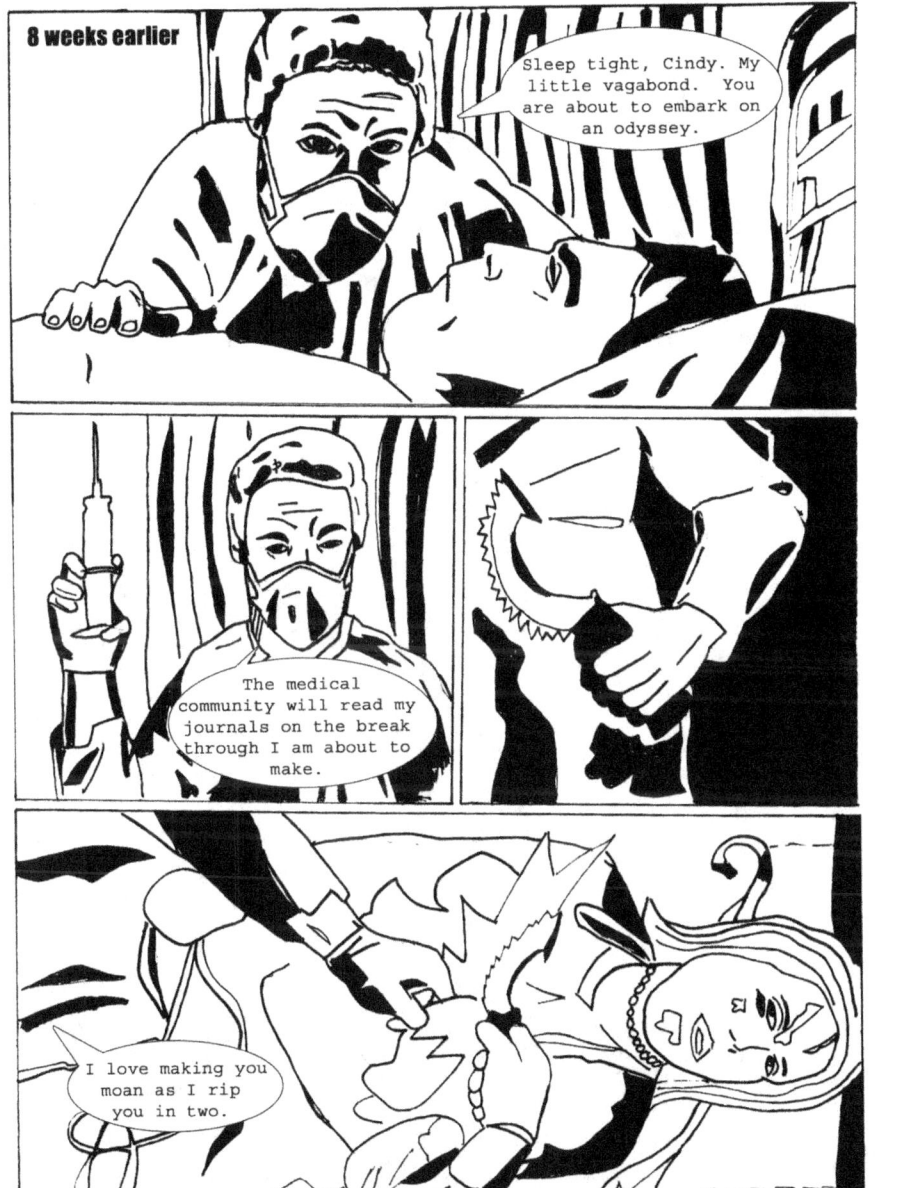

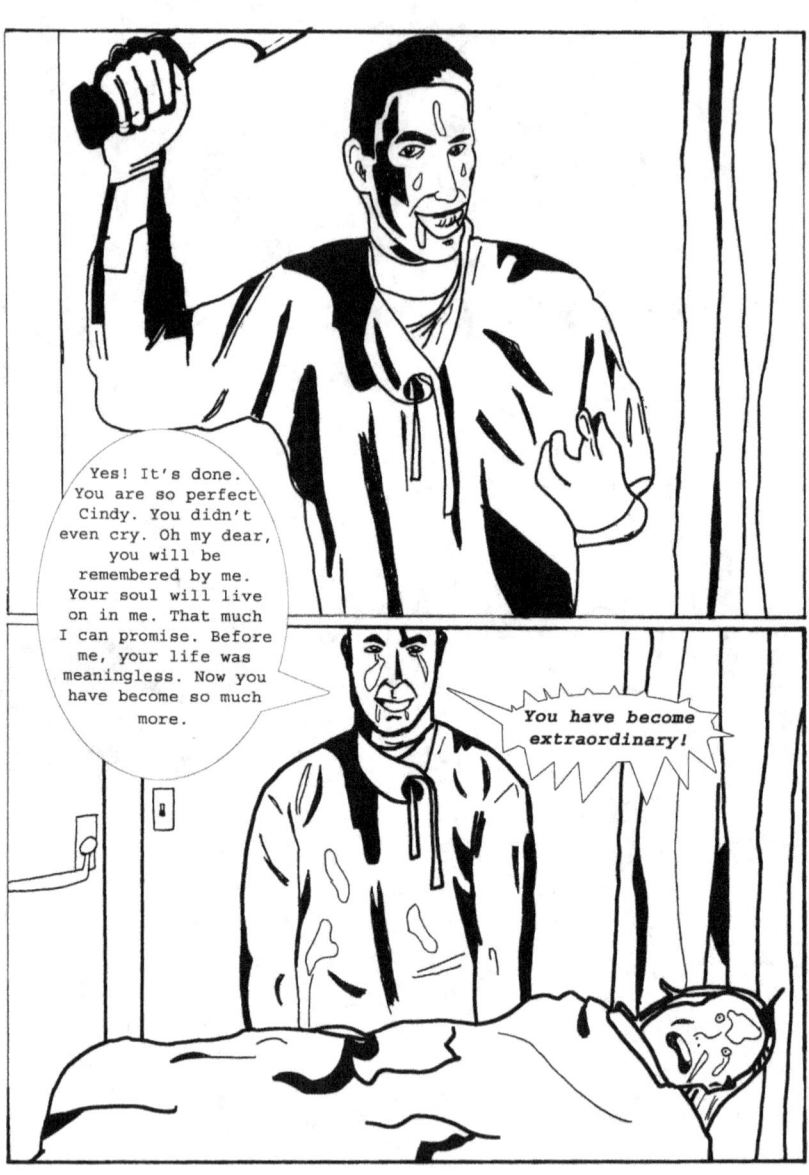

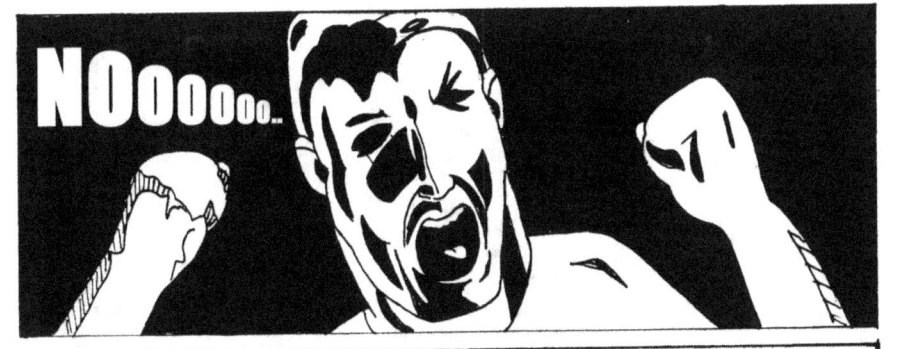

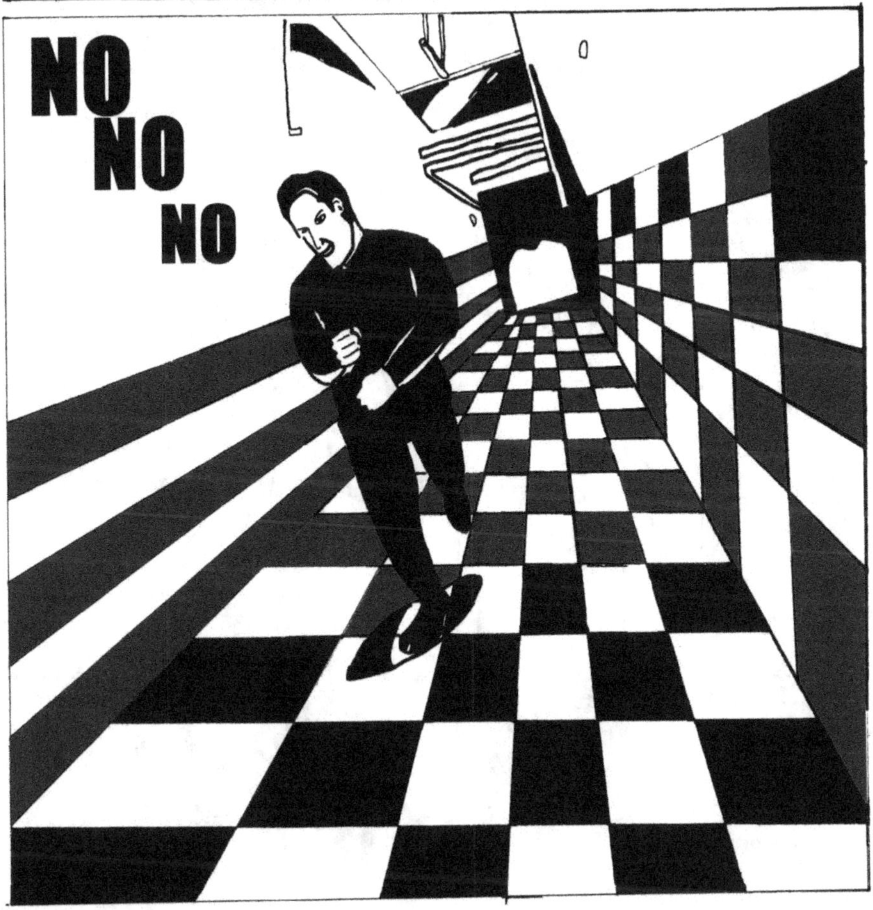

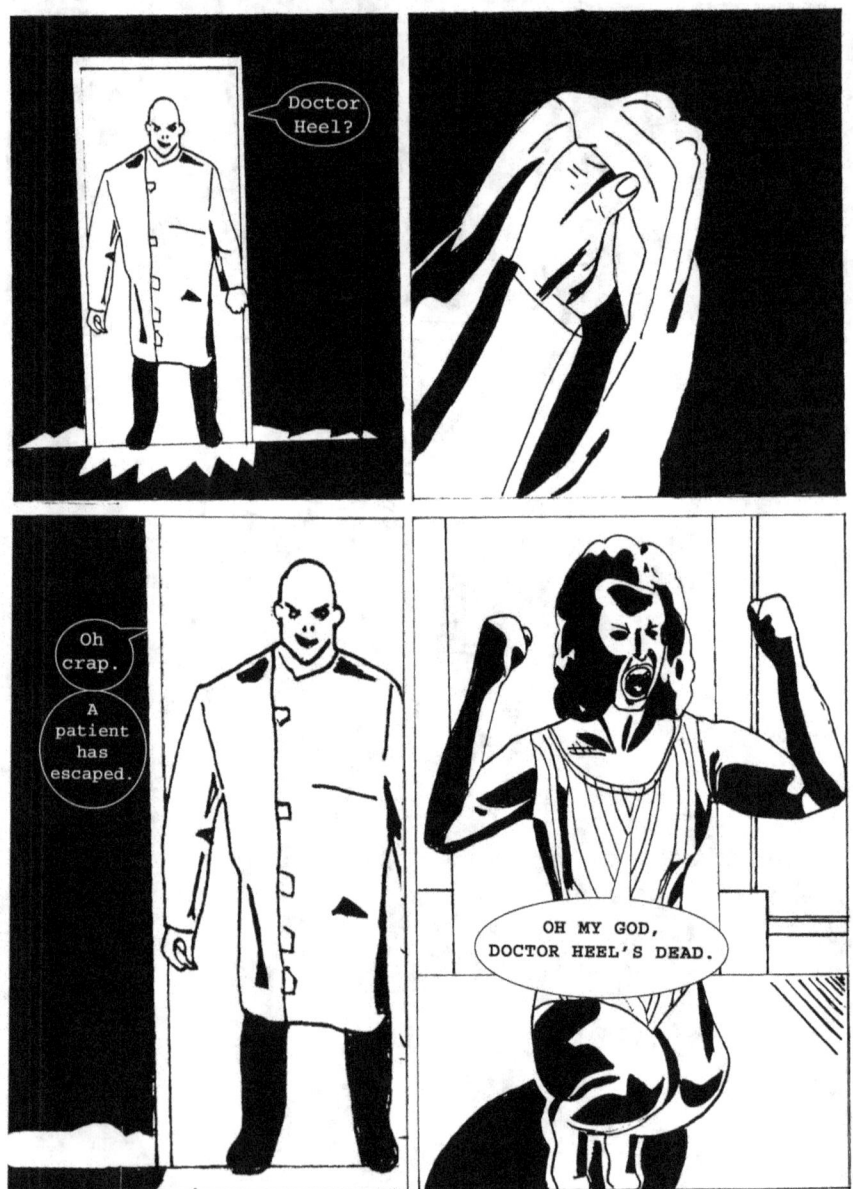

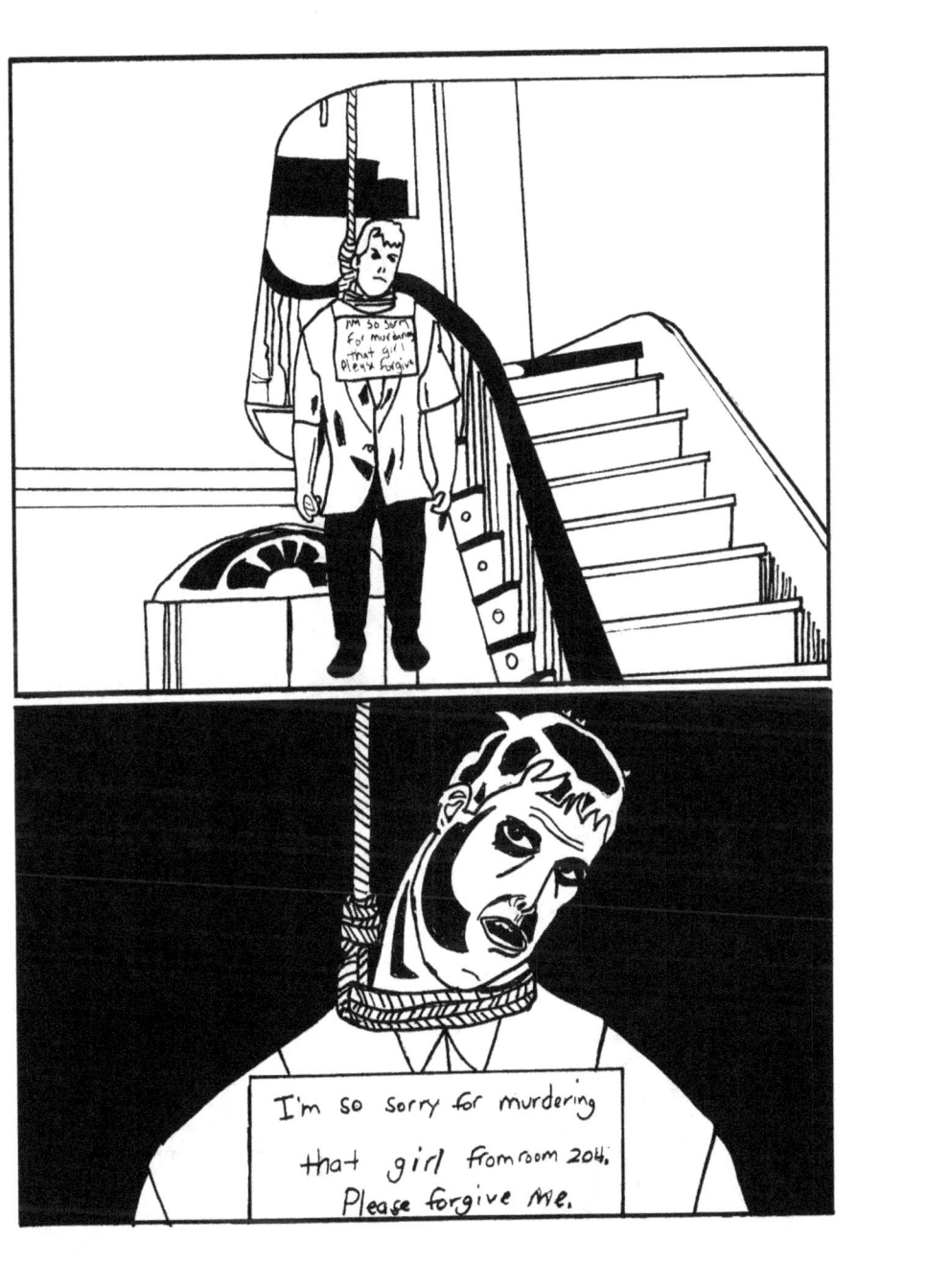

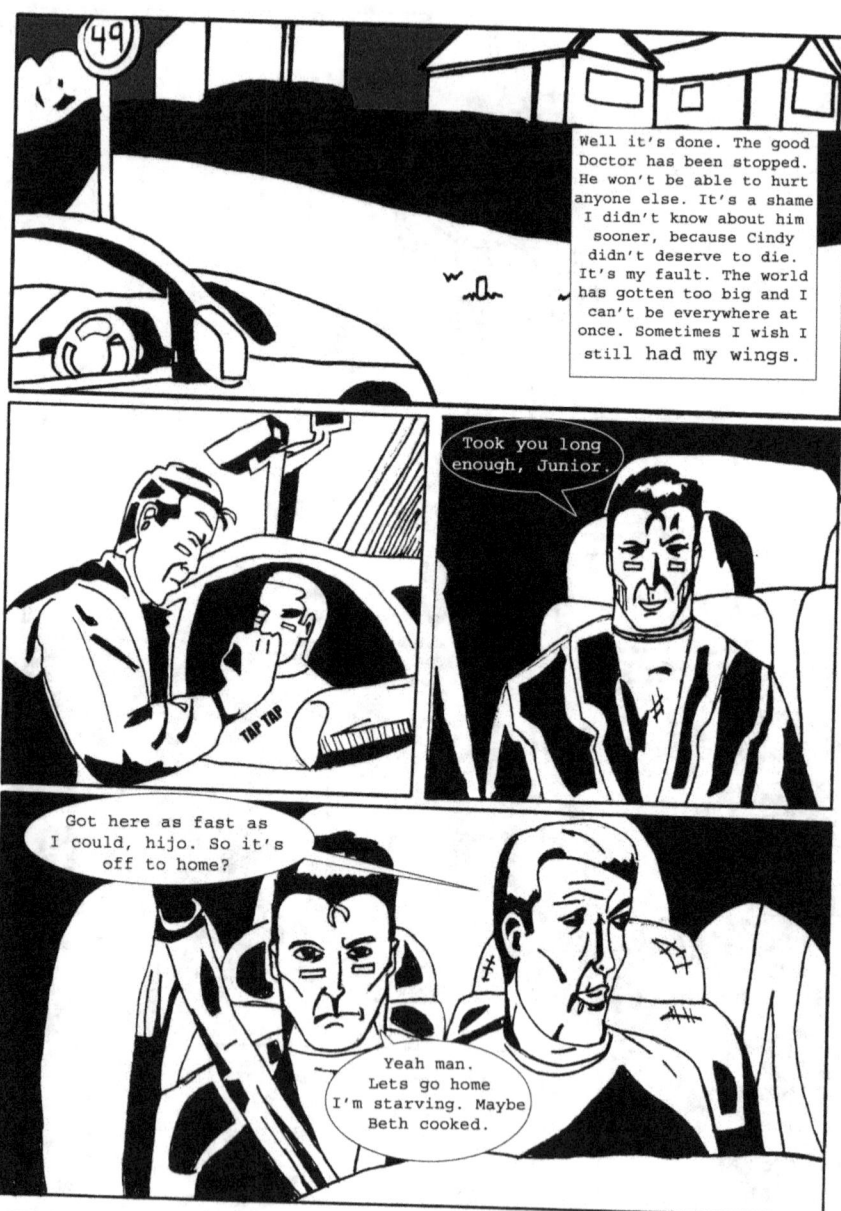

-THE LEGEND OF BOCAS CONTINUES.-

The end.

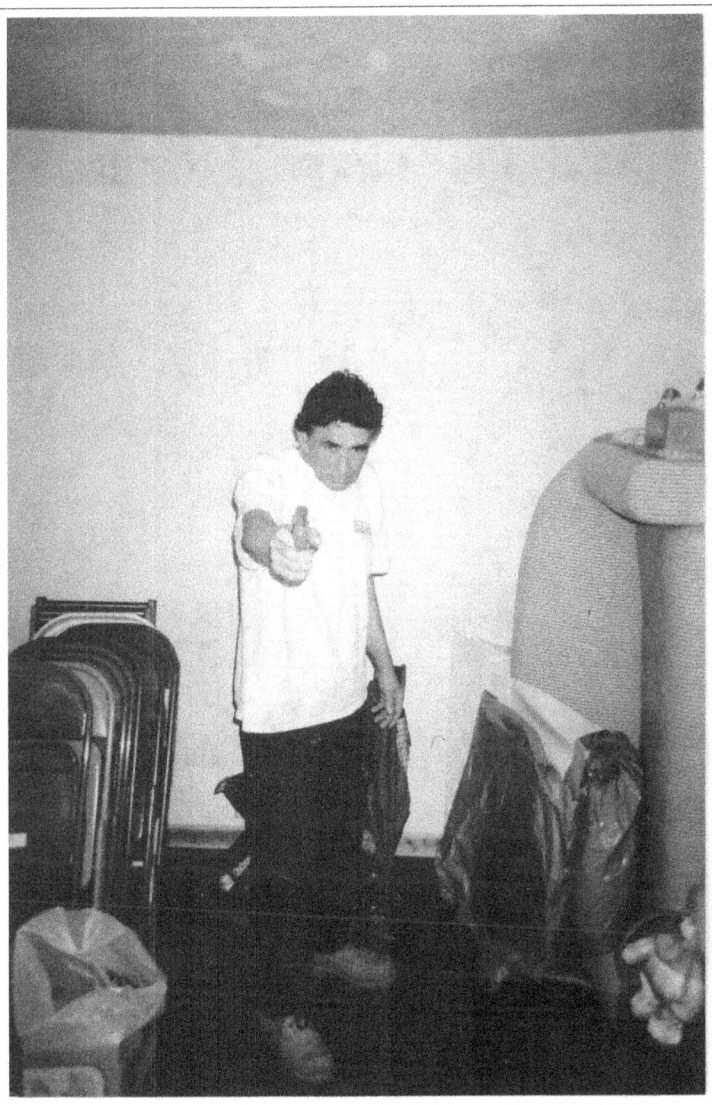

In loving memory of my father, Santiago Estrada. He was the original Bocas model. His memory will always be with me and he will live on through my work!

Santiago "Chago" Estrada
3/31/38-4/25/06

In honor of
Santiago " Chago" Estrada.

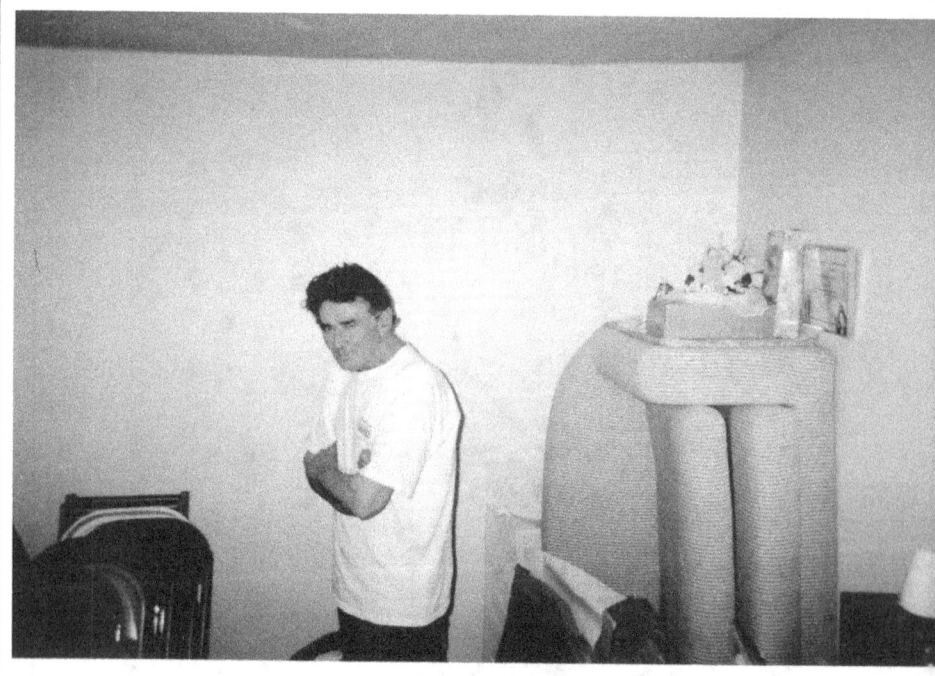

The original Bocas model in his glory.

Santiago "Chago" Estrada
3/31/38-4/25/06

In honor of
Santiago " Chago" Estrada.

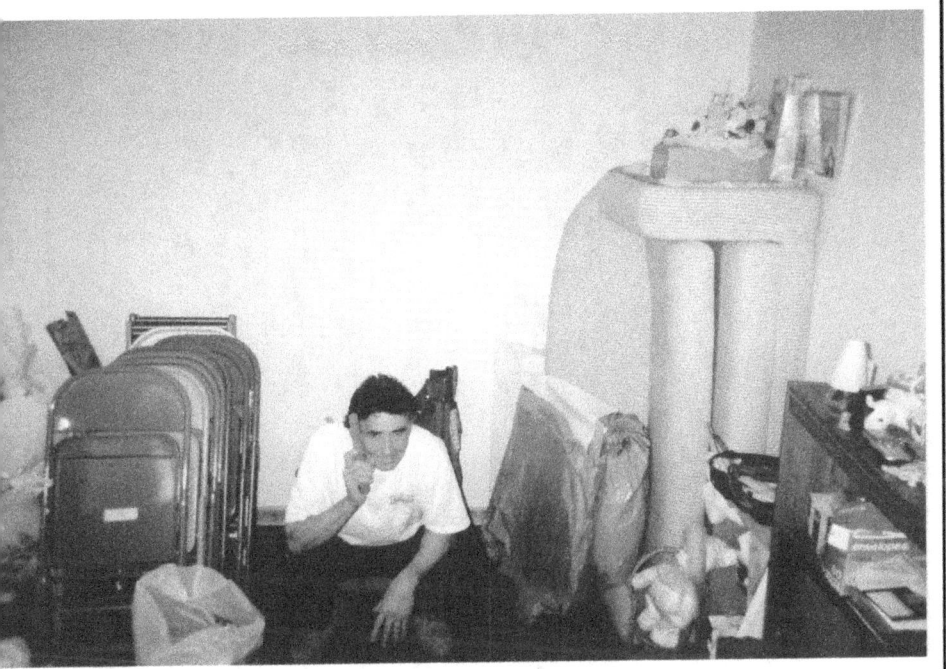

The original Bocas model in his glory.

Santiago "Chago" Estrada
3/31/38-4/25/06

In honor of
Santiago " Chago" Estrada.

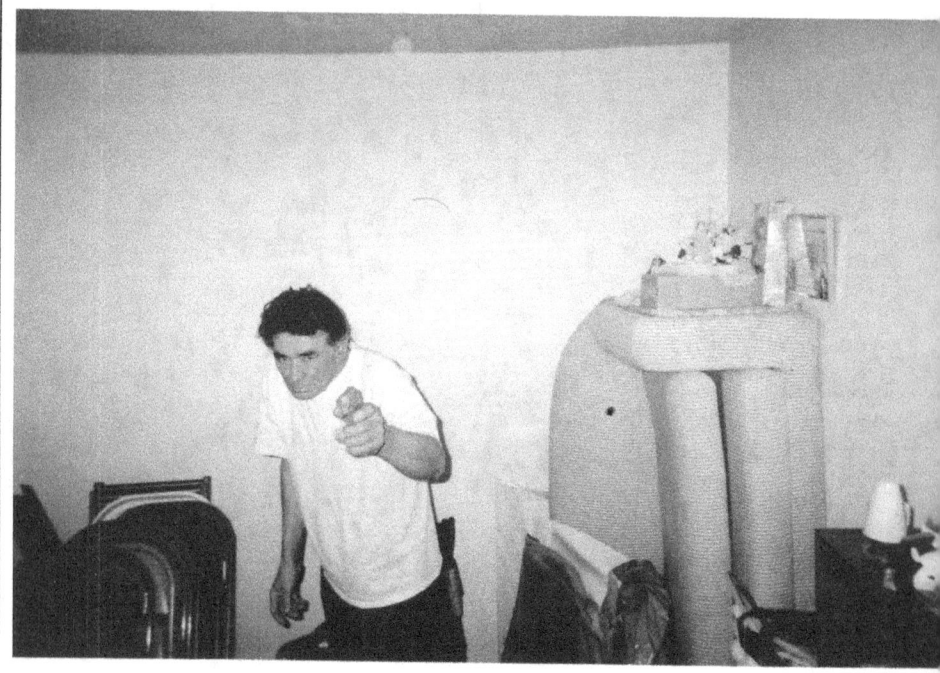

The original Bocas model in his glory.

Santiago "Chago" Estrada
3/31/38-4/25/06

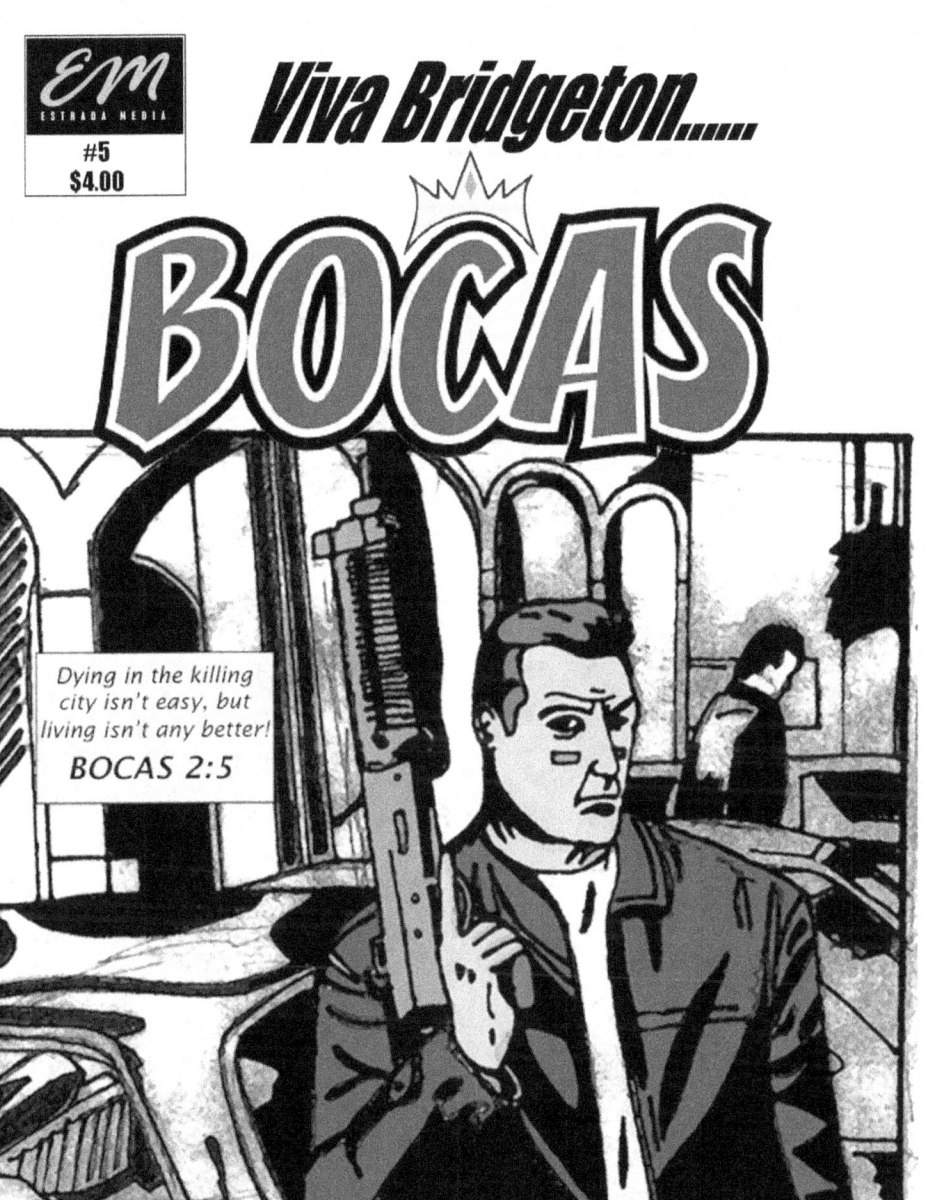

COMING SOON

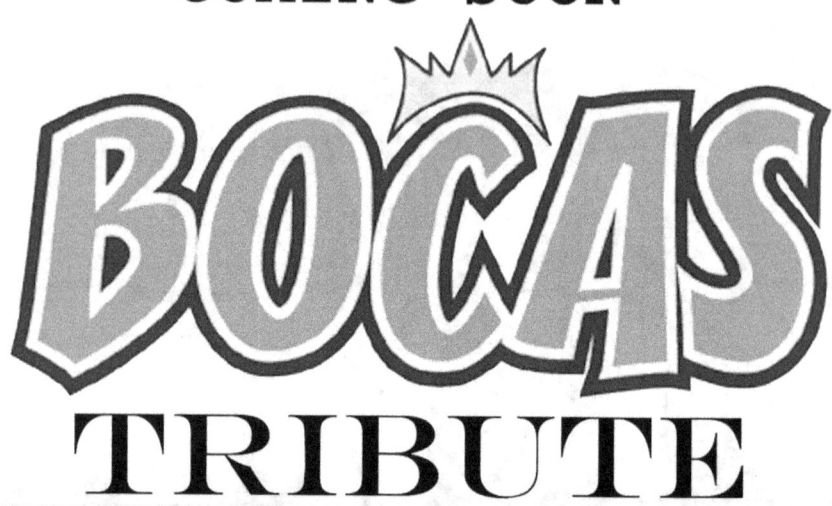

TRIBUTE

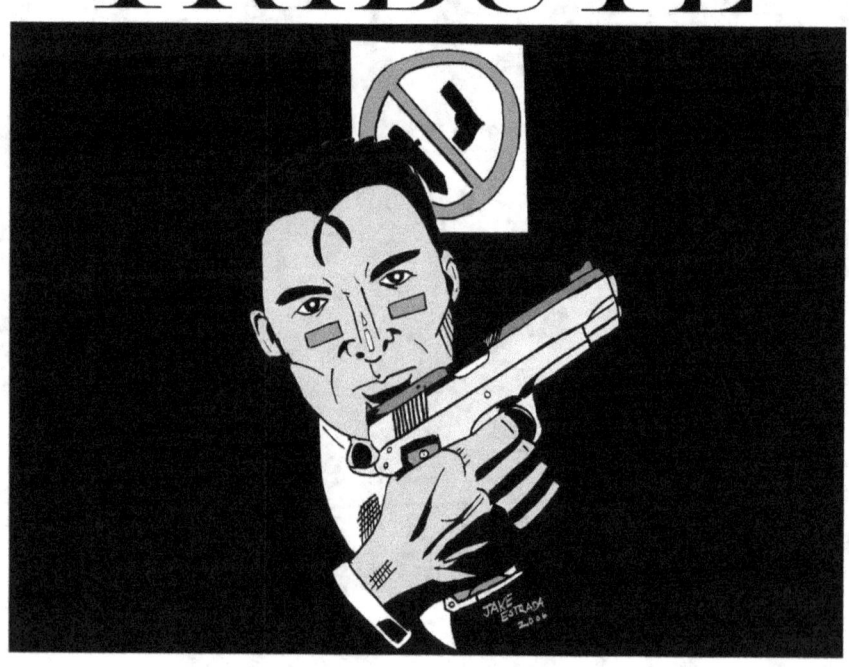